P9-CRX-940

The BANKRUPTCY *Handbook*

Everything You Need to Know to Avoid Bankruptcy, Get Rid of Debt, and Rebuild Your Credit

JOHN VENTURA

Oriole Park Branch
7454 W. Balmoral Ave.
Chicago, IL 60656
312-744-1965
Mon-Thur 9-9
Fri & Sat 9-5; Sun Closed

KAPLAN) PUBLISHING

New York

This publication is designed to provide accurate and authoritative information in regard to the subject matter covered. It is sold with the understanding that the publisher is not engaged in rendering legal, accounting, or other professional service. If legal advice or other expert assistance is required, the services of a competent professional should be sought.

Vice President and Publisher: Maureen McMahon
Editorial Director: Jennifer Farthing
Acquisition Editor: Shannon Berning
Development Editor: Sheryl Gordon
Production Editor: Karina Cueto
Typesetter: PBS & Associates
Cover Designer: Rod Hernandez

© 2008 by John Ventura

Published by Kaplan Publishing, a division of Kaplan, Inc.
1 Liberty Plaza, 24th Floor
New York, NY 10006

All rights reserved. The text of this publication, or any part thereof, may not be reproduced in any manner whatsoever without written permission from the publisher.

Printed in the United States of America

January 2008
10 9 8 7 6 5 4 3 2 1

ISBN-13: 978-1-4277-9599-1

Kaplan Publishing books are available at special quantity discounts to use for sales promotions, employee premiums, or educational purposes. Please email our Special Sales Department to order or for more information at kaplanpublishing@kaplan.com, or write to Kaplan Publishing, 1 Liberty Plaza, 24th Floor, New York, NY 10006.

R0412789915

Oriole Park Branch
7454 W. Balmoral Ave.
Chicago, IL 60656
312-744-1965
Mon-Thur 9-9
Fri & Sat 9-5; Sun Closed

DISCARD

Contents

Introduction

Are you struggling with overwhelming debt and concerned that you may have to file for bankruptcy? Or, have you already decided to file for bankruptcy but you're worried about what's to come? If so, you've picked up the right book. *The Bankruptcy Handbook* provides clear advice and information to help you avoid bankruptcy when possible, explains when bankruptcy is your best option for handling your debts, introduces you to the kinds of bankruptcy most consumers file, and guides you through the bankruptcy process from start to finish. This book also helps you get your financial life back on track once your bankruptcy is over.

I've been a nationally board-certified bankruptcy attorney for close to 30 years, so I've worked with hundreds of consumers who were in your very same situation. As a result, I understand how confusing and scary it can be when you've fallen behind on your debts and just can't get caught up; when you're being threatened by creditors and hounded by debt collectors; and when the thought of bankruptcy has crept into your mind. I also know, however, that knowledge is power. Therefore, after you read this book, you'll feel more in control of your debts, more prepared to make informed decisions about them, and less anxious about what it will be like to file for bankruptcy, if bankruptcy turns out to be the best solution to your financial troubles.

I've divided *The Bankruptcy Handbook* into three sections. The first section, "Avoiding Bankruptcy If You Can," discusses how to get out of debt without filing for bankruptcy. Chapter 1 tells you how to get a handle on your debts by developing a budget, making more money, selling some of your assets, negotiating with your creditors, consolidating your debts, and getting credit counseling. Chapter 2 offers specific advice for managing high-stakes debts, including mortgages, car loans, federal taxes, student loans, and court-ordered child support. The chapter also reviews your options for avoiding an eviction and keeping your utilities on. The final chapter in this section educates you about your legal rights when debt collectors are demanding that you pay what you owe.

The next section, "Considering Bankruptcy When Managing Your Debts Doesn't Work," is essential reading if the information and advice in the first section of the book isn't enough to turn your finances around. Chapter 4 explains when bankruptcy is your best option and exactly what filing for bankruptcy can and can't do for you. Chapter 5 examines the ethical and emotional aspects of bankruptcy. In my experience, most consumers fight to avoid bankruptcy in large part because they believe that they have a moral obligation to pay their debts and because some sectors of our society demonize consumers who end up in bankruptcy. As a result, deciding whether to file can be an emotionally difficult decision. I try to make that decision a little easier by putting bankruptcy in a historical context and by explaining how creditors have used the media to paint unflattering pictures of consumers who file for bankruptcy. I also offer advice for coping with your emotions before, during, and after bankruptcy.

Three other chapters in this section provide specific information about the bankruptcy process. Chapter 6 offers a detailed overview of the two most common types of consumer bankruptcy: a Chapter 7 liquidation of debt and a Chapter 13 reorganization of debt; chapters 8 and 9 provide information on the detailed processes behind both types. Chapter 7 explains why it's important to work with a bankruptcy attorney given the complexity of the bankruptcy process and all of the costly legal land mines you'll face if you decide to act as your own attorney.

The book's final section, "Rebuilding Your Life and Your Finances After Bankruptcy," is devoted to helping you get your finances back on track once your bankruptcy is over. You'll learn how to rebuild your credit and get basic advice about managing your finances to avoid money troubles in the future.

At the end of *The Bankruptcy Handbook* you'll find a glossary of bankruptcy-related terms and sample bankruptcy forms. You'll also find a resources section, which directs you to other books, websites, government agencies, and nonprofit organizations that can help you learn more about dealing with your debts, filing for bankruptcy, and rebuilding your credit after bankruptcy.

Avoiding Bankruptcy If You Can

Managing Your Debts to Avoid Bankruptcy

When you're up to your ears in debt, your finances are moving from bad to worse, and you're having nightmares about bankruptcy, quick and decisive action may prevent those bad dreams from becoming a reality. This chapter reviews the steps you can take to get out of debt and stay out of bankruptcy court, including learning how to live on a budget, making more money, selling some of your assets, negotiating with your creditors, and consolidating your debts.

If you don't feel confident about managing your debts yourself, this chapter also provides an overview of how to find a reputable non-profit credit counseling agency that can help you. In addition, this chapter warns you about actions you should never take when you're struggling with your debts, such as taking out certain types of loans or writing bad checks.

BUILD A GET-OUT-OF-DEBT BUDGET

Your very first step when your finances are in a downward spiral should be to set up a household budget that allocates your dollars toward your most important living expenses and debts. If you already have a budget, review it for changes you can make that will help you meet all of your financial obligations and pay off your debts faster. Those changes may include reducing your spending on nonessentials and even completely eliminating some of your expenses. When your finances improve, you may be able to add them back into your budget.

❗ Hot Tip

The worse the state of your finances, the more aggressive you need to be about reducing your spending. Sure, you may have to give up some of the things you enjoy, but a little sacrifice may be all it takes to turn your finances around so that you can avoid the loss of your assets and stay out of bankruptcy court.

HOW TO SET UP YOUR BUDGET

Begin the budget building process by determining exactly how much you are currently spending. To do this, review your bank statements, check registers, credit card account statements, and any other spending records you may have for the past 12 months. If you are married or live with a partner, your spouse or partner should go through the same exercise.

Next, figure out your current total monthly income, including your monthly take-home pay (your gross income *minus* all tax and health benefit deductions) and any other income you receive on a regular basis, such as rental income, child support and/or spousal support payments, royalties, and the like. Be sure to include your spouse's or partner's monthly income, too.

After you've gathered all this information, use the budget worksheet in Figure 1.1 to organize and record your monthly spending and income information. Take a look at the worksheet on the following page, and read the pages that follow to help you learn how to properly fill it in.

FIGURE 1.1. Sample Monthly Household Budget Worksheet

Use this form to create your own budgeting worksheet, unless you want to use budgeting software, such as *Quicken Basic* or *Deluxe*. Once you've finalized your numbers, you can also use this same form to create your final budget.

If you use this form and some of the expenses listed on it don't apply to you, just ignore them. If you have expenses that are not listed on this form, use the blank lines to record those expenses. Also, if you can't afford to put any money in savings right now, leave that section of your budget blank, too. Once your finances improve, you can revise your budget to reflect the amount you are saving every month.

Monthly Household Income

Your take-home pay	_____
Your spouse's or partner's take-home pay	_____
Child support	_____
Spousal support	_____
Other income	_____
Total Monthly Income	_____

Monthly Expenses

Fixed Expenses

Rent or mortgage payment	_____
Home equity loan payment	_____
Car loan	_____
Any and all monthly insurance payments	_____
Cable	_____
Phone (landline)	_____
Cell phone	_____
Internet service	_____
Child care	_____
Prescription medication	_____
Transportation	_____
Other	_____
Other	_____
Other	_____

Sample Monthly Household Budget Worksheet continues on next page.

Variable Expenses

Utilities _____

Groceries _____

Credit cards _____

Entertainment _____

Dry cleaning _____

Clothing _____

Body/health care _____

Other _____

Other _____

Other _____

Periodic Expenses

Tuition _____

Subscriptions _____

Gifts _____

License renewal; auto inspection/registration _____

Property taxes _____

Income taxes _____

Other _____

Other _____

Other _____

Total Monthly Expenses _____

Monthly Contributions to Your Savings _____

Total Monthly Expenses + Monthly Contributions to Your Savings = _____

Total Monthly Income _____ **– Total Expenses and Contributions** _____ **=** _____

❗Hot Tip

When you record your expenses on the budget worksheet, be sure to record each of your monthly financial obligations regardless of whether you're able to pay them right now. Recording everything is the only way to gain a realistic understanding about the state of your finances.

You'll notice that the worksheet groups your expenses into three different categories: *fixed expenses, variable expenses,* and *periodic expenses.* Let's take a closer look at each.

Fixed Expenses

Fixed expenses are expenses that do not change from month to month. They include your mortgage or rent payment and the payments on your car, your home equity loan, and on any other loans you may have. Your fixed expenses also include the amount you spend every month on such items as insurance, child care, tolls and parking if you drive to work, cable or satellite service, Internet access, court-ordered child support and/or spousal support, a monthly gym membership, and the like.

Variable Expenses

Variable expenses are expenses whose amount changes each month. Common types of variable expenses include groceries, gas for your vehicle, restaurant meals and snacks, entertainment, utilities, dry cleaning and laundry, and spending on clothing and body care services (e.g., manicures and massages).

Periodic Expenses

Periodic expenses are expenses that you only pay once in a while, such as tuition, insurance, auto registration, haircuts, and property taxes. Even though you only pay these kinds of expenses occasionally, every month you should be setting aside the money you will need to pay each of them when they come due. To determine a monthly amount to save for each of your periodic expenses, calculate the total annual cost for each of your periodic expenses, and then divide the amount by 12 (for 12 months) to get a monthly amount. Record the monthly amount on your budget worksheet.

Track Your Miscellaneous Spending for a Month

Most of you probably have a pretty good handle on how much your fixed expenses cost you every month and a general sense of your periodic expenses, but you probably do not have a hint about how much you're spending every month on nonessential, discretionary items like the coffee and bagel you purchase on your way to work each day, your lunch during the workweek, happy hour drinks, clothing, makeup, gifts for family and friends, movies, books, magazines, DVD rentals, and so on. Furthermore, although the amount of money you spend on these kinds of purchases may not seem like a lot—$3 here, $7.50 there—over time, your spending on the "small stuff" can really add up. For example, let's assume that each workday you spend a total of $10 on lunch and a mid-afternoon snack. That daily $10 translates into a total of $50 each week, $200 every month, and $2,400 each year. That's not peanuts! And what do you have to show for it? Probably nothing more than a lower balance in your checking account, a higher balance on your credit cards, and maybe a few extra pounds.

Here's a good way to get a handle on your monthly miscellaneous spending. For one month, carry a notebook with you everywhere you go. Every single time you buy something with cash, a debit card, a check, or a credit card, write down what you bought and how much you spent. It doesn't matter how little something costs—write it down.

! Hot Tip

Recording all of your miscellaneous expenses for a month can be a hassle, no doubt about it, but going through the exercise will make you more aware of exactly what you do with your money, which is an important part of getting your finances under control.

If you are married or if you live with a partner, your spouse or partner should do the same thing. At the end of the month, add up all of the money you spent on nonessentials. You may be surprised at the total. Use the information in your spending notebook to fill in the monthly totals in the variable expenses section of your budget worksheet.

Add and Subtract Your Dollar Amounts

Once you have recorded all of your expense and income information on the budget worksheet, add up all of your expenses and all of your income. Then subtract your total expenses from your total income.

A positive outcome. It's good news if the number you end up with is a positive number, unless the reason for a positive result is either of the following:

1. *Every month you're only paying the minimum amount due on your credit cards.* If you are, it will take you years to pay off your credit card balances, and in the meantime, you're wasting money paying lots of interest on your debts.
2. *You have little or nothing left in your checking account at the end of each month and you're contributing nothing to savings.* Living without a financial cushion means that if you're hit with an unexpected expense, you lose your job, or you experience some other setback, the impact on your life can be disastrous.

If either or both of the above descriptions apply to you, look for expenses in your budget that you can reduce or completely eliminate. That way, each month you can pay more on your debts so you'll have more money left over every month in case of an emergency. It's also possible, depending on how much you are able to cut out of your budget, that you may need to figure out ways to increase

> **Red Alert!**
>
> When you are able to pay your bills each month, but you have little or nothing left over, you're *living paycheck to paycheck*. That's a dangerous way to live because you're always on the brink of a financial crisis.

your income. The "Make More Money" section of this chapter offers some suggestions on how to do that.

A negative outcome. If you got a negative number when you subtracted your monthly expenses from your monthly income, you are spending more than your income each month, and you may be stay-ing financially afloat (just barely, perhaps) by using credit cards and cash advances to pay your essential expenses. Maybe you're running up the balance on your checking account overdraft line of credit, or maybe you're borrowing money from friends or family. You also may be falling farther and farther behind on some of your financial obliga-tions because you can't afford to pay them. In other words, you're on the track to financial ruin, and it's time to change direction.

> **❗Hot Tip**
>
> Once you've gotten your debts under control and you are no longer living on the brink of financial disaster, it's impor-tant to begin building up the balance in your savings account. Financial experts advise that you save a minimum of 10 percent of your take-home pay each month.

HANDLING A BUDGET DEFICIT

If your monthly spending exceeds your monthly income, review your budget worksheet for expenses you can cut or eliminate. Your goals: to reduce your total spending so that you can meet *all* of your financial obligations and to accelerate the rate at which you pay off your high-interest debts. When you're looking for spending cuts, focus first on your variable expenses because they are nonessential, discretionary expenses. In other words, you have direct and total control over them. Here are some suggestions for how you can start to reduce your vari-able spending:

■ Buy in bulk at a warehouse store such as Costco or Sam's Club. However, don't buy items that are apt to spoil before you use them just because the prices are low!

- Plan your meals for the coming week, never go grocery shopping without a list, buy house brands, don't buy preprepared meals or convenience items, reduce the number of times you go to the grocery store each week (the more often you go, the more you are likely to spend), and use coupons.

- Pack your own lunches on workdays—if you have school-age children, pack their lunches, too.

- Give up junk food, sodas, and fast food.

- Make your dinner parties potlucks.

- Give up cigarettes. With the average cost of a pack of cigarettes at $4.40 (taxes included) and the assumption you smoke a pack a day, you'll save $132 per month, or nearly $1,600 each year! Not smoking also will help you reduce the amount you are paying for health insurance if you are not enrolled in a group plan and the amount you pay for teeth cleaning and dry cleaning. An added bonus—your overall health is certain to benefit.

 Red Alert!

Statistics show that compared to non-smokers, the homes and cars of smokers sell for less.

- Check out books and DVDs at your local library rather than buying them (and reading/viewing them once, never to touch them again), or swap these items with friends.

- Contact your utilities for information about how you can reduce your heating, cooling, and water bills. For example, keep your home warmer in the summer and cooler in the winter, set your hot water heater at 120 degrees, use fluorescent lightbulbs, take showers rather than baths, fix leaky faucets, use weather stripping, caulk, and insulation to make your home more airtight, and unplug your TV, cable box, and computer when you leave your home.

- Do your own manicures and pedicures or have a regular "beauty day" with your girlfriends when you give them to one another. You may want to cut and color each other's hair, too.

- Cut your children's hair and your spouse's hair, if you can.

- Give up expensive cosmetics and body care products. There are many inexpensive substitutes available at your local drugstore that will do the job just as well.

> ### ✋ Red Alert!
> Don't treat any of your variable expenses like sacred cows—expenses you would never, ever consider reducing or eliminating. The bigger your budget deficit, the more ruthless you need to be about cutting your budget.

- Shop for clothes at discount stores such as T.J. Maxx, Marshalls, Kohl's, and Target. Also, check out yard sales and resale shops for good deals on items that you need. Avoid recreational shopping.

- Swap clothes with your friends.

- Get rid of nonessential phone services such as caller ID.

- When your doctor writes a prescription for a drug, ask that she make it for a generic drug as long as it is as effective as the regular drug. Also, get your prescriptions filled at the least expensive pharmacy in your area or at an online pharmacy approved by the National Association of Boards of Pharmacy (*www.nabp.net*).

> ### ✋ Red Alert!
> For now, if you are in debt and are contributing any money to savings, stop. It's more important for you to put every penny you have toward reducing your monthly deficit and paying off your high-interest debts as fast as you can. However, once your finances improve and you're no longer living paycheck to paycheck, it's important to begin building your savings.

NEXT STEPS

After you've completed an initial round of cuts, revise your worksheet and tally up the numbers to determine the impact of the cuts you've made. At this point, you may have made enough spending reductions to move your budget into the black. However, if you still haven't made enough adjustments so that you can pay off more each month on your high-interest debts, then try to reduce your spending even more. At this point, in addition to trying to find more ways to reduce your variable spending, you should look for ways to cut back on your fixed and periodic expenses, too. For example, try the following:

- If you are paying on a mortgage, find out if you can lower your monthly payments by refinancing the loan. However, avoid interest-only loans, adjustable-rate mortgages, and mortgages that require you to make a big balloon payment at the end of the loan. Although these kinds of loans may provide you with short-term relief, in the long run they are likely to create new problems. For example, you may face the loss of your home if you can't afford to make your loan payments after the interest-only period ends, if interest rates start to rise, or if you don't have the money you need to make the balloon payment when it comes due.

- If you are a renter, move into a less expensive apartment as soon as your lease is up (if you're on a month-to-month lease, you can move out anytime), or consider some of the other options outlined in chapter 2, including breaking your lease, getting a roommate, and subleasing your apartment to someone else.

- If you have a car loan, sell the car, use the proceeds to pay off the loan, and purchase a less expensive vehicle. Another alternative is to make do without a car, if possible. Chapter 2 provides an in-depth discussion of how to handle your car loan.

- Talk with your insurance agent or broker about ways to reduce your insurance costs.

Staying on Track Once You Are in the Clear

If you are finally able to move your budget into the black and acceler-ate the rate at which you pay off your debts by reducing your spend-ing, you can record the new spending amounts on your budgeting worksheet, relabel it "Monthly Budget," and post it in a visible loca-tion where you and your spouse or partner will be reminded of it daily. Then, at the end of each month, compare what you actually spent to what you budgeted. If you spent more, try to figure out why.

It's possible that you spent more because some of the dollar amounts in your budget are unrealistic. If that's the case, you'll have to increase those amounts. It's also possible that you were hit with an expense that you did not anticipate, such as a car repair fee. However, you may have spent more than you planned because you (and/or your spouse or partner) were not really serious about sticking to your bud-get. If that's the case, it's time to get serious! Although I can't give you a 100-percent guarantee that if you live on a budget you'll avoid bankruptcy, developing a get-out-of-debt budget and then spending according to that budget is absolutely essential to the success of every other action you need to take to get your finances under control.

If you (or your spouse or partner) simply can't stick to a budget, you may have an emotional problem with money, and unless you face up to it and get help, you'll continue to sabotage your budget. Figure 1.2 reviews many of the characteristics commonly associated with emo-tional spending. It also provides information about resources to turn to if you're having problems controlling your spending.

FIGURE 1.2. Are You an Emotional Spender?

Setting up a budget won't help you avoid bankruptcy if you have a spending problem and you don't get the help you need to control it. Sure, you may be able to rein in your spending for a while, but it will only be a matter of time before you overspend again. When that happens, you may undo all of the progress you already made resolving your money troubles.

Here are some of the most common characteristics of an emotional spender:

- You spend money even when you know that you can't afford to and even though you realize that your spending will have negative consequences on your life.

- You spend money to make yourself feel better when you're sad, depressed, or disappointed about something.

- You spend money to reward yourself for completing a project, getting a promotion, or maybe even for sticking with your budget during the previous month.

- No matter how much you buy, you never feel like you have enough.

- You buy items that you never use. In fact, you may never even remove the price tags from some of your purchases.

- You have no idea how much money is in your checking account, how much you spend each month, how much you owe to your creditors, and so on.

- You are constantly in a state of financial crisis.

- You experience a "high" when you spend money, especially when you use a credit card to pay for your purchases.

For a more complete list of the signs of compulsive spending as well as a quiz you can take to help you figure out if you have a spending problem, go to the Debtors Anonymous (DA) website at *www.debtorsanonymous.org*.

If you believe that you have a spending problem, you can get help by contacting any of the following resources:

- Debtors Anonymous (DA). This national organization, which is dedicated to helping compulsive spenders overcome their problem using the methods of Alcoholics Anonymous, has local chapters throughout the country. If there is no local chapter near you or if its meeting times are not convenient, DA also offers help by phone and online. Go to *www.debtorsanonymous.org* to locate the DA chapter closest to your home or job and to learn more about DA.

- A mental health counselor. The website of Mental Health America (previously known as the National Mental Health Association), *www.nmha.org*, is a good resource for learning more about mental health counseling, the various types of mental health counselors, and the cost of various counseling options. You also can use this site to locate a mental health counselor in your area. The American Mental Health Counselors Association's (AMHCA) website at *www.amhca.org* is another good resource.

- A mental health clinic in your community. This is a good resource if you have no health insurance or if your insurance does not cover mental health counseling. Most mental health clinics offer their services on a sliding scale based on income.

MAKE MORE MONEY

Try as you may, it's possible that you won't be able to move your budget into the black and/or pay off your debts faster just by reducing your expenses. If that's the case, it's time to consider other, bigger options, which are discussed next.

Increase Your Work Income

There are several ways to increase the amount of money flowing into your household. For example, you may be able to do the following:

- Work more hours at your current job. If you are paid on an hourly basis or do shift work, let your employer know that you want to work additional hours or would like to add another shift to your schedule.

- Get a second job. A weekend or evening job may be an option.

- Do freelance work. When you freelance, you work for yourself and offer your skills and expertise to potential clients. However, you'll have to market your services to potential clients, bill for your services, and collect from your clients if they don't pay you on a timely basis. Graphic designers, writers, and photographers often freelance.

 Red Alert!

If you are considering earning extra money by freelancing, make sure that you did not sign an agreement with your employer that prohibits you from doing freelance work, or that your employer does not have a general policy that bars employees from freelancing.

- Ask your employer for a raise. It's unlikely that your employer will agree to increase your income just because you're having money troubles, so you'll need a good reason to ask for a raise. Possible good reasons include the following:

  - You are not being paid as much money as your coworkers who have the same amount of responsibility as you do or who have a title that is equivalent to yours.

  - You've been given a significant amount of new responsibility without an increase in income.

  - You have not received a salary increase in at least a year.

  - You just received an excellent performance review.

- If a spouse or partner is not currently working outside the home, have him or her get a job. If your spouse or partner is a stay-at-home parent, talk with one another about the possibility of him or her getting a paid job.

- Look for a new job that pays more. However, unless your skills and knowledge are in demand, it will probably take time to find a new job that pays more than what you are earning now, especially if you live in a rural area or in an economically depressed part of the country.

▼ Hot Tip

Before your spouse or partner looks for a paying job, compare the additional amount of money that you estimate he or she can probably bring in each month to the costs associated with working outside your home. These costs may include transportation to and from work, child care, work clothes, dry cleaning, and lunches during the workweek. After you make this comparison, you may conclude that your household will net little or nothing extra each month if your spouse or partner gets a paying job.

Sell Some of Your Assets or Give Them Back to Your Secured Creditors

Another option when you're having problems making ends meet is to sell assets that you rarely, if ever, use and for which there is a market—items that someone else might find of value. Selling them is a particularly good idea if you are still paying on any of the assets and if you can sell them for enough money to wipe out at least what you still owe on them. Examples of assets you may want to sell include the following:

- Your car, if you can get to work by using public transportation, riding your bike, carpooling, or walking

- A boat, motorcycle, RV, or recreational watercraft

- Real estate, other than your home

- Fine art

- Antiques

- Fine jewelry

- A rare book collection, a stamp collection, etc.

If you plan to sell the assets yourself, research their current market values so that you know how much they are worth, and then use that information to set your asking prices. If you want to sell a difficult to value item or an asset that you believe is worth a substantial amount, it's a good idea to hire a professional appraiser. To find an appraiser in your area who specializes in placing a value on the kind of item you want to sell, go to the appraiser locator page on the website of the American Society of Appraisers at *www.appraisers. org/findappraiser.*

❗ Hot Tip

If you are really anxious to sell some of your assets, they may sell faster if you price them a little below market value.

Returning the assets that collateralize your debts to the creditors to whom you owe the debts is another way to reduce the amount of money you are spending each month. If you do, the creditors will sell the assets and then apply the sales proceeds to the outstanding balances on the debts. However, if any of the assets don't sell for enough to pay the full amount that you owe on a debt, your creditors can look to you to pay the deficiency.

✋ Red Alert!

If you sell an asset that you are still paying on and it does not sell for enough to pay off the outstanding balance on your debt, you'll have to pay the balance due (the deficiency) to complete the sale.

If the amount of the deficiency you owe is not substantial, the creditor may be willing to forgive it, which means that you won't have to pay the money. The same is true if the creditor decides that it will be difficult if not impossible to collect the deficiency from you given the state of your finances.

Negotiate Lower Payments with Your Creditors

One way to reduce your monthly spending and keep up with your debts is to ask your creditors to let you reduce the amount of money you must pay them each month. You may ask them to do this on a permanent basis or just on a temporary basis depending on your situation. There are several options your creditors have to allow you to reduce the amount you have to pay to them:

- They can lower your monthly payments by increasing the number of months you have to pay off your debts. By spreading out your debt over a longer period of time, the amount of your monthly payments on the debt will go down.

- They can decrease the interest rates on your debts.

- They can allow you to make interest-only payments for a while.

Also, if you are behind on any of your debts, your creditors may agree to let you pay off the amounts that are past due over time rather than in lump sums.

Some up-front homework is essential before you contact your creditors about reducing your monthly payments. As part of that homework, complete the Debt Analysis Worksheet in Figure 1.3. Among other things, the form asks you to organize your debts according to whether they are secured debts, priority unsecured debts, or unsecured debts. It's important to make this distinction because you have the most to lose if you do not pay your priority unsecured debts and your secured debts. Therefore, if you have fallen behind on any of those debts, they are the ones that you need to negotiate first. Assuming you have any money to spare after you have contacted these creditors, you should then contact the creditors that are associated with your less important debts. The "Understanding Which Debts Are Most Important" section explains the reasons for this advice.

Once you've filled in the worksheet, review your budget to determine exactly how much you can afford to pay on each debt, starting first with the ones that are most important so that you know what concessions you need from your creditors.

FIGURE 1.3. Debt Analysis Worksheet

Use this form to help you prepare to contact your creditors to negotiate lower debt payments with them.

Name of Creditor/Outstanding Balance/Monthly Payment/Interest Rate/Secured or Unsecured/ Amount Past Due

■ Secured Debts

_____

_____

_____

■ Priority Unsecured Debts

_____

_____

_____

■ Other Unsecured Debts

_____

_____

_____

_____

Understanding Which Debts Are Most Important

Although you should always try to keep up with all of your debts, sometimes it may be impossible because you owe too much relative to your income. If this is the case, it is imperative that you pay your secured and your priority unsecured debts before your other debts. That's because of the potential consequences you face if you don't pay those debts.

Here are examples of secured debts and what's likely to happen if you don't pay them:

- Mortgage. You will lose your home in a foreclosure.

- Home equity loan or line of credit. You may lose your home.

- Car loan. Your car will be repossessed.

- Other secured loans. You will lose the assets that collateralize the loans.

 Red Alert!

All it may take for your car to be repossessed is just one missed car payment. Adding insult to injury, you may not receive advance notice that the repossession is about to happen nor be given an opportunity to get caught up on your loan in order to avoid the loss of your car.

Here are examples of unsecured debts that you should treat as top priorities and what might happen if you don't keep up with them:

- Your rent. You will be evicted.

- Child support obligation. Your state's Child Support Enforcement Agency may try to collect the payments that are past due by garnishing (taking) your wages, putting liens on some of your assets, seizing the funds in your bank account, canceling your driver's or professional license, or intercepting (taking) your state and federal tax refunds, among other things. Also, the parent to whom you are supposed to be paying child support may hire a private child support collection agency to collect the money that you owe.

- Federal income taxes. The IRS may put a tax lien on one or more of your assets, take some of your assets (including the money in your bank account), and/or garnish your wages.

- Property taxes. The taxing authority may put a lien on your real estate, and if you don't pay your tax debt, the taxing authority will take your property, eventually auction it off, and then apply the sale proceeds to the debt. If any balance remains on your tax debt, the taxing authority will expect you to pay it.

- Federal student loans. When you fall too far behind on your student loans, the full amount of the outstanding loan balances—not just the past due amounts—will be due in full. To collect those balances, your federal tax refunds may be seized and applied to the debts (your state tax refunds may be seized, too, depending on your state), your wages may be garnished, you may be denied a professional license, you will be ineligible for receiving any more federal financial aid (even if you are applying for aid on behalf of your college-age child), and you may lose your eligibility for other types of federal loans, such as a loan from the Federal Housing Administration or the Veterans Administration.

Less important debts. Examples of your least important debts include unsecured debts such as credit card debts, past due medical bills, and the money you may owe to your attorney, certified pulic accountant, or some other professional. When you don't pay these kinds of debts, some of your creditors may sue you at some point, assuming they decide that you owe them enough to merit the time and expense of a lawsuit and assuming you are not judgment-proof. Being *judgment-proof* means that you have no assets that a creditor can take if it wins its lawsuit and that your state does not allow wage garnishment. (Pennsylvania, South Carolina, and Texas do not permit wage garnishment.) When your wages are garnished as a result of a lawsuit, the court issues an order requiring your employer to take a set amount of money out of your paychecks in order to pay whatever amount of money the court decides you must pay the creditor who filed the lawsuit and won.

If any of your unsecured creditors decide not to sue you, they will write off your debt as uncollectible and you'll probably never hear from them again. However, the fact that your debts were written off may show up as damaging information in your credit histories. It will depend on whether the creditors report that information to one or more of the credit reporting agencies.

> **❗ Hot Tip**
>
> If you file for bankruptcy, most of your unsecured debts, but not your priority unsecured debts, will be discharged, or wiped out.

Consolidate Your Debts

Debt consolidation involves using new debt to pay off old debt. When you owe too much to your creditors, it can be a good way to lower the total amount of money that you have to pay on your debts each month. However, it's not a smart move unless the following guidelines are met:

- The total amount that you must pay each month on the new consolidated debt is less than the combined amount that you are currently paying on all of the debts that you would pay off.

- The interest rate on the new debt is lower than the rates on the debts that you would pay off.

- When you consolidate, you don't trade fixed-rate debt for variable-rate debt. When a debt has a variable rate, the rate is pegged to another interest rate, such as the prime rate as published in *The Wall Street Journal.* Therefore, when that other rate goes up, the interest rate on your debt goes up, too, and when that other rate goes down, your rate goes down, as well. Unfortunately, there is no way to predict which direction your interest rate will move. Worst-case scenario: While you are paying off a variable-rate debt, its interest rate will increase so much that you will end up paying more on that debt than what you were paying before on each of the debts that you consolidated.

■ You can pay off the new consolidated debt within a three- to five-year period (the amount of time you would have to pay off the debt if you filed a Chapter 13 reorganization bankruptcy), and you are committed to not taking on any new debt until you do.

There are several ways to consolidate your debts:

Transfer your credit card balances. Transferring higher interest credit card debt to a card with a lower rate of interest is a quick and easy way to consolidate. However, don't make such a transfer unless you understand all of the terms of credit associated with it. For example, be clear about how long the lower rate lasts. If it will increase eventually, be aware of what the new rate will be. Also, make sure you understand the amount of the balance transfer fee and any other fees you may have to pay, and be clear about the method the credit card company will use to calculate the minimum amount you must pay each month on the transferred debt. The adjusted balance or average daily balance methods are best. Avoid transferring debt to a credit card that uses the two-cycle average daily balance method.

Use a cash advance from one of your credit cards. Another quick and easy debt consolidation method is to get a cash advance from one of your credit cards that is large enough to pay off the balances on your other credit cards. (You also can use a credit card cash advance to pay off other kinds of debts, too.) However, because most cash advances have very high interest rates, this method is usually not a wise way to consolidate your debt.

Red Alert!

Never transfer credit card debts to another card if the rate on that card will eventually be as high or higher than the current rates on the credit card debts you want to transfer, unless you are sure that you can pay off the transferred debt before the higher rate kicks in.

Use a bank loan. If you consolidate debt using the proceeds from a bank loan, it may be a loan that your bank is marketing as a debt consolidation loan or it may be a home equity loan (or line of credit). Or, you may obtain a new mortgage that is large enough to pay off the balance on your existing mortgage and to pay off some of your other debts, as well. Here is an overview of how each kind of loan works:

- Debt consolidation loan. This kind of loan may be secured or unsecured. A secured debt is a debt that you have collateralized (guaranteed payment on) by letting the lender put a lien on one of your assets. When a debt is collateralized and you don't pay it, the lender can take the asset you used as collateral. An unsecured debt is one that you simply promise to repay. In other words, you have not secured it with an asset that you own. If your finances are in bad shape, and especially if you want to borrow a significant amount of money, the lender will probably require that you collateralize your debt consolidation loan. As a result, if you don't keep up with the loan payments, you'll lose the collateral.

- Home equity loan. Getting a home equity loan involves borrowing against the amount of equity (the difference between what your home is worth now—its market value—and the outstanding balance on your mortgage) that you have in your home and letting the lender put a lien on your home. The lien entitles the lender to take your home if you fall too far behind on your loan payments.

 Red Alert!

Most reputable lenders will not allow you to borrow any more than 80 percent of your home's equity. If a lender encourages you to borrow more than that amount, don't do business with that lender. The lender is probably gambling that if you borrow more than 80 percent, you won't be able to keep up with your loan payments, and the lender will end up with your home.

Refinance your home and get cash out This debt consolidation method involves getting a new mortgage that is larger than the outstanding balance on your current mortgage. The lender will use the proceeds from the new loan to pay off your existing mortgage and then will either issue you a check for the difference or pay off some of your other debts for you using the extra funds. Consolidating debt using this method does not make sense in the following cases:

- If you've been paying on your current mortgage for more than 10 years, assuming you've got a 30-year mortgage. The reason is that in the early years of a mortgage, your monthly payments primarily go toward paying interest on the loan, but once you've been paying on your mortgage for at least 10 years, you will have begun whittling down the amount of the loan principal, too. Therefore, each month that you make a loan payment, the closer you will be to paying off your mortgage and the more equity you will have in your home. However, if you refinance your mortgage once you've begun paying on principal, you'll lose all of your equity and you'll have a brand-new mortgage to start paying off.

- If your new loan payments will be larger than your payments are now. This could be true depending on how much you still owe on your current mortgage, the interest rate on the new mortgage, and the amount of extra money you want to borrow.

- If you are trading a conventional mortgage for an interest-only mortgage. The problem with an interest-only mortgage is that although your payments on the new loan during the interest-only period (5 or 10 years usually) will be relatively low, they will skyrocket once the interest-only period ends and you're required to start paying on the loan principal, too. If you can't keep up with your mortgage payments once you have to begin paying interest and principal, you will be at risk of losing your home.

- If you are trading a fixed-rate mortgage for one with a variable rate. Depending on how much the rate increases on your new loan, your mortgage payments could end up being higher than the payments were on your old mortgage, and eventually the payments could become unaffordable.

Borrow against your life insurance policy or from your 401(k) retirement plan. Getting a loan from your whole life insurance policy—a type of policy that has a savings component that can grow in value over time—or borrowing from your 401(k) plan are two other debt consolidation options. Although there are no applications to fill out or credit checks to go through, and even though you'll receive the loan proceeds relatively quickly, there are some serious potential drawbacks associated with each:

- When you borrow against the cash value of the policy, you don't ever have to repay the loan, and if you do, you don't have to adhere to any sort of set payment schedule. However, if you die before you have repaid the loan, the outstanding balance will be deducted from the policy proceeds that are paid to the beneficiary of your policy—your spouse or partner, probably. As a result, that person will receive less money. This would be a problem if your beneficiary needs the full amount of the policy proceeds to help pay his or her bills after your death.

- If you are employed, you may be participating in a 401(k) retirement plan. (If you're employed by a nonprofit organization, you may be contributing to a 403(b) plan, which is similar to a 401(k) plan.) Although the purpose of the plan is to help you finance your retirement, most plans allow you to borrow from your 401(k) account before you reach retirement age. Usually, you can take out up to 50 percent of your account's value or $50,000, whichever is less, and you'll be expected to repay the funds within five years. However, if you don't repay the full amount of the loan within this time period, and assuming you were younger than 59½ when you got the loan, you'll have to pay a 10 percent penalty on whatever is unpaid. Also, the IRS will treat the balance due as earned income, which means that you could end up owing considerably more to the agency on April 15 compared to what you would owe if you had repaid the loan in full by the deadline. Furthermore, if you can't afford to pay your tax debt, the IRS will use its considerable powers to collect the money that you still owe. Meanwhile, your tax debt will be growing rapidly due to interest and penalties.

 Red Alert!

If you can't afford to pay the IRS what you owe, you can file for bankruptcy to prevent the IRS from garnishing your wages or putting a lien on one or more of your assets. How- ever, you cannot use bankruptcy to discharge your tax debt. In other words, you will eventually have to pay it.

Borrow money from someone you know. Borrowing the money that you need to consolidate your debts from a friend or family member may seem like a great option—no loan application to fill out, no credit check, and probably no loan interest and penalties to pay—however, if you can't repay the loan, your relationship with the lender may be ruined.

Get Help from a Reputable Nonprofit Credit Counseling Agency

If you are confused about the best way to deal with your debts and want help evaluating your options, schedule an appointment with

---

❗ Hot Tips

Don't borrow money from a friend or family member who has a hard time telling you no, especially if you know that she does not have a lot of money. That person may agree to loan you money even if she really can't afford to, and as a result may develop financial problems; or your friend or family member may have to do without something she really needs.

If you borrow money from someone you know, it's a good idea to secure the loan by giving the lender a lien on one of your assets so that he will become a secured creditor. That way, if you file for bankruptcy before you've repaid the loan, the lender will be better positioned to get his money back through your bankruptcy. Most unsecured creditors receive nothing in a bankruptcy.

Red Alert!

Beware! Some for-profit companies choose names in order to appear like they are nonprofits.

a nonprofit credit counseling agency. (The agency can also help you develop a budget for your household.) Be sure to work with a reputable nonprofit agency—many agencies (especially for-profit agencies) are not on the up-and-up. They prey on consumers who are anxious to find a solution to their money troubles by charging a lot for their services, which are often of minimal value, and they might give those consumers misleading and even dangerous advice about how to get out of debt. As a result, consumers who work with these kinds of agencies often end up worse off than they were before. Figure 1.4 provides advice for finding a nonprofit credit counseling agency you can trust.

Counselors who work for reputable nonprofit credit counseling agencies are trained and certified to help consumers with their debt problems. The counselor will review your budget (or help you to set one up) to determine the expenses you can cut, and will advise you about other

! Hot Tip

The website of the U.S. Bankruptcy Trustees at *www.usdoj.gov/ust/eo/bapcpa/ccde* provides a directory of federally approved credit counseling agencies. However, being federally approved is no guarantee that an agency will provide you with the services you need at a price you can afford.

steps you should take to get out of debt and to avoid bankruptcy. Among other things, the counselor may suggest that you participate in a debt management plan (DMP) that the agency will set up for you. If you agree to a DMP, the counselor will contact each of your unsecured creditors to try to get them to agree to let you pay less on your debts each month than you are currently obligated to pay. Once the counselor gets agreements from as many of those creditors as possible and you sign off on your DMP, each month you'll send the amounts you've agreed to pay to each of those creditors to the counseling agency, which in turn will pay the creditors.

After you've identified one or more credit counseling agencies that you might want to work with, contact your state's attorney general's office and your local better business bureau. Find out if either of them have any complaints on file about the agency. The phone number for your state's attorney general's office is located in the Blue Pages of your local phone book, and you can find the phone number for your area's better business bureau in your local business pages.

> **Red Alert!**
>
> Credit counseling agencies will not negotiate with your secured creditors. Also, they may not negotiate tax debts that you cannot discharge (wipe out) through bankruptcy either.

LOANS TO AVOID

When you are desperate to stay out of bankruptcy, you might learn about loans that sound like the answer to your prayers. Be careful! Most loans that sound too good to be true will make your financial situation worse, not better. Examples of these kinds of loans follow.

Advance Fee Loans

As you may have guessed from its name, to get this kind of loan you must pay the lender money up front, something no reputable lender will do (although a reputable lender may ask you to pay an application fee). The risk of paying an advance fee lender money up front is that it might take the money and disappear. And, if it does give you a loan, the loan will have a very high interest rate and expensive fees.

FIGURE 1.4. Tips for Finding a Good Credit Counseling Agency

Here are some questions to ask credit counselors working for the nonprofit credit counseling agencies you are considering hiring. Analyzing their answers to these questions will help you to determine which one will do the best job for you, and will help ensure that you do not agree to work with a for-profit agency that is trying to disguise itself as a nonprofit.

- **Is your agency federally approved?** Being federally approved is not a 100-percent guarantee that an agency will do a good job for you, but you can use the question as an initial screening tool because being federally approved means that the agency has met certain minimum federal standards.

- **What services do you offer?** The agency you work with should provide debt counseling, should offer classes on such personal finance topics as budgeting, saving, and debt management, and should give you the option of participating in a DMP. Be sure to steer clear of organizations that push a DMP as your only or your best option for getting out of debt without first spending at least an hour analyzing your finances.

- **Do you offer free printed educational information about budgeting and other aspects of financial management?** Reputable organizations not only provide their clients with this information in the form of brochures, fact sheets, and/or workbooks, but they also offer free or low-cost financial management workshops. Avoid organizations that don't have any printed information or that charge for it.

- **In addition to helping me solve my immediate problem, will you help me develop a plan for avoiding problems in the future?** Good credit counseling agencies will.

- **What are your fees?** Most good, nonprofit credit counseling agencies charge very little for their services, and if your income is quite low, they may not charge you anything at all. Disreputable credit counseling agencies, on the other hand, often charge substantial fees for their services—either large up-front fees or many smaller fees over time. Before you agree to work with an agency or sign any paperwork provided by the agency, get a list of all of the fees you will be charged. Don't work with an agency that won't provide such a list.

Tips for Finding a Good Credit Counseling Agency continues on next page.

■ **If I decide to work with your agency, will I be provided a formal written contract to sign?** Don't work with a credit counseling agency that won't provide a contract. When you meet with a credit counselor, ask for a sample contract, and then take time to review it at your home or office. Make sure that the contract, includes all of the services the agency will provide to you, an itemized list of the cost of its services, and information on the duration of its services.

■ **What training and education do counselors at your agency receive? Are they accredited or certified by an outside organization?** It's best to work with an agency whose counselors are trained by a nonaffiliated party.

■ **How are counselors at this agency compensated?** Reputable credit counseling agencies either pay their counselors a salary or an hourly fee. Some agencies, however, pay their counselors according to the dollar value of the services the counselors convince consumers to buy. As a result, those counselors are little more than salespeople.

■ **Are the counselors at this agency licensed to offer your services in my state?** Many states license credit counseling agencies. Contact your state's attorney general's office to find out if your state is one of them. If it is, find out which government office does the licensing, and then contact that office to learn whether the credit counseling agency you are thinking about working with has an up-to-date license.

■ **How will this agency keep my personal and financial information confidential and secure?** If you get no answer to this question or if the answer you receive is not convincing, find another credit counseling agency to work with.

■ **Can I see the agency's IRS approval of nonprofit status letter?** If the agency does not have such a letter or claims that it does not know where the letter is, it may be because the agency is a for-profit business that is posing as a nonprofit. Steer clear!

Finance Company Loans

Finance companies are in the business of giving high-interest loans to consumers who can't qualify for a regular loan from a bank, savings and loan, or credit union. Although many finance companies are totally forthcoming about the terms of their loans, others are not. Instead, they bury critical details about their loans in the fine print in their loan agreements. As a result, unless you read that fine print before you sign a finance company's agreement, you may not realize that you've given the company the right to take some of your household goods if you fall behind on your loan payments.

Car Title Loans

If your car is totally paid for, some lenders will loan you a small fraction of what it's worth. The loan will have a very high rate of interest, will be secured by your vehicle, and will probably have just a 30-day term—which means that if you can't repay the full amount of the loan at the end of the 30 days, the lender can take your car. However, the lender may allow you to roll over the loan for another month, and if you can't repay the loan at the end of the second month, you may be able to roll it over again. How many months you can roll it over is determined by your state's car title loan law. Once you've rolled over your loan the maximum number of times, the lender is entitled to take your car unless you pay everything that you owe to it.

Payday Loans

A payday loan is a very small loan, usually with an interest rate of at least 50 percent, that is made on a very short-term basis—from one payday to the next—by some finance companies, check cashing companies, and other nontraditional lenders. To get a payday loan, you give the lender a personal check for the amount of money you want to borrow plus the amount of the lender's fee, which is usually a percentage of the loan amount. You promise to repay the loan on your next payday. In return, the lender holds on to the check and gives you the amount of money you want to borrow. If you repay the loan when you receive your next paycheck, the lender gives you back your personal check. However, if you can't repay the payday loan, you can roll it over (renew it) until the following payday in exchange for paying the lender another fee. In fact, you can do that time after time after time. If you do, however, you'll dramatically increase the total cost of your loan because of all of the interest and fees you will pay.

Tax Refund Loan

A tax refund loan is a relatively small high-interest loan—no more than $5,000—that is made against your future federal income tax refund. Tax preparation firms, finance companies, check cashing companies, and even some car lenders and retailers make this kind of loan. To get a tax preparation loan you must pay the lender an up-front fee, which will increase the overall cost of the loan. When the IRS issues your tax refund, it will deposit the money in a special account set up by the tax refund lender. After deducting its fee from the amount of your refund, the lender will pay you whatever money may be left.

OTHER MISTAKES TO AVOID WHEN YOU HAVE TOO MUCH DEBT

Besides avoiding risky loans, there are other things you should never do when you are having problems paying your debts:

- Never write a bad check. Never write a check that you can't cover, gambling that by the time the check hits your bank, there will be enough money in your account to pay it. If you are wrong and your check bounces, the business to whom you wrote it may decide to press charges against you if you can't make good on the check. If you are prosecuted and found guilty, you may be given an opportunity to pay the amount of the check and all related fees, including the plaintiff's legal fees and expenses, but you may also be put on probation or sent to your county jail. Your punishment will depend on the laws of your state, on whether you've been found guilty of passing a bad check before, and on whether the court decides that you knowingly wrote a bad check or simply made an honest mistake.

- Never work with a debt negotiation firm. This kind of firm claims that it will contact your unsecured creditors—mostly credit card companies—to get them to agree to let you pay off your unsecured debts for between 10 percent and 50 percent of their outstanding balances. If you work with one of these firms, you will be instructed to stop paying the creditors that the firm has promised to contact and to begin sending your payments to the debt negotiation firm instead. In turn, the firm will promise to deposit your payments in a special account and use them to pay your creditors according to the terms of the agreements it negotiates with them. However, if you follow the instructions of the debt negotiation firm and it doesn't do what it has promised, your creditors won't get paid, the amount that you owe to them will increase due to late fees and interest, or they may turn your accounts over to debt collectors. And if you don't get control of the situation, some of the creditors may eventually sue for the money that you owe to them. Meanwhile, your credit histories will show that you've defaulted on the debts.

  Even if a debt negotiation firm does what it promises to do, you will probably be charged a substantial amount of money for its services. Most likely, you'll have to pay a steep initial fee, a monthly service fee, and a final fee, which will be a percentage of the money that the firm will claim it has saved you.

In this chapter, you gained essential information about what to do when you are having trouble paying your debts and your day-to-day living expenses and want to avoid bankruptcy. You also learned how a credit counseling agency can help if you want professional assistance evaluating your debt management options, and you learned how to find a good agency. You also got the lowdown on loans to avoid when you are looking for a solution to your debt problems, and you found out about other actions you should avoid taking because they will cause your financial situation to go from bad to worse.

The next chapter of this book deepens your knowledge of debt management by explaining the risks of not paying your most important financial obligations such as your mortgage or rent, your car loan, and your federal taxes, and by discussing what you can do to try to avoid the very serious consequences of defaulting on such debts.

Debts That Merit Your Special Attention

As you learned in chapter 1, certain debts are more important than others because of the serious consequences you may suffer if you don't pay them. These debts include secured loans such as a car loan and a mortgage, and some unsecured debts such as federal income taxes, federal student loans, and court-ordered child support. If you can't afford to pay everything that you owe, it's critical that you do everything you can to keep up with your most important debts—even if that means not paying some of your other debts.

This chapter underscores that advice by explaining the risks you take when you don't pay the debts that belong at the top of your to-be-paid pile. It also provides specific advice and information for how to deal with each of those debts and explains when filing for bankruptcy is your best alternative. In addition, this chapter tells you what will happen if you don't keep up with your rent and utilities. It will guide you through the eviction process and lay out your options for avoiding an eviction and for keeping your utilities on.

MANAGING YOUR PAST DUE CAR LOAN

Having your car repossessed would be disastrous if you need it to get to and from work and to take care of your family's needs—driving your kids to school, going grocery shopping, getting to and from the doctor's office, and so on. However, even if you miss just *one* loan payment, your car may be repossessed without any advance notice whatsoever from the lender or any opportunity to get caught up on your past due payments. So, aside from keeping up with your car payments, what can you do to try to avoid a repossession?

Your Options for Avoiding Repossession

You have several options available to you to keep your car from getting repossessed:

- Contact your lender to see if you can get the lender to agree to lower the amount of your monthly payments. Review your budget first so you know exactly how much you can realistically afford to pay. For example, you may decide that you need to make interest-only or reduced payments for a period of time (the lender probably won't agree to anything longer than three months) while you are trying to get back on your financial feet, or you may decide that you need to extend the term of your car loan in order to permanently reduce the amount of your monthly payments. If the lender agrees to your request, get all of the terms of your agreement in writing before you begin paying on the agreement. Depending on exactly what you and the lender decide, the written agreement should indicate the following items:

  - The start and end dates of the agreement
  - The amount you must pay to the lender each month
  - The applicable interest rate
  - When each of your payments will be due
  - The penalty for being late with a payment

– How you must pay the difference between what you will pay each month under the new agreement and what you would have paid under your previous agreement with the lender. For example, the lender may want you to pay this difference in a

> ## ❗ Hot Tip
>
> Some car loan agreements give you the right to avoid repossession by paying the amount of your loan arrearage in a lump sum, that is, by paying the total amount that is past due.

lump sum once the period of reduced payments ends, or it may allow you to pay the amount over time or at the end of your loan.

– How you must make the payments you may have already missed. The lender may agree to let you pay them in a lump sum at the end of your loan or may require you to pay the past due amount over time.

– When you will be considered to have defaulted on the agreement and the consequences of defaulting.

 Red Alerts!

Most car lenders won't give you any breaks on your car loan if you've already fallen behind on the payments. Even so, it's a good idea to ask the lender for what you need to hold on to your car, because there's always a chance that your lender will agree to your request.

Some car loan agreements include a provision that entitles the lender to *call* the loan under certain conditions. If your loan is *called*, you'll either have to pay the loan's outstanding balance in full immediately or you'll lose your car.

■ Sell your car before you miss any car payments and apply the sale proceeds to the balance due on your loan. This is a good option if you don't need a car and you can sell it for more than what you still owe on it. Or, if you know that your vehicle will sell for less than what you owe to the lender, you'll be able to come up with the difference. If you can't, you won't be able to complete the sale (meaning you can't transfer title of the car to the buyer).

■ Find someone to assume your car loan, if your loan agreement allows an assumption. The person who assumes your loan will take possession of your car in exchange for agreeing to finish paying off the note.

🖐 Red Alert!

Your lender may be unwilling to take you off of the note if you find someone to assume your car loan. If that's the case, and you go through with the assumption anyway and the person who takes over your loan misses a car payment, the lender can look to you for the money. If your former car is repossessed and auctioned off, the lender can hold you responsible for paying the loan deficiency if the car sells for less than the loan's outstanding balance.

■ Give your car back to the lender in a voluntary repossession. Although a *voluntary repossession* means that a repo man won't take your car, the process that follows will be much like a regular repossession. (That process is described in the next section of this chapter.) However, because you willingly returned your car to the lender, you won't have to reimburse the lender for the cost of taking it from you, although you will still have to pay the lender for the costs it incurs while storing your car and auctioning it off.

❗ Hot Tip

Before you give your car back through a voluntary repossession, try to get the lender to give you some concessions. For example, maybe the lender will agree not to hold you liable for any loan deficiency that may exist after your car is auctioned off, or not to report the voluntary repossession to any of the credit reporting agencies (CRAs) to which it reports. If the lender gives you any concessions, try to get them in writing before you give back your car.

- File for bankruptcy. Bankruptcy will halt the repossession your lender may be planning. If you file for Chapter 13 bankruptcy, you can keep your car by paying off the outstanding balance on your car loan during the three to five years that your Chapter 13 bankruptcy will last. Chapters 6 and 9 discuss the Chapter 13 bankruptcy process.

How a Repossession Works

If you are not able to avoid a repossession, your auto lender will probably hire an auto repossession firm to take your car. It can be taken at any time: at night, during the day when you're at work, while you're shopping in a mall, at a doctor's appointment, visiting your child's school, etc.

 Red Alert!

A repo man is legally entitled to come onto your property to take your car, and can even enter your garage assuming it's not locked.

If you see the repo man who has arrived to take your car, you can do the following:

- Tell the repo man to go away and to leave your vehicle alone. The repo man may do that, but you can expect him to show up again sometime later to take your car. He will get it eventually. If the repo man leaves without your car, contact a consumer law attorney immediately. The attorney may find problems with your car loan paperwork that can be used to stop the repossession and maybe help you hold on to your car. Also, at the meeting, you can discuss using bankruptcy to stop the repossession.

- Let the repo man take your car, but not before getting his business card. If he doesn't have one, ask for his name, phone number, and the name of the company he works for, and then contact a consumer law attorney right away. Share with the attorney all of the information the repo man provided to you. Also, ask the repo man for a copy of any legal documents he may have related to the repossession. If he gives you any, share them with your attorney, too. The attorney may find problems in the documents that can be used to get your car returned to you.

Do not try to physically prevent the repo man from taking your car—if you do, you could be arrested and charged with assault. Also, if someone who claims to be a law enforcement official or some other kind of government official accompanies the repo man, ask to see that person's identification. Although he could be there to serve you with a court order requiring you to turn your car over to the repo man, it's unusual for a government official to participate in a repossession. If the person claiming to be a government official cannot provide you with proof of his official status, then he may be violating the federal Fair Debt Collection Practices Act by pretending to be someone else in order to intimidate you into letting the repo man have your car. Get in touch with a consumer law attorney immediately.

If the Repo Man Violates Your Legal Rights

The previous section discussed some ways that a repo man might violate your repossession rights. Other ways he might be out of legal bounds are if he threatens you with violence, becomes physical with you in any way, or uses profanity or bullying tactics when speaking to you.

If you believe that a repo man has violated your legal rights, call the police right away. Then, as soon as the immediate problem has been resolved, contact a consumer law attorney.

❗ Hot Tip

If there are any witnesses to the repossession of your car, get their names and contact information. Your attorney may want to talk to them if you sue the auto repossession firm that employs the repo man; and if your case goes to trial, the witnesses may be called to testify. Also, maintain a detailed record of all your repossession-related expenses—for example, any expenses you incurred getting to and from work or getting your kids to and from school without your car, your repossession-related legal expenses, any medical bills you might have incurred because you developed emotional problems as a result of the repossession, and so on. If you sue and win your lawsuit, the court may order the auto repossession firm to reimburse you for those expenses.

What Happens Once Your Car Is Repossessed

After your car has been repossessed, the lender will auction it off. In most states, you must be given advance notice of when and where the auction will take place so that you can try to buy your car back if you want.

If you don't buy back your car the lender will sell it to someone else, and the auction proceeds will be applied to the outstanding balance on your loan, your loan delinquency fees, and to all of the costs that the lender incurred repossessing, storing, and selling your car. It's very likely, however, that your car will not sell for enough to cover the total amount of these costs, which means that you'll have to pay the deficiency. If the lender agrees to let you pay the deficiency over time, get the terms of your agreement in writing before you pay the lender any money. Among other things, the agreement should address the amount of your installment payments, when the agreement begins and ends, the rate of interest that will apply to the deficiency, whether you must make a balloon payment at the end of the agreement, when you'll be considered in default of the agreement, and the consequences of a default.

How to Keep Your Car After It Has Been Repossessed

Depending on the state you live in, after your car is repossessed but before the date that it's scheduled to be auctioned off, you may be able

! Hot Tip

If your car lender insists that you pay the deficiency in a lump sum, *don't* do this if paying it means that you won't have the money you need to cover your mortgage or rent obligation, to buy your family groceries, or to keep your utilities running. The deficiency will be an unsecured debt, which means that if you don't pay it, the lender will have to take you to court to try to collect the debt. If the amount of the deficiency is not large, the lender may decide it's not worth the cost and hassle of a lawsuit. Meanwhile, if your finances improve, you may be able to pay the deficiency; but if they continue to deteriorate and you file for bankruptcy, you may be able to get the debt discharged.

to get your car back by redeeming your car or reinstating your car loan. Here is how each option works:

Redeem your car. When you redeem your car, you buy it back by paying in one lump sum the outstanding balance on your car loan, all late fees, and all of the lender's repossession costs within a certain period of time. The amount of time will depend on the law in your state, assuming your state gives you the right to redeem.

Reinstate your car loan. If you agree to reinstate your loan, you must begin paying on it according to the terms of your original loan agreement. However, before you can reinstate the loan, you and the lender must reach an agreement regarding how you will pay the amount that is past due on the loan as well as all of the late fees that you owe and all of the lender's repossession costs. The lender may require that you pay everything in a lump sum, or it may allow you to pay it over time by adding a little extra money to each of your loan payments or by adding the amount to the end of your loan.

MINIMIZING THE IMPACT OF A PAST DUE MORTGAGE

There is little worse than losing your home in a foreclosure. Just imagine having to give up what is probably your most valuable asset, losing all of the equity that you've built up in your home, and having to uproot your family. (Your equity is the difference between what your home is currently worth and what you still owe on your mortgage.) Furthermore, a foreclosure will do serious damage to your credit histories and to your credit scores.

❗Hot Tip

Contact a house counseling agency approved by Housing and Urban Development (HUD) if you want help figuring out how to avoid a foreclosure. A counselor with this agency will even contact your lender on your behalf. Go to *www.hud.gov/offices/hsg/sfh/hcc/hcs.cfm* to locate the HUD-approved housing counseling agency nearest you.

Obviously, you should do everything possible to avoid a foreclosure by following the advice in chapter 1, including living on a budget, reducing your spending, negotiating lower payments on your other debts, and consolidating your debts. However, if you take those actions and you still can't afford to keep up with your mortgage and catch up on the payments you've missed, it's time to take other steps. These steps may include the following:

- Contact the loss mitigation or workout department of your mortgage lender or mortgage servicer to discuss possible ways for you to pay the arrearage on your mortgage. The arrearage is the amount of your loan that is past due. (Most national mortgage lenders contract with mortgage service companies to service their loans—these companies collect and process your monthly mortgage payments. If a mortgage service company is managing your loan, you must negotiate with it, not with your lender.) Possible options include paying the arrearage over time by adding a portion of the past due amount to each of your future mortgage payments or paying it as a lump sum at the end of your loan.

> **❗ Hot Tip**
>
> If you are sure that the problems that caused you to fall behind on your mortgage are over, you may want to borrow the money you need to get caught up on the loan from a friend or relative. However, do not ask for the money unless you are absolutely sure that you can repay it and unless you and the friend or relative work out all of the details on the loan and put them in writing.

> **✋ Red Alert!**
>
> If the mortgage lender or servicer agrees that you can pay off your mortgage arrearage over time, you'll also have to pay each of your future mortgage payments as they come due. In other words, while you are paying off the arrearage, the monthly amount that you will have to pay on your home will be higher than the payments you agreed to make when you signed your mortgage agreement.

- Refinance your current mortgage. If mortgage interest rates are going down and if you have a lot of equity in your home, consider paying off your existing loan and your arrearage by getting a new, lower interest mortgage that will cost you less each month. However, don't refinance by trading a fixed-rate mortgage for one with an adjustable

> **▼ Hot Tips**
>
> If you refinance your mortgage, apply for a 10-year or 15-year mortgage rather than a traditional 30-year loan, assuming you can afford the payments on a short-term loan. This is especially good advice if you are close to retirement age, because it's best if you don't have to spend your retirement years burdened by a mortgage.

rate or for an interest-only loan. If interest rates start to rise, or once the interest-only period ends and you have to begin paying interest *and* principal on the new loan, you may not be able to keep up with the mortgage payments. As a result, you may end up right back where you started—worrying about a foreclosure.

- Rent out your home. Letting someone else live in your home as your tenant can be a good way to hold on to your home, assuming that you can rent it out for enough money to cover your mortgage payments and the cost of your homeowners' insurance and property taxes (if these costs are not included in your mortgage payments) and assuming that you can find a cheaper place to live. If you decide to pursue this option, carefully screen

 Red Alert!

Refinancing your home is an important decision with a lot of complicated variables to evaluate, especially when you are considering refinancing because you're experiencing money troubles and are concerned about the possibility of foreclosure. Therefore, it's a good idea to discuss what you are considering with a HUD-approved housing counseling agency or with a financial advisor who has given you good advice in the past. Otherwise, you may do something that will make your financial situation worse, and you'll lose your home in the end.

potential tenants, or better yet, use a rental agent. In exchange for a fee (e.g., your tenant's deposit), the rental agent will show your home, screen all rental applicants, provide you with information about the recommended applicants, and prepare a landlord-friendly lease for you and your tenant to sign.

- Find someone to assume your mortgage. When someone assumes your loan, that person agrees to take over all of your mortgage obligations. In return, you move out of your home. Not all mortgage agreements allow assumptions.

- Sell your home. Ideally, if you put your home on the market, it will sell for enough money to pay off everything that you owe on your mortgage. If it doesn't (or if you know before you put your home up for sale that it's not going to sell for enough to pay everything), ask your lender if you can *short sell* your home, or sell it for less. The lender or loan servicer may agree to a short sale to avoid incurring the cost of a foreclosure. If it does, ask the lender for a written statement saying that you won't owe the loan deficiency. You won't owe the deficiency because the lender will have concluded that getting some money now by letting you short sell your home is a better deal for it than going through the expense and the hassle of a foreclosure and auction of the home. However, in agreeing to let you short sell your home, the lender will protect itself by setting a minimum amount of money you must get for your home. If you can't sell it for at least that much, you won't be able to complete the sale, and a foreclosure will move forward.

❗ Hot Tip

Working with a real estate agent is essential when you are selling your home in order to avoid a foreclosure. This is because your mortgage lender or loan servicer will not put the foreclosure process on hold while you're trying to find a buyer for your home. There-fore, you'll need to find one as quickly as possible so you can complete the sale before your home's foreclosure date. The best way to do that is to work with a real estate professional rather than trying to sell your home yourself.

■ Give your home back to the mortgage lender or loan servicer. This is *not* a good option if you've built up a lot of equity in your home because you've been paying on your mortgage for a long time. When you give your home back—deed it back— you lose all of your equity. There are also other reasons, for trying to avoid this option. For example, when you deed back your home, your credit histories will be damaged nearly as much as if your home was foreclosed. Also, the lender or loan servicer will require you to pay for a home appraisal, and if the appraisal indicates that your home won't sell for enough to pay the outstanding balance on your mortgage and all of the costs associated with auctioning off your home, you will have to pay the deficiency. Under those circumstances, it's possible that the lender or loan servicer will refuse to let you deed back your home. Or it may agree to let you, and agree to let you pay less than the full amount of any deficiency, if the lender or loan servicer believes that by doing so it will end up with more money than it would get through a foreclosure.

 Red Alert!

You will probably get more money for your home if you sell it with the help of a real estate agent rather than letting the lender or loan servicer auction it off.

■ File for bankruptcy. If a foreclosure is imminent, you can stop it dead in its tracks by filing for bankruptcy. If you file a Chapter 13 reorganization bankruptcy, you'll get three to five years to pay the amount of your mortgage arrearage, all delinquency fees, and any foreclosure-related costs your mortgage lender or servicer may have already incurred; however, you'll have to make all of your future loan payments as they come due at the same time. If you file a Chapter 7 liquidation bankruptcy, you'll lose your home, but you won't have to pay the mortgage arrearage, delinquency fees, foreclosure costs, or any deficiency. Later chapters will go into more specifics about the different types of bankruptcy.

Get Legal Advice When You Are Facing Foreclosure

Run, don't walk, to the office of a consumer law attorney as soon as you begin having problems keeping up with your mortgage and are worried about the possibility of foreclosure. The attorney can do the following:

- Explain how foreclosures work in your state, including the timetable of events that will lead up to a foreclosure. Having this information is very important—unless you take certain actions by very specific deadlines, the foreclosure process will move forward and the options you have for avoiding the loss of your home will dwindle and become less attractive. Figure 2.1 discusses the two types of foreclosures and provides a general foreclosure timetable, although the timetable that applies to foreclosures in your state may be a little different.

- Help you assess your options for avoiding a foreclosure and determine which option is best.

- Negotiate with your mortgage lender or loan servicer if you don't feel up to the job.

- Review your loan paperwork for problems that your attorney may be able to use to stop the foreclosure process. For example, the attorney may discover that your mortgage lender does not have an enforceable lien on your home or that before you signed your loan paperwork, you were not provided all of the federally required disclosures, among other possible problems.

❗ Hot Tip

If you've already received paperwork related to the foreclosure of your home, your attorney can determine if the mortgage lender or loan servicer followed all of the required foreclosure procedures and sent you all of the required notices by the appropriate deadlines. Your attorney can use anything that may not have been done or may not have been done right to slow down the foreclosure process so that you have more time to figure out what to do about your mortgage loan.

FIGURE 2.1. The Foreclosure Process and Timeline

The foreclosure clock begins ticking as soon as you miss your first mortgage payment. However, the timeline for the foreclosure process depends on a number of factors, including whether foreclosures in your state are *statutory* or *judicial*. Contact your state's attorney general's office or the office of a consumer law attorney to find out which type of foreclosure applies in your state.

If foreclosures in your state are *statutory,* the lender or loan servicer does not have to go to court to get permission to take your home. Therefore, the foreclosure process will move forward fairly quickly once it begins. In contrast, in states where foreclosures are *judicial,* the process will be a lot slower because the lender or loan servicer will have to sue you in order to get the court's permission to take your home. From start to finish, a judicial foreclosure could take as long as a year.

Although the specific details of the foreclosure law in your state and maybe even the policies of your lender will affect how quickly you could lose your home, in general the foreclosure process works like this:

1. After your mortgage is between 45 and 60 days past due and assuming that you and your mortgage lender or loan servicer have not worked out a way for you to get caught up, your mortgage will be turned over to an attorney who will send you an official loan delinquency notice. The notice, which may be called a Notice of Default, a Notice of Delinquency, or something else, will tell you the exact amount of money you must pay to get current on your mortgage. Prior to receiving the delinquency notice, you will receive other notices from your mortgage lender or loan servicer asking you to either pay what you owe or to get in touch. Over time, the tone of the notices will grow increasingly serious and ominous.

2. Once your mortgage is at least 60 days past due, and assuming that you've still not worked out a way to pay the past due amount, you'll probably receive a Notice of Acceleration. (The name of the notice may be different depending on your state.) This notice marks the official start of the foreclosure process. It will inform you that you now owe the full amount of the outstanding balance on your mortgage, not just the past due amount, and it will indicate when and where your home will be auctioned off if you don't pay the balance.

The Foreclosure Process and Timeline continues on next page

3. When your mortgage is 90 to 100 days past due, you may still be able to avoid the loss of your home if the mortgage lender or loan servicer agrees to let you resume paying your mortgage according to the terms of your loan agreement. If it does, you'll also have to pay the full amount of your loan arrearage and all late fees, and you'll have to reimburse the lender or loan servicer for all of the foreclosure-related expenses it's already incurred.

4. Once your loan is 90 to 100 days past due, there is no time to dillydally around trying to decide what to do, especially if foreclosures in your state are statutory. You are quickly running out of time to avoid the loss of your home.

5. Sometime after you receive a Notice of Acceleration, your home will be sold in a public auction. The sale proceeds will be applied to the balance due on your mortgage loan, to all of the late fees that you owe, and to all of the lender's or loan servicer's foreclosure costs. If your home doesn't sell for enough to pay everything that you owe (and it probably won't because usually there are not a lot of bidders for foreclosed property), you will have to pay the deficiency.

6. After your home has been sold, if you have not already moved out, a sheriff, constable, or marshal will come to your home with a foreclosure notice telling you that you must move out right away. The law enforcement official will put your furniture and other personal belongings in storage, and you'll have to pay the storage fee before you can get them back. This will happen after the new owner of your home (probably your mortgage company) has filed a *forcible entry and detainer action* in your local justice of the peace court and has gotten an order from the judge to evict you.

DEALING WITH YOUR IRS TAX DEBT

If you don't pay the amount of federal taxes that you owe by April 15 of each year, the IRS will begin sending you a series of notices asking you to pay up. Each notice will sound more ominous than the previous one. You also may be contacted by a debt collector that the IRS has hired to collect past due taxes.

Getting on the wrong side of Uncle Sam by ignoring its notices or the efforts of a debt collector to contact you is dangerous, because the IRS has virtually unlimited powers to collect what you owe. Figure 2.2 reviews the consequences you may face if you do not deal with the issue. Also, the amount of your outstanding tax debt will rapidly increase due to interest and penalties.

If you can't afford to pay your taxes in a lump sum when they come due, your best option is to pay what you owe over time through an installment agreement with the IRS. Another option, if even an installment agreement will not work for you, is to ask the IRS to let you settle your debt for less through an *Offer in Compromise.* Both of these options are discussed in more detail below.

❗ Hot Tip

When you owe money to the IRS, dealing with the agency can be stressful and the forms you'll have to complete can be confusing. Under the circumstances, the assistance of an experienced certified public accountant (CPA) who specializes in tax issues will be invaluable.

Pay Your Tax Debt Through an Installment Plan

If you can't pay your federal tax debt by April 15, your first option should be to set up an installment payment plan by completing IRS Form 9465, Installment Agreement Request. You may have to fill out other forms, too, depending on how much you owe to the agency. When you fill out this form, you must indicate how much you want to pay on your tax debt each month and how you'll make your pay-

FIGURE 2.2. If the IRS Decides to Try to Collect Past Due Federal Taxes from You

If you fall behind on your federal taxes and you don't contact the IRS to work out a way to pay your debt, the agency may decide to use its considerable powers to collect the money that you owe. Factors that will help determine whether it will try to collect from you include the amount of your tax debt (the larger the debt, the more likely that the IRS will try to collect it from you), whether you own any assets that the IRS could take, and your overall financial condition, among other considerations.

If the IRS decides to collect from you, it may do the following:

■ Put a federal tax lien on your assets. You won't be able to sell, transfer, or borrow against your assets without working out a way with the IRS to clear up your tax debt. As long as you continue to owe money to the IRS, the tax lien will also apply to any assets you may acquire in the future.

■ Seize or levy your assets, including your home, other residences or buildings you may own, and undeveloped land. The IRS may also take your personal property such as your car, boat, RV, motorcycle, fine art, fine jewelry, and the like. It will sell the assets it seizes and apply the sales proceeds to your tax debt.

■ Seize the money in your bank and retirement accounts, your commissions, any rental, royalty, or dividend income you may be receiving, and the cash value of your life insurance policy. In addition, it may garnish your wages. The money that the IRS collects through these measures will be used to pay down your tax debt.

If the money that the IRS collects from you is not sufficient to pay the total amount of your tax debt, you will continue to owe the outstanding balance to the IRS. The IRS will monitor your financial situation so that it will know if your financial situation improves—for example, you start making more money, you acquire a new asset, or you receive an inheritance—so it can try to collect from you again.

Although the statute of limitations on a federal tax debt is 10 years, when the 10-year mark is drawing near, the IRS is likely to file a new lien so that it will get another 10 years to collect from you if you continue to owe a substantial amount of money to the agency.

Given the serious and possibly long-lived consequences of owing past due taxes to the IRS, when the IRS sends you a notice threatening to take steps to collect its money, get in touch with a tax CPA or with a bankruptcy attorney right away. Ignoring the IRS is foolhardy.

ments. The IRS prefers that you either have them automatically debited from your bank account or deducted from your paychecks.

If you owe less than $10,000, the IRS will automatically approve your installment request, assuming the following:

- Over the past five years, you either filed each of your tax returns on time or you filed extension requests asking for more time to file.

- Over the past five years, you paid any income taxes you owed to the IRS on time.

- The amount of your monthly payments is large enough that you'll pay the full amount of your tax debt plus interest and penalties within three years.

- The agency believes that you can actually afford to make the installment payments.

If you owe more than $10,000 but less than $25,000, the IRS will probably okay your request for an installment plan, assuming that the amount of the monthly payments you are proposing is large enough to wipe out your tax debt, plus interest and penalties, within five years. If you need more than five years to pay off the debt, you'll have to complete a second form called an IRS 433-A, Collection Information

🖐 Red Alert!

When the IRS reviews the information on your Collection Information Statement to figure out how much you can afford to pay in monthly installments, it won't consider all of your expenses, but only those that it deems *essential*. For example, it won't consider how much you are paying each month on your credit card payments or on any other unsecured debts you owe. Also, when it comes to your essential expenses, it may not recognize the amounts that you are actually spending on each of those expenses. Instead, it will assign a set amount for each of those expenses based on your family size and your area of the country. As a result, it's very likely that the IRS will decide that you can pay considerably more on your tax debt each month than you believe is realistic.

Statement, which asks you about your assets, your monthly expenses, and your income. The IRS will use the information on this form to determine how much it thinks you can afford to pay every month and to help it collect what you owe if you don't live up to the terms of your installment agreement.

If you owe the IRS more than $25,000, you'll have to complete both the Installment Agreement Request and the Collection Information Statement. The IRS may also require that you provide it with additional information about your finances.

When you use an installment plan to pay off your tax debt, it is essential that you do the following:

- Make each of your installment payments on time.

- Pay the full amount that is due on each payment.

- File all of your future tax returns on time while your installment plan is in effect (or file an extension to file on time), and pay the IRS the taxes that you owe on those returns by April 15.

If you don't comply with these requirements, the IRS will probably cancel your installment agreement and demand that you pay the full amount of your tax debt right away. If you don't, the agency will try to collect the money that you owe.

Make an Offer in Compromise

When you ask the IRS to accept your Offer in Compromise, you're asking to be allowed to settle your tax debt for less than its full amount. However, the IRS prefers that you pay your debt in installments, so it won't consider your offer unless, after reviewing your Collection Information Statement, it decides that at least one of the following applies to you:

- It's unlikely that the agency will ever be able to collect the full amount that you owe.

- The full amount of your tax debt shouldn't be collected because of a serious situation in your life—you've become permanently disabled, for example.

- You've proven to the IRS that you do not owe the money it wants you to pay.

Also, the IRS won't approve your Offer in Compromise unless you've filed all of your tax returns for the previous five years.

To make an Offer in Compromise, you must fill out IRS Form 656, which is actually a series of forms and worksheets. In addition, you must pay a $150 fee, and when you file your request, you must also make a partial, nonrefundable payment on your offer as a sign of good faith. If you propose paying the offer amount in a single lump-sum payment, your nonrefundable payment must be 20 percent of your total offer, and if you propose to pay the offer amount over time, the nonrefundable payment must be the first of those payments.

If the IRS approves your Offer in Compromise and you've promised to pay the settlement amount in a lump sum, the money will be due in full within 90 days. If the IRS agrees to let you pay the settlement amount over time through installments, you'll probably have 24 months to complete your payments. However, if you need more time, the IRS may let you pay the settlement amount in installments over whatever number of months still remains on the 10-year statute of limitations for collecting your tax debt. (The statute of limitations is the total amount of time that the IRS has to collect a past due tax debt.

 Red Alert!

Assuming you are paying your settlement amount in installments, during the years that your Offer in Compromise is in effect, you must file each of your tax returns (or extensions to file) by April 15, and you must pay any taxes you owe by April 15 of each year, as well. If you don't, the IRS can cancel your agreement and demand that you immediately pay the outstanding balance on the settlement amount in one lump sum. If you don't, the agency will take steps to collect the money from you.

While the agency is considering your request, it will put the statute of limitations on hold, and then once it decides what to do, the statute of limitations will start running again.)

If the IRS rejects your Offer in Compromise, it's probably because it believes that your offer was too low. If that's the case, the agency's rejection notice will tell you what would be an acceptable offer. If you can afford to pay that amount, then you may want to respond with a new Offer in Compromise. Another option is to appeal the agency's decision. While your appeal is being processed, the IRS cannot try to collect the money that you owe; however, interest and penalties on your tax debt will be accruing. If you are unhappy with the outcome of your appeal, you can request a judicial review of the agency's decision. You must request this within 30 days of the date that the IRS issues its decision regarding your appeal. If the court's review of your case ends in a decision that favors the IRS, you're out of options. (You can use the same appeals and judicial review processes if your request for an installment plan is denied.)

If the IRS wants you to make a bigger Offer in Compromise than you can afford, and if your appeal and request for a judicial review don't work out as you hoped, then it's time to consider bankruptcy. If you decide to file and your tax debt is less than three years old, you'll have to file a Chapter 13 reorganization bankruptcy. Otherwise, you may be able to file for Chapter 7, but it will depend on the outcome of something called the *means test*, which you'll learn about in chapter 6.

❗ Hot Tip

If you need help resolving a problem with the IRS, contact the office of the Taxpayer Advocate Service (TAS). This independent office within the IRS has responsibility for protecting taxpayers' rights. To request help from the TAS, fill out IRS Form 911, Application for Taxpayer Assistance Order. You can obtain this form at the IRS website at *www.irs.gov,* by calling 800-829-3767, or by visiting the IRS office closest to you. If you want to speak with a TAS representative, contact the TAS office in your state. For contact information, go to *www.irs.gov/advocate,* click on "Contact Your Advocate" and then on "View Local Taxpayer Advocates by State," or call 877-777-4778. The IRS must suspend certain kinds of collection actions while the TAS is trying to resolve your problem with the agency.

FIGURING OUT WHAT TO DO ABOUT YOUR PAST DUE STUDENT LOANS

When you sign a federal student loan agreement, you agree to begin repaying the loan as soon the loan's grace period expires, which is after you graduate from college or trade school or when you leave school without finishing your course of study. If you don't begin repaying the loan, or if you begin paying on the loan and then fall behind on your payments, at some point you will be considered in default. Exactly when you will be considered in default will depend on your particular type of federal student loan. For example, if the loan is part of the Federal Family Education Loan Program (FFELP) or the Direct Loan Program (DLP), you'll be in default when your loan is at least 270 days past due. If you have a Perkins Loan, you'll be in default if you miss just one payment.

As soon as you are in default, you will face serious consequences that go beyond the consequences that are associated with not paying most other kinds of unsecured loans. For example, unless you figure out a way to deal with your student loan debt, your federal income tax refunds may be seized, you will not be entitled to any additional federal student aid in the future (not even assistance that you apply on behalf of your children), and you may become ineligible for other types of federal loans, such as a mortgage from the Federal Housing Administration or a loan from the Veterans Administration. Furthermore, with one exception, you can't wipe out your student loan debt by filing for bankruptcy. The exception is if you qualify for a hardship discharge, but that's extremely difficult to get. Your financial situation must be very, very bad and you must be able to prove to the bankruptcy court that you made a good faith effort to pay your student

---

 Red Alert!

As a result of the 2005 changes to the federal bankruptcy law, loans that you obtain from a nongovernmental entity or from a for-profit organization to help finance your education are nondischargeable in bankruptcy, just like federal student loans. In other words, even though you've filed for bankruptcy, you'll still have to pay those debts when your bankruptcy is over.

loan debt before you filed. A bankruptcy judge will decide if you can get a hardship discharge after a hearing on the matter.

What You Can Do to Avoid Defaulting on Your Student Loan

If you are concerned about defaulting on your federal student loan, you may be able to catch up on your past due loan payments by pursuing one or more of the get-out-of-debt options that were discussed in the previous chapter. However, when it comes to dealing with a past due federal student loan, you have other options, including getting a loan deferment, forbearance, getting your loan cancelled, or filing for bankruptcy.

Deferments and forbearance. Getting your loan payments deferred and getting forbearance are two possible ways to avoid a default. Here are explanations of each option:

1. Loan deferment. When your loan is deferred, the lender or loan servicer agrees to suspend your loan payments for a limited period of time—no longer than three years. The theory is that the deferment period will give you an opportunity to get your finances in order (by finding a job, paying off other debts, and so on) so that when the deferment period ends, you'll be able to keep up with your student loan payments. However, depending on your particular type of loan, interest and penalties will accrue during the deferment period, which means that at the end of the period, you'll have a larger debt to repay than you did at the start of the period. It's up to your lender to determine the specific criteria you must meet to be eligible for a deferment. Usually, at least one of the following criteria will apply:
    - You are currently enrolled in an eligible school at least half-time.
    - You are unemployed.
    - You are serving in the military.
    - You are in a graduate fellowship program.

- You are disabled and participating in a rehabilitation training program.
- Having to pay on your loan will create an economic hardship in your life.

 Red Alert!

While you are waiting to find out if you qualify for a loan deferment, continue paying on your loan. Otherwise, the lender may determine that you've defaulted on the loan, and you'll be ineligible for a deferment and for forbearance as a result.

---

2. Forbearance. If your lender agrees to give you forbearance, your loan payments will be postponed or the amount of your payments will be reduced—usually for no more than three years. However, interest will accrue on your outstanding debt during the forbearance period.

Your lender or loan servicer may agree to give you forbearance because of any of the following:
- You are participating in a medical or dental internship or residency.
- Your monthly loan payments are equal to or greater than 20 percent of your gross monthly income (your income before taxes and other deductions).
- You cannot keep up with your loan payments because you're in poor health or because you have some other personal problem.

 Red Alert!

If you've already defaulted on your student loan, you are automatically ineligible for a loan cancellation.

Cancelling your loan. You can only cancel your federal student loan under very limited circumstances. Some examples include if you are totally and permanently disabled and can't earn a living, or if you are a full-time teacher. However, being unable to find a job post-school or mismanaging your finances are not acceptable reasons. For more information about getting a DLP loan cancelled, call the Direct Loan Servicing Center at 800-848-0979. If you want to get a FFELP cancelled, call the lender or agency that is holding your loan. If you want to cancel a Perkins Loan, contact the school that gave you the loan.

Filing for bankruptcy. Filing for bankruptcy is another option when you've fallen behind on your student loan and you can't use a deferment, forbearance, or a loan cancellation to avoid a default. If you file for Chapter 13, you'll get three to five years to pay off the amount that you still owe on your student loan principal, but you'll have to pay all accrued interest and late fees that are past due after you are out of bankruptcy. Also, while you are in a Chapter 13 bankruptcy, you'll have to continue to pay each of your loan payments as they come due. If you file a Chapter 7 liquidation bankruptcy, however, you won't have to pay on the loan while you are in bankruptcy, but you will have to resume making payments as soon as your bankruptcy is over. Again, I will go into much more detail about the types of bankruptcy in later chapters.

If You Default on Your Student Loan

All is not lost if you end up defaulting on your student loan because you may be able to *rehabilitate* the loan. When you rehabilitate a loan, you get current on it according to the terms of your original agreement with the lender. If you complete the rehabilitation, your loan will no longer be in default, you won't have to worry about the lender or loan servicer taking action to collect on the loan, the fact that you defaulted on your student loan will be removed from your credit reports, and you'll preserve your eligibility for additional student loans for yourself and for your children in the future.

To be able to rehabilitate your loan, you and your lender or loan servicer must reach an agreement on all of the following:

- The duration of the loan rehabilitation period. You will probably be required to make a certain number of consecutive loan payments of an agreed upon amount over a specific period of time. The number of payments and the duration of the rehabilitation period will depend on the particular type of federal student loan that is past due. At the end of the rehabilitation period, you'll have to resume making your regular loan payments.

- The amount of your loan payments during the rehabilitation period. Your payments will include your regular payment as well as a portion of your loan arrearage.

HANDLING YOUR CHILD SUPPORT PAYMENTS

When you get behind on your court-ordered child support obligation, you may not only jeopardize the well-being of your minor children, but you may also be putting yourself at risk for some very unpleasant consequences. For example, the parent to whom you owe the child support may ask the Child Support Enforcement (CSE) office in the state where the support court order was issued to help him or her collect your past due payments. If that happens, the office will contact you about getting caught up. If you can't afford to pay everything that you owe all at once, the CSE office may let you pay the debt in installments. In this case, however, the CSE office may put a lien on one of your assets in order to guarantee payment. As a result, your child support debt will become a secured debt.

If you can't work out a way to pay your past due child support, or if you ignore the efforts of the CSE office to contact you, it may decide to take one or more of the following actions. What it decides to do will depend in part on how much past due child support you owe, how long the money has been past due, and the policies of the state that ordered you to pay the support. The actions the CSE office may take include the following:

- Put a lien on your bank and/or investment accounts. Also, the funds in those accounts may be taken (*levied*) to pay your debt.

- Put a lien on some of your other assets so that you cannot borrow against them, sell them, or transfer them to someone else without paying your child support debt first.

- Seize some of your assets (but not your home or your car), sell them, and apply the proceeds to your debt.

- Garnish your wages, if wage garnishment is legal in your state. Pennsylvania, South Carolina, and Texas prohibit wage garnishment.

- Take the money you receive in an insurance settlement or as a result of a lawsuit or a workers' compensation claim that you may have filed.

- Take your state or federal tax refund.

- Turn your debt over to the IRS so it can try to collect what you owe in past due child support.

- Suspend or cancel your professional or driver's license.

- Sue you for the money that you owe.

- Put you in jail until you pay what you owe.

Instead of contacting the CSE office, the other parent of your minor children may decide to hire a private child support collection agency to collect the past due child support that you owe. He or she may hire such an agency because it tends to get faster results than the government or because contacting the CSE office has not yielded good results.

If you are contacted by a private child support collection agency, you will be given an opportunity to pay what you owe either in a lump sum or through installment payments. If you can't afford to pay what you owe all at once and are unable to work out the terms of an installment payment plan, the agency may sue you in order to get the court's permission to garnish your wages, put liens on some of your assets, or freeze some of your assets so that you can't do anything with them, among other things.

 Red Alert!

Some attorneys are in the business of help-ing parents collect the past due child support that they are owed. Attorneys who offer this service have at their disposal all of the same tools that a private child support collection agency can use.

AVOIDING AN EVICTION

If you are a renter, your monthly rent is an obligation that belongs at the top of your bills-to-be-paid list because you'll be evicted if you fall too far behind on your rent payments. The easiest way to try to avoid an eviction is to contact your landlord as soon as you know that you're not going to be able to pay your rent or as soon as you've fallen behind. Ask your landlord for a temporary reduction in your rent and/or if you can pay your past due rent over time by adding an additional amount to your future rent payments. If you've always paid your rent on time until now, your landlord may agree to what you've asked. Also, you're more apt to get what you've asked for if you're renting from a small landlord and you deal with one another directly rather than if you're renting from a large apartment rental company.

If your landlord agrees to the concessions you've asked for, get all of the terms of your agreement in writing so that down the road there will be no misunderstandings between the two of you regarding your agreement. Depending on the terms, the written agreement should address the following matters:

- The amount of the reduced payments

- The period during which you will make the reduced payments

- How you must pay the difference between the total amount of the reduced payments and what you should have paid

- How you will catch up on any rent payments that are past due: in a lump sum, by adding a little extra to each of your rent payments once the period of reduced payments ends, or by deducting the difference from your security deposit when you move out of your rental

- Whether you must pay the landlord an additional security deposit

- When you will be considered in default of the agreement and the consequences of a default

You may have other options for avoiding an eviction, including getting a roommate, terminating your lease, breaking your lease, subleasing your apartment, or letting someone assume your lease.

Getting a Roommate

Getting a roommate is an option assuming your lease allows you to have one. If it doesn't, you could explain to your landlord why you'd like a roommate. The landlord may give you the go ahead to help ensure a steady stream of income from your apartment and to avoid the expense and hassle of an eviction.

❗ Hot Tip

Before you get a roommate, read your lease so you are clear about any rights your landlord may have with regard to a roommate. For example, your landlord may have the right to approve the person you want to live with before that individual moves in. Your landlord may also have the right to cancel your existing lease and give you and your roommate a new lease listing the two of you as cotenants. As cotenants, you'll each have an equal responsibility for living up to the terms of the lease.

If you don't already have someone in mind to be your roommate, take time to think about the qualities you do and don't want in one. This exercise will help ensure that you end up sharing your space with someone who is compatible with you in terms of your lifestyle and personality. You should also ask each prospective roommate to complete a rental application. There are many sample rental applications on the Internet that you can use as is or can customize to your needs. Visit *www.ilrg.com/forms/rentlapp.html* and *www.legaldocs.com/rent-app_1.aspx* to see a few. It's also a good idea to run a credit check on whomever you are seriously considering as a roommate, so you can be sure that the person has a good financial track record. Also, contact that person's current landlord and references.

Once you've found a roommate, the two of you should spend some time discussing all of the practical details of living happily under one roof, such as who will take out the trash and how you will share responsibility for keeping your apartment clean and for mowing your lawn and for shoveling snow, assuming your landlord does not take care of those things. You should also discuss how the rent will be paid each month—for example, each of you writes a check to your landlord or your roommate pays you and then you pay your landlord—and so on. Put all of the terms of your relationship in a written agreement that both you and your roommate sign. You'll find some sample roommate agreements at *www.roommateclick.com/doc_links_sample_roommate.htm* and *www.tenantresourcecenter.org/pdf/roommate_agreement_form.pdf*.

Terminating Your Lease

Another option is to terminate your lease, assuming you have a month-to-month lease. When your lease is month to month, you can end it whenever you want as long as you give notice to your landlord as required in the lease.

Breaking Your Lease

Breaking your lease involves moving out before the term of your lease is up. However, even though you won't be living in your apartment anymore, if you break your lease, you are usually obligated to continue paying rent either until the term of the lease is up or until your

> **❗ Hot Tip**
>
> Read your lease before you break it so you will be clear about whether there is a specific process you must follow and what you will and won't be obligated to pay for.

landlord finds someone to move in to your apartment. Also, if you've already missed some of your rent payments by the time that you break the lease, your landlord will deduct the amount of the arrearage from your security deposit along with any late fees and other expenses your landlord is entitled to according to your lease. For example, your landlord is probably entitled to deduct the cost of repairing any damage you may have done to your apartment and the cost of advertising for a tenant to replace you.

Subleasing Your Apartment

When you sublease your apartment, you move out and someone else moves in and takes over your lease responsibilities. To pursue this option, your lease must either specifically allow subleasing or your landlord must give you permission to sublease. Take note: If your lease allows it, it probably requires you to get up-front permission from your landlord before you sublease. It may also give your landlord the right to approve or disapprove the person to whom you want to sublease.

There is a big drawback associated with subleasing—as long as your lease is in effect, you'll continue to be responsible for ensuring that all of your lease terms are met. This means that if the person who subleases falls behind on the rent or damages the apartment, your landlord can look to *you* to pay the past due rent and the cost of repairing the damage. One way to protect yourself from such problems is to require potential subtenants to complete a subleasing application.

Be sure to confirm that all of the information on the application is accurate and run a credit check on each applicant. Another way is to require the person you choose to move in to your apartment to sign a sublease agreement. The agreement should indicate the amount of the monthly rent, when the rent is due, the duration of the agreement, the amount of any security deposit your landlord may require the subtenant to pay, the process that must be followed if the subtenant wants to break the agreement, any penalties the subtenant would have to pay if the agreement is broken, and the consequences of not living up to the terms of the agreement.

Let Someone Assume Your Lease

This alternative is preferable to subleasing your apartment because when someone assumes your lease, your name is taken off the lease and the other person becomes legally liable for living up to all of the lease terms. Check your lease to see if it allows someone to assume it. If it doesn't, talk with your landlord about whether it's a possibility.

File for Bankruptcy

If you file for bankruptcy before an eviction has begun, your landlord can't begin the eviction process. However, if an eviction has already begun by the time that you file for bankruptcy, then the landlord can move forward.

 Red Alert!

When you file for bankruptcy, you'll have just 30 days after your bankruptcy begins to get caught up on your past due rent. If you can't come up with the money you need within the required time frame, you'll face eviction despite your bankruptcy. Therefore, filing may only give you a temporary reprieve from an eviction.

✋ Red Alert!

If you receive a "Notice to Vacate," moving out right away will not eliminate your obligation to pay your landlord all of the past due rent that you owe as well as any fees that your landlord may be entitled to. If you can't pay all of it, your landlord may sue you for the money after you move out.

If an Eviction Begins

Although the eviction process varies somewhat from state to state, generally it will work like this:

1. Once you've fallen too far behind on your rent, your landlord will send you either a "Notice to Pay," which gives you one last chance to avoid an eviction, or a "Notice to Vacate," which tells you that you must be out by a specific day. If you receive a "Notice to Pay," you may want to go ahead and pay the money, assuming you can come up with it, so that you don't have to make an emergency move and so you can avoid having an eviction in your credit histories. You will also buy yourself a little time to review your options for avoiding an eviction in the future and to pursue the options that make the most sense for you, assuming you believe that coming up with your rent each month is going to be an ongoing struggle.

❗ Hot Tip

If you receive a "Notice to Pay" and you disagree with the amount of money that the notice says you owe, contact your landlord in writing to dispute the amount. In your letter, clearly state why the amount is incorrect, indicate the correct amount, and include copies of any evidence you have that helps prove your point, such as cancelled checks, receipts, correspondence, and the like. After making a copy of the letter for your files, send it and copies of whatever documentation you have to your landlord via certified mail with a return receipt requested.

---

2. Assuming that the eviction process moves forward, your land-lord will file a *complaint* with the court explaining why you should be evicted. The court will be the small claims court for your area, your local housing court, a justice of the peace court, or some other lower-level court.

3. The court will send you a *summons*, which is an official notice informing you that an eviction has begun and which tells you when your eviction hearing will take place.

4. Once you receive the summons, you'll have to decide how to respond. It's best not to make this decision alone, so set up an appointment with a landlord-tenant attorney if you are not already working with one. If your income is very low, you may be able to get legal help from your local Legal Aid Society. Your area's nonprofit Tenant Council may be another resource.

You may decide to respond to the summons in any of the following ways:

–   Try to reach a settlement with your landlord. Your landlord may be willing to stop the eviction process in exchange for your agreeing to do certain things by certain dates. Get all of the terms and conditions of a settlement in writing.

–   Fight the eviction. If you want to fight, you will either have to file an *answer* or *response* to your landlord's lawsuit by the deadline indicated in the summons, or you will have to just show up on the day of the hearing to state your case. It will depend on how things work in the court where the hearing will take place. An answer or response is a written statement to the court in which you deny the allegations that were made in the complaint filed by your landlord and explain your side of the issue you are being sued over.

–   Do nothing. If you don't respond to the summons and you don't show up in court, the judge will probably award your landlord a *default judgment* against you. The judgment gives your landlord the right to evict you.

KEEPING YOUR UTILITIES ON

Having utility services, such as heat and air-conditioning, water, wastewater, and electricity, is essential to the well-being of you and your family. Therefore, if you have fallen behind on any of your utility bills and are being threatened with termination of service, it's important to know what to do. Your options include the following:

- Contact the utility to try to work out a plan for getting caught up. If the amount that you owe is not substantial and you can afford to get caught up relatively quickly, you may be able to set up an installment payment plan over the phone by calling the

 Red Alert!

Depending on your state, if you can't live up to the terms of your agreement with the utility, it can refuse to negotiate another agreement with you.

utility's customer service office. If the person you speak with tells you that you need to pay more than you are offering to pay in installments and you don't think you can afford to pay more, let the customer service representative know. You will probably be told that you must fill out an application if you want to make lower installment payments and that the utility will review the information on the application to decide how much your payments must be. To make that decision, the utility will consider how much you owe, your overall financial condition, and whether you have had a good history of paying on your account, among other things.

If you and the utility reach an agreement about how you will pay off what you owe, the utility will send you a written agreement restating everything to which you agreed. If the agreement contains anything that you don't remember okaying or anything that

 Hot Tip

If the utility you are having problems with is not regulated by the PUC, the commission will be able to tell you who does regulate it.

> **❗ Hot Tip**
>
> Your utility may maintain a fund that can help you when you're having problems keeping up with your utility bill, so that your service will not be terminated. Contact the utility to find out if it has such a fund, and if it does, whether you qualify for help from the fund.
>
> Also, some PUCs maintain similar emergency funds for consumers. In addition, your local utility as well as the PUC in your state should be able to refer you to other sources of help for paying your utility bills.

you don't understand, contact the utility customer service office again. Don't sign the agreement until all of your questions have been answered to your satisfaction.

- If you are unable to reach a payment agreement with the first person you talk to at the utility, ask to speak with that person's supervisor. The supervisor may have more latitude to negotiate with you. If you are not able to work out an affordable payment plan with the supervisor either, you can appeal the utility's decision with your state's Public Utility Commission (PUC), which regulates investor-owned, for-profit utilities in most states. If you do, the utility must suspend any pending termination action while your appeal is being decided. Contact your PUC to find out how to initiate an appeal.

- Get help keeping your utility service on by tapping resources in your community that help people in your situation. These resources include churches and charitable organizations that assist consumers who are having problems paying their essential expenses; your local, county, or state human services or housing agency; or the federally funded Low Income Home Energy Assistance Program (LIHEAP). (To learn about the LIHEAP in your area, go to *www.acf.hhs.gov/programs/liheap/grantees.*) However, to get assistance from most of these resources, you will have to prove that your household income is below a certain amount.

- File for bankruptcy. You can use bankruptcy to get rid of your past due utility debt, but to keep your service on, you'll have to pay a *reasonable deposit* to the utility within 20 days of filing for bankruptcy. A reasonable deposit is usually two- to three-months' worth of utility payments.

This chapter explained why when money is tight, you should pay certain kinds of debts—your most important debts such as your mortgage, car loan, and your child support obligation—before other kinds of debts, and you learned the consequences of falling too far behind on these debts. You also found out about your options for handling your most important debts when you are having problems keeping up with them.

The next chapter offers advice and guidance for what to do when you are contacted by debt collectors. It also fills you in on your federal debt collection rights and explains exactly what debt collectors can and can't do to you—despite what they tell you they are going to do.

Knowing How to Handle
Debt Collectors

3

Debt collectors can make your life miserable when you are struggling to keep up with your financial obligations and have fallen behind on some of your debts. However, the federal Fair Debt Collection Practices Act (FDCPA) protects you by placing limits on what debt collectors can do to collect the money they say you owe. It also gives you certain rights with regard to how you can respond to them. This chapter explains your debt collection rights and the restrictions that the FDCPA places on debt collectors. It also tells you what may happen if you don't pay the debt that a debt collector is trying to collect from you.

HOW DEBT COLLECTORS WORK

When you fall behind on a debt, the creditor to whom you owe the money will probably send you a series of notices asking you to pay what you owe. Eventually, if you don't pay the full amount that is past due or if the creditor does not agree to let you pay the arrearage over time or to let you settle your debt for less, the creditor will probably turn your debt over to a debt collector.

Red Alert!

If a debt collector seems friendly and understanding about your financial situation, don't delude yourself into thinking that he is genuinely concerned about your money troubles. The debt collector is probably just trying to get you to let down your guard so you will share information about your finances that he can use to collect from you. Examples of information you should never share with a debt collector include the name of your bank, your bank account numbers, information about the assets you own, and the name of your employer. If a debt collector asks you for any of this information, politely respond, "I'm sorry, but I won't share that information with you." The FDCPA does not require you to make the debt collector's job easy.

The first time that the debt collector contacts you by phone, she may be very friendly; but unless you immediately agree to pay the debt, the debt collector will probably become increasingly hostile and demanding with each subsequent call. Some debt collectors, however, are aggressive from the get-go.

Debt collectors have a financial motivation to be persistent and demanding because most get a percentage from the creditors for which they are working of whatever money they collect. Therefore, the more they collect, the more they make; and if they collect nothing, they get nothing for their efforts. However, some debt collectors are in the business of purchasing past due debts from creditors. They are demanding because they want to maximize the return on their investment by collecting as much as possible on the debts that they've purchased.

UNDERSTANDING WHAT DEBT COLLECTORS CAN'T DO TO COLLECT FROM YOU

The FDCPA clearly limits the actions that a debt collector can take to try to collect past due debts from you. For example, the law prohibits debt collectors from:

- Repeatedly contacting you about a debt within a relatively short period of time (e.g, during one morning or afternoon) in an effort to wear you down.

- Calling you earlier than 8 AM or later than 9 PM, unless you tell them that it's okay to call you then.

- Calling you at a time that you tell them is inconvenient.

- Calling you anytime on a Sunday.

- Calling you at work if you tell them that your employer doesn't want you contacted there.

- Contacting your employer about the money that you owe, unless the debt collector is trying to collect past due child support from you.

- Continuing to call you if you tell them not to call you anymore. However, telling them not to contact you anymore does not mean that debt collectors won't continue trying to collect the money that you owe, especially if you owe a lot of money. For example, they may sue you for the money.

- Telling your friends, relatives, or neighbors that you owe a debt in order to embarrass you into paying it. However, the FDCPA does allow debt collectors to contact them to find out how to get in touch with you—where you live and your phone number—although debt collectors are not allowed to say why they want the information.

- Sending you information about a past due debt using a postcard or an envelope that clearly indicates that it was sent by a debt collector.

- Using an envelope that appears to have been sent by a court or by a government agency.

- Using profanity or abusive language when they talk to you.

- Promising to ruin your reputation if you don't pay what you owe.

- Threatening to throw you in jail. You can't be sent to jail for not paying your debts, with the exception of past due court-ordered child support, depending on the state that issued the court order.

- Threatening to sue you over an unpaid debt unless they actually intend to follow through on their threat.

> **❗ Hot Tip**
>
> Some states have their own debt collection laws, and those laws may apply to in-house as well as outside debt collectors. Also, your state may have other laws that can help protect you from abusive or harassing debt collection efforts by both types of debt collectors. You can find out if your state has these laws by calling a consumer law attorney or your state's attorney general's office.

- Requiring you to accept their collect calls.

WHAT MAY HAPPEN IF YOU DON'T PAY THE DEBT THAT A COLLECTOR WANTS YOU TO PAY

When a debt collector contacts you about a past due unsecured debt that you may owe (such as a past due credit card bill or medical debt) and you don't agree to pay the debt, despite the debt collector's ominous warnings and threats, it may do nothing else to try to collect from you. What the debt collector does next will largely be determined by the following:

- The amount of the debt. If the debt is relatively small and the debt collector concludes that it won't be easy to collect the money from you, the debt collector may decide to give up on you and move on to "greener pastures." Even so, the fact that your account was turned over to collections is likely to show up in your credit histories, which will make it a lot harder to get new credit at reasonable terms in the future. If the amount of the debt is substantial, however, you should expect the debt collector to be more persistent and maybe even to sue you for the money.

🖐 Red Alert!

The FDCPA only applies to outside debt collectors—debt collectors who are hired by creditors or who purchase past due debts from creditors—and to attorneys who collect past due debts for their clients. The law does *not* apply to debt collectors who are the employees of creditors, which means that those kinds of debt collectors are not covered by the FDCPA when they are trying to collect money from you. If you are not sure whether the debt collector who contacts you about a debt is an outside debt collector or an employee of the creditor to whom you owe the debt, ask the debt collector whom she is employed by.

- Whether you are judgment-proof. When you are *judgment-proof* it means that if you are sued for the money you owe and you lose the lawsuit, the debt collector won't be able to collect the money judgment (the amount of money that the judge says you must pay to the debt collector) because you have no assets to collect and your state doesn't allow wage garnishment. Currently, Pennsylvania, South Carolina, and Texas don't permit it. (When your wages are garnished, the court orders your employer to take a certain amount of money out of each of your paychecks so that the funds can be applied to your debt.) When a debt collector knows that you are judgment-proof, it probably won't waste its time and money suing you. Again, however, the fact that your debt was turned over to a debt collector will seriously damage your credit histories. It's also possible that if your financial situation improves and the statue of limitations on collecting the debt that you owe has not expired, a debt collector could try to collect the money that you owe sometime down the road.

❗ Hot Tip

Get in touch with a consumer law attorney immediately if a debt collector threatens to sue you or to take an asset that collateralizes one of your debts.

If you are not judgment-proof, however, and if the debt collector sues you and wins the lawsuit, the debt collector may ask the court for permission to collect what you owe by:

- Garnishing your wages.
- Putting a judgment lien on one of your assets. When there is a lien on an asset that you own, you can't transfer the asset into someone else's name, sell the asset, or use it as loan collateral unless you pay the amount of the lien.
- Seizing one of your assets. The asset will be sold in a public auction and the sale proceeds will be applied to your debt. If the proceeds are not enough to pay the debt in full, you'll have to pay the outstanding balance (the deficiency).

 Red Alert!

If a debt collector is trying to collect a secured debt and you don't agree to pay it, the creditor will eventually take the asset that collateralizes the debt from you through a foreclosure or repossession. However, if the debt collector purchased that debt from the creditor, then the debt collector will be the one to initiate the foreclosure or repossession because the lien on the collateral will have transferred from the creditor to the debt collector.

HOW TO RESPOND TO A DEBT COLLECTOR

When a debt collector contacts you for the first time about a debt that you owe, the FDCPA requires it to send you a written statement within five days. The notice must indicate the amount of the debt and the name of the creditor to which you owe it. (If the debt collector purchased the debt from your original creditor, then the notice will indicate that you owe the money to the debt collector.) The notice must also inform you of your right to request written verification of the debt and to dispute the debt.

Regardless of whether you agree that you owe the debt, it's a good idea to request that the debt collector verify in writing the total amount of the debt and the original amount of the debt, and itemize all of the interest, late fees, and collection fees it says that you owe. Put the request in writing and send your letter via certified mail with a

return receipt requested. Once you
receive written verification, if you
don't believe that you owe the debt
or if you disagree with the amount
of the debt, follow the directions
found later in this chapter.

> **▼ Hot Tip**
>
> If you agree that you owe a debt but you
> can't afford to pay it, asking for written
> verification buys you time to figure out
> what to do about it.

If You Agree That You Owe a Debt

If you agree that you owe a debt, you can pay it or you can tell the
debt collector that you can't afford to pay it and that you don't want
to be contacted again. When you're deciding what to do, however,
remember that you should never pay a low-priority debt if doing so
will jeopardize your ability to pay your essential living expenses and/
or your secured and priority unsecured debts. Chapters 1 and 2 discuss which are your most important debts and the consequences of
not paying them.

If you can't afford to pay the debt in a lump sum, you can do the
following:

- Ask the debt collector to let you pay it in installments. When
  you work out the terms of your installment agreement, don't
  agree to make payments that are bigger than you feel comfortable with. Also, don't give the debt collector any money until
  all of the terms of the agreement are spelled out in writing.
  Among other things, the agreement should specify the duration of the installment plan, the amount of each of your installment payments, the applicable interest rate, whether you'll
  have to make a balloon payment at the end of the plan, when
  you will be in default of the agreement, and the consequences
  of a default. If the debt collector refuses to prepare a written
  agreement, prepare one yourself, date and sign it, and send a
  copy to the debt collector.

- Try to settle your debt for less. When you do this, you clear up
  the debt by paying less than the total amount that you owe.

Red Alert!

Always pay a debt collector with a money order or a cashier's check, not with one of your personal checks. The risk of using a personal check is that if the debt collector is unscrupulous, the information printed on your check can be used to have money transferred from your bank account into the debt collec- tor's own account. Also, never have money electronically transferred from your account to the debt collector's account because there is a chance that the debt collector could obtain your account information via this payment method, too.

The debt collector may agree to your request if it decides that the chance of collecting the full amount of your debt is slim to none, assuming that the debt collector feels that your settlement offer is reasonable. For example, if you owe $3,000 on a debt and you offer to settle it for $125, the debt collector will probably reject your offer.

❗Hot Tip

When you are discussing the possibility of settling an unsecured debt, casually mentioning to the debt collector that you may have to file for bankruptcy if you are not able to agree on a settlement amount may make the debt collector more interested in working something out with you. This is because if you do file for bankruptcy, the debt collector knows it will probably end up with little to nothing for its efforts. Do not use this same strategy with any of your secured creditors! If you do, the creditors may immediately take your collateral.

If You Can't Afford to Pay a Debt That You Owe

If you agree that you owe a debt but you don't have the money to pay the debt in a lump sum, over time, or through a settlement agreement, or if paying the debt means that you won't have the money you need to cover more important debts and/or all of your essential living expenses, send the debt collector a certified letter, return receipt requested, stating that you cannot afford to pay the debt and that you do not want the debt collector to contact you again. Although the letter won't get rid of the debt, it will stop the debt collector's calls and letters. The FDCPA says that the debt collector must cease all contact with you after receiving your letter except to confirm that it won't contact you again or to inform you of an action that it is about to take in order to collect your debt. For example, the debt collector may decide to sue you to get the court's permission to garnish your wages, put a lien on one of your assets, or seize an asset that you own.

> **❗ Hot Tip**
>
> Even if you plan on paying a debt that a debt collector contacts you about, the FDCPA says that you can ask the debt collector not to contact you about it again. Put your request in writing and send the letter via certified mail with a return receipt requested.

If You Don't Agree That You Owe a Debt

If you don't believe that you owe the money that a debt collector contacts you about or if you disagree with the amount of the debt, send the debt collector a letter stating so within 30 days of the date that it contacts you about it for the very first time. According to the FDCPA, the debt collector must either provide you with written proof that you owe the money or stop contacting you.

 Red Alert!

There is a potential downside to settling a debt for less. The IRS will treat the difference between the total amount that you owe on the debt and the settlement amount as taxable income. As a result, when April 15 rolls around, you could end up owing more to the IRS than you would have if you had not settled the debt. However, if you are *insolvent,* settling the debt may have no impact on the amount of taxes that you owe. Generally speaking, when you are insolvent you do not have enough money to meet your financial obligations. However, the IRS uses very specific criteria to determine whether you are insolvent. Consult with a certified public account (CPA) who specializes in tax issues to find out if you are insolvent by IRS standards.

If You Think That a Debt Collector Has Violated the FDCPA

If you believe that a debt collector has violated the FDCPA, even in a small way, file a complaint with the Federal Trade Commission (FTC), the office that enforces the FDCPA among other federal consumer laws. You can file your complaint online at *www.ftc.gov*, by calling 800-382-4357, or by writing to: Consumer Response Center, FTC, 600 Pennsylvania Avenue NW, Washington, DC 20580. The FTC won't help you resolve your problem with the debt collector, but if it receives enough complaints like yours, it may file a lawsuit against the debt collection agency that employs the debt collector.

If your state has its own debt collection law, file a similar complaint with your state's attorney general's office. Again, the office won't help you resolve your problem, but your complaint might help the office build a legal case against the debt collection agency that employs the debt collector. You can find out if your state has such a law and about your rights under the law by calling your state's attorney general's office, by contacting a consumer law attorney, or by visiting the website of the Privacy Rights Clearinghouse at *www.privacyrights.org*.

You should also get in touch with a consumer law attorney when a debt collector violates your federal or state debt collection rights, especially if the violation is ongoing or especially serious—the debt collector has been calling you day and night, has contacted some of your family members to discuss your debt, or has been using abusive language or threatening to put you in jail. All it may take to convince the debt collector that it better back off and abide by the law is a letter from your attorney.

Depending on the nature of the debt collector's violation of the law, the attorney may suggest filing a lawsuit. Most attorneys who handle such cases will represent you on a contingent-fee basis, which means that you won't have to pay the attorney an up-front fee. Instead, if you win your case, the court will order the debt collection agency to pay your attorney's fees, and if you lose, you won't owe the attorney any money for her time and effort. However, you will probably have to reimburse the attorney for your court costs and for any expenses she incurred handling your case. Make sure that all of the terms of your agreement with the attorney, including how your attorney will be paid and what expenses you'll be liable for, are spelled out in a written agreement before you begin working together.

If you move forward with a lawsuit and your state has its own debt collection law, your attorney

> **❗ Hot Tip**
>
> If the first consumer law attorney you meet with won't work on a contingent-fee basis, look for one who will. If you can't find an attorney who will work with you that way, it's probably because you have a weak case that is not worth pursuing.

will decide whether to file the lawsuit in state or federal court. The decision will be based on the nature of the debt collector's violation, on which law offers you more legal remedies, and on which option allows you to sue for the greatest amount of money.

Under the FDCPA, you can sue for actual and punitive damages and you can ask the court to order the debt collector to reimburse you for your attorney's fees and court costs if you win your lawsuit. If you sue for actual damages, you'll be asking the court to compensate you for the harm that the debt collector inflicted on you—the wages you may have lost if you had to take unpaid time off from work to deal with your debt collection problem, the out-of-pocket expenses you may have incurred trying to resolve the problem (such as postage, photocopying, and long-distance phone calls), and any pain and humiliation you may have experienced because of the debt collector's actions. If you sue for punitive damages, you will be asking the court to order the debt collector to pay you additional money to discourage it from violating the law again.

Now that you've read this chapter, you're armed you with the information you need to gain the upper hand over debt collectors. You know how debt collectors work and what they can't do to try to collect money from you, you are aware of your options for responding to debt collectors when they get in touch with you, and you have a basic understanding of what to do if a debt collector violates your legal rights.

The next chapter is the first in a series of chapters that addresses some aspect of bankruptcy. These are important chapters to read if your efforts to manage your debts and avoid bankruptcy don't seem to be working. For example, the next chapter explains when filing for bankruptcy does and doesn't make sense, and it highlights the advantages and disadvantages of filing for bankruptcy.

Considering Bankruptcy When Managing Your Debts Doesn't Work

Knowing When Filing for Bankruptcy Is Your Best Bet

4

Filing for bankruptcy is a big step that will affect your finances for years to come. The fact that you filed will remain in your credit histories for as long as 10 years, depending on whether you file for Chapter 7 or Chapter 13 bankruptcy; and while it is there, it will be more difficult for you to get new credit at affordable terms, qualify for a job, purchase insurance, and rent a place to live, among other possible consequences. Even so, sometimes filing for bankruptcy is your best option.

This chapter helps you understand when filing for bankruptcy is and isn't a good idea. Among other things, it summarizes the key advantages and disadvantages of filing, explains what bankruptcy can and can't do for you, and debunks some of the more common misconceptions about bankruptcy. For more detailed information about filing for bankruptcy, read chapters 6, 8, and 9.

WHEN BANKRUPTCY MAKES SENSE

Just thinking about filing for bankruptcy may tie up your stomach in knots and make you want to stay in bed with the covers pulled over your head. Your reaction is understandable, because even though consumer bankruptcy is a lot more commonplace than it used to be, there is still a social stigma associated with filing, and having to file can make you feel like a failure. Even so, filing for bankruptcy is a smart money move when you've tried everything you can to resolve your money problems and you're still overwhelmed by debt. It's an especially good move if you have a lot of unsecured debt (such as credit card and medical bills), because bankruptcy discharges or wipes out most types of unsecured debts. If you're at risk for losing assets (such as your home and your car), as soon as you file, your creditors can't continue trying to collect from you.

Here are some specific examples of when you should run, not walk, to the office of a bankruptcy attorney, who can help you evaluate your situation and determine whether filing for bankruptcy is your best move:

> ! **Hot Tip**
>
> Generally, the less income you have, the more debts you can discharge (wipe out through bankruptcy); and the more assets that you own and want to keep, the more bankruptcy makes sense.

- You are about to lose your home in a foreclosure.

- You believe that you are at risk for having your car repossessed.

- Your creditors are threatening you with legal action.

- The IRS is threatening to collect your past due federal taxes by garnishing your wages, putting a lien on one of your assets, intercepting your federal tax refund, or taking some other action.

> 🖐 **Red Alert!**
>
> As you learned in chapter 2, in most states your car can be repossessed without any advance warning. Also, if your car loan agreement is like most, it gives your auto lender the right to take your vehicle if you miss just a single payment on your loan.

- Your wages are already being garnished. Filing for bankruptcy will stop the garnishment, and you may even be able to get back some of the money that has already been taken out of your paychecks.

- Your state's Child Support Enforcement Office is about to seize one of your assets, take money from your bank account, intercept your state or federal tax refund, or take some other action to collect your past due child support debt.

Red Alert!

Don't decide for yourself whether bankruptcy is right for you. Always get the advice of a consumer bankruptcy attorney. Chapter 7 tells you how to find a reputable one.

WHEN FILING FOR BANKRUPTCY DOESN'T MAKE SENSE

Sometimes, even when you are overwhelmed by debt, there may be no reason to spend your time and money filing for bankruptcy. Examples of when you *shouldn't* file include:

- You are over 65 years of age, you are receiving Social Security benefits, you are not working, and you have no assets.

- You are over 65 years of age and you are still working, but you live in a state that doesn't allow wage garnishment. These states are Pennsylvania, South Carolina, and Texas.

- You are permanently disabled and unable to work, your only source of income is government benefits, and either all of your assets are exempt or you have no assets. Exempt assets are assets that are protected from the collection actions of your creditors. They typically include your car (up to a certain dollar value), your household goods and clothing, the tools you need to earn a living, and any money you may have in a qualified retirement plan (such as a 401(k) account). Chapter 6 provides more information about exempt and nonexempt assets.

THE PROS AND CONS OF FILING

There are positives and negatives associated with filing for bankruptcy. Some apply to both a Chapter 7 liquidation bankruptcy and a Chapter 13 reorganization bankruptcy, but others only apply to one or the other. It's important to understand the advantages and the disadvantages of bankruptcy so that if you decide to file, you'll take that step with your eyes wide open. The rest of this section provides you with an overview of bankruptcy's pros and cons.

The Advantages of Bankruptcy

Generally, filing for bankruptcy offers you the following benefits:

- Your creditors will have to stop trying to collect from you because of the automatic stay, which will go into effect as soon as you file the required paperwork to begin your bankruptcy. As a result, you'll receive no more threatening calls and letters from your creditors and from debt collectors; lawsuits that have been filed against you will be put on hold; and you won't have to worry about losing any of the assets that collateralize your secured debts as a result of a foreclosure or a repossession. However, if any of your secured creditors get the court's permission to lift the stay, they'll be able to take their collateral while you are in bankruptcy. The automatic stay will end once your bankruptcy is over.

- You can use bankruptcy to reduce the total amount of money that you owe to some of your creditors.

- Bankruptcy will wipe out the outstanding balances on some kinds of debts. Be aware, however, other kinds of debts will survive your bankruptcy and you'll have to pay them once your bankruptcy, is over. Chapter 6 discusses the kinds of debts that survive bankruptcy.

- Bankruptcy helps you hold on to your car and to your home. While you can't use bankruptcy to reduce the outstanding balances on your car loan or mortgage, you can use it to help you keep them. There is one exception—if you financed the purchase of your car more than 910 days before the start of your bankruptcy, then you may be able to reduce the remaining balance.

The Disadvantages of Bankruptcy

Some of the most important disadvantages of bankruptcy include the following:

- You may lose your nonexempt assets.

- Your credit histories will be damaged and your FICO scores will plummet. (Your FICO scores are the kinds of credit scores that most mortgage companies and other major national creditors use to make decisions about you.) As a result, it will be impossible to get new credit at affordable terms and you may have trouble getting a job, especially if the job involves handling money, managing an employer's finances, and the like. In addition, you may have a harder time finding a home or apartment to rent (most larger landlords will run a credit check on you, which will alert them to your bankruptcy) and purchasing adequate insurance, among other possible negative consequences. The truth is, however, that if your finances are in such bad shape that you are considering bankruptcy, your credit histories and your FICO scores are already badly damaged. Figure 4.1 explains the importance of having positive account paying information in your credit histories and high FICO scores.

- Going through a bankruptcy can be stressful. However, if your finances are in such bad shape that you are thinking about filing, you're probably already stressed out.

- It costs money to file for bankruptcy. For example, you'll have to pay a filing fee to the court when you initiate your bankruptcy, and you'll need to hire a bankruptcy attorney. (Representing yourself is always an option, but it's not a good idea given the complexities of the bankruptcy process.) Chapter 6 discusses how much it costs to file for bankruptcy and chapter 7 discusses how much you should expect to pay an attorney.

■ Bankruptcy involves completing a lot of detailed paperwork and many complicated legal procedures. You also may have to attend some court hearings. If you've ever dealt with the legal system before, you know well that all of this can be both confusing and intimidating. Hopefully, after reading this book, you'll have a better idea about what to expect so you won't feel overwhelmed by the bankruptcy process.

■ Your bankruptcy will be in the public records. This means that anyone who is nosy enough to want to find out if you ever filed can check the records of the federal district bankruptcy court in your area or use the Internet to access a public records database, such as *publicrecords.com.*

🖐 Red Alert!

The federal bankruptcy law states that you cannot be discriminated against because you filed for bankruptcy. In reality, however, when creditors, insurance companies, landlords, and others know that you've filed, it's very likely that they will be influenced by that fact when they are making decisions about you, especially if your bankruptcy is relatively recent.

Your *FICO scores* are three-digit numbers that are derived from the information in your credit histories. If the information in each of your credit histories is positive, then your scores will be high, but if your credit histories are full of negatives, just the opposite will be true. A growing number of creditors, employers, insurance companies, and landlords are using your FICO scores to make decisions about you rather than reviewing the information in your credit histories. Chapter 10, "Rebuilding Your Credit After Bankruptcy," explains how to order your credit history from each of the three national credit reporting agencies. It also tells you how to order your FICO scores.

FIGURE 4.1. How Your Credit History Information and Your FICO Scores Affect Your Life

Your credit history is a detailed account-by-account portrait of how you've managed your credit over time. If you've managed your credit responsibly and you have not experienced any financial setbacks that have made it difficult for you to keep up with your debts, your credit history will be full of positive information. As a result, you'll be able to qualify for credit at affordable terms, it will be easier for you to obtain the insurance you need, employers won't be reluctant to hire or promote you because of your finances, and landlords won't refuse to rent to you out of concern that you won't be able to keep up with your rent. Quite the opposite will be true, however, if your credit history shows that you've been late paying on your accounts, you've defaulted on some of your financial obligations, some of your debts have been turned over to debt collectors, your home has been foreclosed on, your car has been repossessed, you've been sued by your creditors, and so on.

Three national credit reporting agencies—Equifax, Experian, and TransUnion—collect information about your credit accounts and your bill paying habits and maintain that information in their computerized databases. In turn, many creditors, employers, and landlords, as well as some government agencies review the information to help make decisions about you. For example:

■ Creditors use your credit history information to decide whether to give you credit and the terms of any credit they may extend. They also use it to help them decide if they should increase or lower your credit limits, raise the interest rates on your accounts, or cancel the accounts.

■ Employers consider the information in your credit histories when they are deciding whether to hire you, promote you, fire you, or demote you.

■ Insurance companies take your credit history information into account when they are deciding whether to sell you insurance and how much to charge you for the insurance.

■ Landlords review that information to help them decide if they want to rent to you.

■ Government agencies review your credit history before they issue you a security clearance or a special license.

COMMON MISCONCEPTIONS ABOUT BANKRUPTCY

Like many consumers, you may have misconceptions about bankruptcy that can get in the way of making a wise decision about whether to file and what to expect if you do. This information will set you straight by debunking the following most common bankruptcy misconceptions:

- All of my debts will be wiped out (discharged) if I file for bankruptcy. Not necessarily. Some kinds of debts survive bankruptcy, which means that you'll have to pay them when your bankruptcy is over. These debts include court-ordered child and/or spousal support, federal student loans, and most taxes, although you may be able to discharge a federal income tax debt that is more than three years old. The next section of this chapter, along with chapter 6, provides more detailed information about the kinds of debts that survive bankruptcy.

- I'll never be able to get credit again. Not true. You'll still be able to get credit, but at first the credit you qualify for won't have attractive terms. For example, you'll be charged high rates of interest, the amount of credit that you can get will be limited, and you may not be able to qualify for an unsecured loan. However, as the years pass, your bankruptcy will have less and less impact on your finances, assuming that you manage your money responsibly. As a result, it will become easier to qualify for credit with attractive terms. Also, after 7 years, a Chapter 13 bankruptcy won't show up in your credit histories anymore. A Chapter 7 will disappear after 10 years.

- If I file for bankruptcy, I'll be left with nothing. No, you won't be destitute. The property exemption law of your state will let you keep some of your assets. Also, depending on the kind of bankruptcy you file and the overall state of your finances, you may not lose a single asset.

- I can handle my own bankruptcy. Technically, that's true. However, given the complexity of the bankruptcy process, acting as your own lawyer is a really bad idea. When you represent yourself, you may lose assets that an attorney would be able to help you hold on to, and you may end up having to pay more on your debts than you would if you were working with an attorney. Also, you may unintentionally create legal problems for yourself that could even cause your bankruptcy to be dismissed. Bottom line: As a non-attorney, it would be virtually impossible for you to understand all of the complex rules that apply to bankruptcy.

- My friends and neighbors will know that I filed for bankruptcy. That's unlikely, although anyone who wants to can go to the federal courthouse and find out if you've filed. However, most people you know are probably way too busy to do that.

- If I file for bankruptcy once, I won't ever be able to file again. Hopefully, you'll never need to file for bankruptcy again! However, if you do develop serious money troubles after your bankruptcy is over, you can file for another bankruptcy, although there are limits on how soon you can do that. For example, if you've just completed a Chapter 7 bankruptcy, you can't file another one for eight years. If you've completed a Chapter 13 bankruptcy, you'll have to wait for two years before you can file again. There is one exception—you won't be able to file another bankruptcy at all if a bankruptcy judge determines that you committed bankruptcy fraud. Chapter 6 provides additional information on how soon after one bankruptcy you can file another.

- I'm a failure if I file for bankruptcy. Not true! If you are like most people who end up in bankruptcy, you got there because you're overwhelmed by debt as a result of a problem that you did not create—someone in your family had a serious medical condition and you're left with a mountain of medical bills you can't pay, you lost your job, a divorce has devastated your finances—and you've spent months if not years struggling to make ends meet to avoid having to file.

WHAT BANKRUPTCY WON'T DO FOR YOU

Although bankruptcy will give you relief from the collection actions of your creditors, wipe out some kinds of debts, and help you hold on to your assets, if you file a Chapter 7, there are things that bankruptcy can't do. For example, it won't do the following:

- Get rid of your court-ordered obligation to pay child and/or spousal support.

- Discharge the balance due on your mortgage and your car loan.

- Erase most tax debts.

- Eliminate your obligation to repay your federal student loans.

- Protect you, while you are in bankruptcy, from any of your secured creditors who get permission from the court to take back an asset that is collateralizing the debt that you owe to them.

- Prevent you from being criminally prosecuted.

Although you should always make the decision about whether to file for bankruptcy with the help of a consumer bankruptcy attorney, this chapter has helped prepare you to make that decision by educating you about the basics of bankruptcy, including when filing is a wise move and the advantages and disadvantages of bankruptcy. It also has provided you with an overview of the two most common kinds of consumer bankruptcy, explained how filing will affect your credit histories and your credit scores, and debunked common misconceptions about bankruptcy that could cause you not to file even though filing is your best alternative. The next chapter addresses some of the ethical concerns you may have about filing. It also discusses some of the emotions you may be feeling now that you are thinking about bankruptcy and provides advice to help you deal with them.

Grappling with the Ethical and Emotional Aspects of Bankruptcy

5

After reading the previous chapter, you may be starting to understand the benefits of bankruptcy from a dollars-and-cents perspective. Even so, you may still find yourself resisting the idea of filing. Maybe you feel ashamed that you're having money problems and you don't want to be labeled as a financial failure, or maybe you believe that filing for bankruptcy is morally wrong. You tell yourself, "The debt is mine. I incurred it. So shouldn't I pay it?"

For centuries now, society has been debating whether filing for bankruptcy is an ethical step to take when you're drowning in debt. On one side of that debate are those who believe that debtors who owe too much should be reviled and made to pay their debts no matter what; and on the other side are those who believe that well-intentioned people sometimes make mistakes with their money or have bad luck, and that they should be given another chance by having their debts forgiven. These two perspectives have shaped our modern-day laws about credit and bankruptcy, and have affected the way that the media portrays bankruptcy.

If you're struggling to decide whether bankruptcy is the morally right step for you to take, this chapter won't solve your dilemma. It will, however, provide a historical and ethical framework for thinking about what you should do. It also addresses some harmful myths about people who file for bankruptcy that may be shaping your thinking.

If you decide to file for bankruptcy, this chapter offers insights into the emotions you may experience as you go through the process. It also suggests ways to cope with these emotions so they don't compromise your ability to make wise decisions as you go through the bankruptcy process and so they don't create problems in your relationships that make it difficult for you to focus at work or to engage fully in life.

PUTTING BANKRUPTCY IN A HISTORICAL CONTEXT

Whether debt should be forgiven has been a hot issue for hundreds of thousands of years. Even the Old Testament reflects on the controversy. For example, this passage from Deuteronomy argues for forgiveness: "At the end of every seven years, you are to cancel the debts of those who owe you money. This is how it is done. Everyone who has lent money to his neighbor must not try to collect the money: the Lord himself has declared the debt canceled." This passage from Psalm 37:21, "The wicked borrow and do not repay, but the righteous give generously," reflects the other side of the issue.

Together, the two biblical passages clearly encapsulate the opposing attitudes toward bankruptcy that prevailed in England before the U. S. colonies were established and that have prevailed in this country since its earliest days. Today, those attitudes continue to influence how we think about bankruptcy and shape our federal bankruptcy laws, with consumers and consumer advocates on one side and creditors and others who feel like consumers' debts should never be forgiven on the other.

When the U.S. Constitution was written in 1776, it included a provision for bankruptcy. However, it was not until 1800 that Congress passed this country's first bankruptcy law in response to economic fallout from rampant land speculation. The law, which applied only to businesses, allowed companies to get rid of all of their debts. However, pressure from creditors caused Congress to repeal the law 3 years later. Then, in 1841, a new federal bankruptcy law that applied to both consumers and businesses was passed, but 2 years later it, too, was repealed due to creditor pressure. A third law was enacted in 1867, but 11 years later, disgruntled creditors killed it, as well.

In 1898, Congress passed a fourth bankruptcy law. This law provided the foundation for future bankruptcy laws in this country. It introduced the concept of protecting bankrupt debtors from the collection actions of their creditors as well as the concept of allowing debtors to reorganize their debts through bankruptcy in order to make it easier for them to pay their creditors.

During the Great Depression, a number of other bankruptcy laws were passed. These new laws were shaped primarily by bankruptcy attorneys and judges in contrast to the bankruptcy laws of the past, which were largely influenced by creditors and the financial community. The new laws culminated in the Chandler Act of 1938, which gave consumers two formal options for dealing with their debts through bankruptcy: a liquidation bankruptcy or a debt reorganization bankruptcy. With its passage, the key features of modern bankruptcy law were established. Then, in 1978, another law was passed that made it easier for consumers and businesses to file for bankruptcy and to reorganize their debts. In an interesting coincidence, that very same year the U.S. Supreme Court made a ruling that effectively removed the cap on the amount of interest that creditors could charge consumers. The ruling had the effect of encouraging creditors to extend more credit to consumers, even consumers whose finances were iffy. Many consumer advocates and policy makers point to this change as one of the primary reasons for the high rates of consumer credit card debt and consumer bankruptcies we've seen in recent decades.

In 1994, yet another important bankruptcy law was passed to enhance the rights of creditors in bankruptcy at the expense of consumers. This law reduced the kinds of debts that a bankrupt consumer could get discharged through bankruptcy. Then, in 2005, working hand-in-hand with creditors—mostly credit card companies—Congress passed the

Bankruptcy Abuse Prevention and Consumer Protection Act (BAP-CPA). This law made things even tougher for bankrupt consumers and businesses. A key premise of this law is that too many consumers abuse the bankruptcy process by wiping out their debts through a Chapter 7 bankruptcy rather than paying off their debts over time through a Chapter 13 reorganization. Among other measures, the BAPCPA implemented a financial means test in order to force more consumers into Chapter 13, increased the kinds of debts that cannot be wiped out in bankruptcy, and gave bankruptcy judges many more reasons to dismiss a consumer's bankruptcy. These measures are discussed in detail in chapters 6, 8, and 9.

CONSIDERING THE ETHICS OF BANKRUPTCY

The biblical passages quoted earlier in this chapter, coupled with the expansions and contractions of debtors' rights as reflected by the various bankruptcy laws that have been passed and then repealed or amended over the years, demonstrate the two basic ways that our society thinks and has always thought about consumers who file for bankruptcy. On the one hand, many creditors and some of the media portray them as morally irresponsible spendthrifts who are looking for an easy way out of debt. On the other hand, consumer bankruptcy attorneys and consumer advocates point out that the majority of consumers who file for bankruptcy didn't get head over heels in debt because they were frivolous spenders. Rather, they often had experienced a serious setback in life, spent months (even years) struggling to pay what they owed, and filed only after they had run out of options and were faced with the loss of their home or their car or the garnishment of their wages, for example. These experts cite several reasons as to why consumers most often end up in bankruptcy, which are detailed next.

Job Loss

Many consumers use up their savings and max out their credit cards while they are looking for new jobs.

Lower Paying Jobs

Some consumers who lose their jobs end up in new jobs that pay them less than they were earning before or that offer them few if any of the benefits they used to have, such as health insurance. However, because the financial obligations of these consumers stay the same, many of them end up living paycheck to paycheck, which means that even the smallest setback in their lives can trigger a financial crisis.

Medical Bills

Many consumers are forced into bankruptcy because someone in their family is hospitalized or has a serious ongoing illness and they either have no insurance or their insurance pays just a small fraction of the medical bills. Others become disabled and either can't continue working full-time or can't work at all, making it impossible for them to keep up with mounting medical bills.

Divorce

Getting divorced is a financially devastating experience for many people, women especially, because divorce often means that their incomes plummet, and they end up saddled with a lot of debt. Also, a high percentage of divorcees who are entitled to receive child and/or spousal support (women usually) never receive the payments or receive them only occasionally.

Creditors at Fault?

Many bankruptcy attorneys and consumer advocates also make a convincing case that it's creditors, especially credit card companies, who are morally challenged—not bankrupt consumers. They point out that many of the very same creditors who vocally demonize consumers who file for bankruptcy make it very easy for these consumers to get credit, are not always 100 percent up front about the terms of that credit, and have no qualms about reaping huge profits by charging the consumers such high fees and interest rates—as high as 28 percent—that the consumers end up spending years trying to pay off even relatively small balances. Although many of these creditors try to justify their high fees and interest rates by claiming that they are simply protecting themselves against the risk of extending credit to consumers, the overall default rate on credit cards has hovered at around a mere 4 percent for years. Given this very low default rate, the explanation credit card companies use to explain their high rates and fees does not ring true. Pure greed seems to be a better one.

SEEING THROUGH THE MYTHS ABOUT PEOPLE WHO FILE FOR BANKRUPTCY

Over the years, a lot of harmful myths have developed about consumers who file for bankruptcy. These myths tend to contribute to the shame, guilt, embarrassment, and profound sense of failure that many consumers feel when they are overwhelmed by debt and are thinking about bankruptcy. In many cases, these myths also make it more difficult for consumers to think clearly about the best way to deal with financial problems. Even if they eventually decide that their best option is bankruptcy, the decision can be gut-wrenching for them because of all the negative information they've absorbed.

Here's a look at three of the most prevalent and harmful bankruptcy myths, together with what's really true:

1. Myth: Consumers who file for bankruptcy are bad people.

   Fact: Most people who file for bankruptcy are good, hardworking people who have fallen on tough times.

2. Myth: Consumers who file for bankruptcy are taking the easy way out of debt.

Fact: Ask anyone who has filed, especially since the passage of the BAPCPA, and 99.9 percent of them will tell you that there is nothing easy about bankruptcy. It costs money, it is an emotionally difficult experience, working with an attorney and diving into the legal system is stressful, and pulling together all of the required financial information and documentation is very time-consuming. Furthermore, the fact that those consumers have filed for bankruptcy will follow them for as long as 10 years (the amount of time that the federal Fair Credit Reporting Act says a bankruptcy can be reported)—although the three national credit reporting agencies report Chapter 13 bankruptcies for just 7 years.

3. Myth: If I file for bankruptcy, I will never be able to get credit again.

   Fact: This is a myth that creditors and debt collectors try to perpetuate to scare consumers into paying their debts and not filing for bankruptcy. The truth is that you will be able to get small amounts of new credit after your bankruptcy, although initially the credit will have a high interest rate and you'll probably have to collateralize it with an asset that you own. However, no reputable mortgage lender will help you finance the purchase of a home right away. Eventually, though, as your bankruptcy recedes into the past and assuming you've done a good job of managing your new credit, you'll qualify for credit with more attractive terms and for a mortgage, too.

HANDLING YOUR EMOTIONS BEFORE AND DURING BANKRUPTCY

Few problems in life are more stressful than not having enough money to meet all of your financial obligations. Being short of money can create tension and conflict in your relationship with your spouse or partner, interfere with your sleep, make it more difficult to be productive at work, and may even cause you to self-medicate by abusing alcohol or drugs. Furthermore, if you file for bankruptcy, although initially you may feel like a big load has been lifted from your shoulders, that sense of relief may not last for long—the stressful bankruptcy process is likely to engender a whole new set of worries and emotions for you to cope with. For example, although your rational self may tell you that you did the right thing, you may also feel fear for the future, shame, sadness, and a sense of failure. Also, you may become depressed, which will make it more difficult for you to handle your day-to-day responsibilities and to make sound decisions as you move through the bankruptcy process.

If you experience any of these feelings, you are not alone. Millions of other consumers who have been in your same situation have felt them, too. Many of them found the following advice to be helpful:

- Acknowledge that you are not the first person to file for bankruptcy and that you won't be the last. Countless successful people have filed for bankruptcy and gone on to achieve additional successes in life. Here are just a few:
  - John Connally, former governor of Texas
  - Francis Ford Coppola, Oscar-winning movie producer and director
  - Henry Ford, auto manufacturer
  - Milton Hershey, founder of Hershey Foods, chocolate maker
  - Ulysses S. Grant, U.S. president
  - Larry King, television talk show host
  - Michael Jackson, singer
  - Thomas Jefferson, founding father and U.S. president
  - M.C. Hammer, rapper
  - Cindy Lauper, singer
  - Willie Nelson, singer
  - Tom Petty, rock and roll singer
  - Lynn Redgrave, actress
  - Donald Trump, businessman and former host of *The Apprentice*
  - Mark Twain (Samuel L. Clemens), novelist
  - Walt Disney, creator of Mickey Mouse

- Acknowledge why your financial problems developed, accept responsibility for whatever role you may have played in creating them, forgive yourself, and move forward.

- Cope with your emotions in healthy ways: exercise, do yoga or Tai Chi, find quiet time for yourself during each day (even if it's only 10 or 15 minutes), get enough sleep, and spend time with the people who care about you and who can give you emotional support.

- Focus on the future. Although it can be difficult to think about the future when you are distracted by the here and now of your bankruptcy, try not to lose sight of why you filed—to deal with your debts and to get a financial fresh start in life.

Pay close attention to any signs that you may be depressed, and get help from a mental health therapist if you think that you are or if your spouse or partner or someone else who cares about you suggests that you need help coping. Being depressed is nothing to be embarrassed about. It's a common response to an emotionally overwhelming problem. The signs of depression include loss of interest in the things that you care about, sadness that you can't shake, crying or anger, sleeping all of the time or trouble sleeping, loss of appetite, and feelings of worthlessness and/or hopelessness. Although occasionally we may all experience some of these feelings for a day or two or even a week, if time goes on and you don't feel better, or if your feelings begin to create more problems in your life and make it difficult for you to function day-to-day, schedule an appointment with a mental health professional.

In the end, the decision about whether you should file for bankruptcy is yours to make. Although a credit counseling agency and a bankruptcy attorney can advise you about what to do from a financial and legal perspective, it's up to you to decide if filing for bankruptcy is right for you. However, don't allow yourself to be influenced by what credi-

> **Red Alert!**
>
> If you are having suicidal thoughts, call the National Suicide Prevention Hotline at 800-273-8255.

tors and the media may say about consumers who go bankrupt. They have their own agenda and their comments have little or nothing to do with reality.

In this chapter, you learned about the history of bankruptcy law, about the ethical issues that may arise when you are trying to decide whether filing for bankruptcy is a step you want to take, and about common but harmful myths about bankruptcy and the people who file for bankruptcy. Hopefully, this information has helped you clarify your thoughts.

This chapter also discussed some of the emotions you may be feeling as you think about filing, as well as emotions you may feel if you do file, and it provided you with advice on how to cope with these emotions. Otherwise, if your emotions "get the best of you," you may find it difficult to think clearly and you may make bad decisions as a result.

The next chapter is loaded with more important information that you should have when you are thinking about filing or if you've already decided to file. For example, the chapter introduces you to the two most common types of consumer bankruptcy—a Chapter 7 liquidation and a Chapter 13 reorganization—and provides an overview of how each process works, together with the pros and cons of the two types of bankruptcy. It also explains the role of the bankruptcy trustee, the bankruptcy judge, your attorney, and your creditors in bankruptcy; it introduces you to key bankruptcy concepts you should know about; and it highlights the many different legal forms that will have to be filled out and filed with the court if you file for bankruptcy. It also explains that some kinds of debts will survive your bankruptcy and that you'll still have to pay them when your bankruptcy is over.

An Overview of the Bathkruptcy Process

This chapter is the first of three chapters detailing the bankruptcy process. It highlights the different kinds of consumer bankruptcies and tells you who is eligible to file for each, introduces you to the "cast of characters" you'll meet when you file, and explains how every bankruptcy begins. It also tells you about the many bankruptcy forms that must be filled out and filed with the court at the start of your bankruptcy and explains some of the key concepts fundamental to a Chapter 7 or a Chapter 13 bankruptcy—the two most common kinds of consumer bankruptcy. Finally, this chapter explains the differences and similarities between both kinds of bankruptcy and tells you what will happen once your bankruptcy is over.

Once you have read this chapter, turn to chapter 8 if you want to learn more about the Chapter 7 bankruptcy process. For more information about how a Chapter 13 bankruptcy works, read chapter 9.

GETTING A HANDLE ON THE DIFFERENT TYPES OF CONSUMER BANKRUPTCY

Most consumers who file for bankruptcy file either a Chapter 7 liquidation of debt or a Chapter 13 reorganization of debt. This book focuses on these two types of consumer bankruptcy.

1. Chapter 7 liquidation of debt. Consumers can file for this kind of bankruptcy in order to discharge or wipe out most of their debts. Any type of business can also file this kind of bankruptcy.
2. Chapter 13 bankruptcy reorganization of debt. Consumers who file this kind of bankruptcy get three to five years to pay most of their debts. Businesses run as sole proprietorships that want to stay in business can also file for Chapter 13.

In addition, there are other types of consumer bankruptcy, such as the following:

- Chapter 11 reorganization of debt. Consumers (as well as sole proprietorships) who have more than a certain dollar amount of unsecured and/or secured debt must file this kind of bankruptcy if they want to reorganize their debts. They cannot file a Chapter 13 reorganization. If you owe more than $336,970 in unsecured debt and more than $1,010,650 in secured debt, and you want to reorganize your debts instead of liquidating them, you'll have to file for Chapter 11. This kind of bankruptcy is much more expensive, more time-consuming, and more difficult to complete than a Chapter 13, and many consumers who file for Chapter 11 end up having to convert their bankruptcy to a Chapter 7 liquidation.

- Chapter 12 reorganization of debt. This is a special kind of reorganization bankruptcy reserved for family farmers.

MEET THE CAST OF CHARACTERS IN YOUR BANKRUPTCY

Regardless of the kind of bankruptcy that you file, once it begins and you start moving through the bankruptcy process, you will encounter a "cast of characters," each of whom will play a very specific role in your bankruptcy.

A Federally Approved Credit Counseling Agency

> **❗Hot Tip**
>
> You can file for bankruptcy without a Certificate of Compliance if you are on active duty in the military and stationed in a combat zone or if you are disabled or incapacitated and the court determines that, because of your condition, you can't complete the prebankruptcy counseling.

In 2005, Congress passed the federal Bankruptcy Abuse Prevention and Consumer Protection Act (BAPCPA), which amended the existing bankruptcy law. The BAPCPA requires you to meet with a federally approved credit counseling agency some time during the 180 days (six months) prior to beginning your bankruptcy. An agency counselor will educate you about the consequences of filing for bankruptcy and will determine if there is anything you can do to avoid bankruptcy, such as live on a stricter budget, consolidate your debts, or participate in a debt management program (a debt payment plan negotiated by the credit counseling agency). The prebankruptcy counseling session will last about one hour and will probably cost about $50.

If the counselor concludes that bankruptcy is your best option, you will be given a Certificate of Compliance, which entitles you to file. Give the certificate to your attorney.

 Red Alert!

To date, statistics show that most consumers who receive prebankruptcy counseling from a federally approved credit counseling agency are in such bad financial shape that there is nothing that they can do to avoid bankruptcy.

> **❢ Hot Tip**
>
> If you cannot afford to pay for prebankruptcy counseling and/or for the post-filing class, ask the credit counseling organization if it will waive its fee.

The BAPCPA also requires that you complete a post-filing debtor education class while you are in bankruptcy. Federally approved credit counseling agencies also offer this class, which will teach you how to develop a budget, manage your money, and use credit. Once you've completed this class, you'll receive a second certificate. The class will last about two hours and will probably cost somewhere between $50 and $100.

To locate a federally approved credit counseling agency in your area, go to *www.usdoj.gov/ust/eo/bapcpa/ccde/cc_approved.htm*. If there is no federally approved agency near you, some agencies offer counseling by phone or online.

> **❢ Hot Tip**
>
> If you need to file for bankruptcy on an emergency basis, for example, because your home is about to be foreclosed on or your car is about to be repossessed, and you haven't yet completed the required credit counseling to obtain a "Certificate of Compliance," your bankruptcy attorney will probably let you receive the counseling over the Internet using one of the attorney's office computers, and the credit counseling agency will email or fax the certificate to your attorney's office.

Bankruptcy Trustee

When your bankruptcy begins, a trustee will be assigned to your case by the office of the bankruptcy clerk for the court where your case has been filed. The trustee will probably be a private attorney, an accountant, or someone with extensive business experience. The U.S. Trustee Program, which works for the U.S. Department of Justice, will monitor the activities of the trustee. Regardless of whether you file a Chapter 7 or a Chapter 13 bankruptcy, the trustee will do the following:

- Ensure that your creditors will receive as much as you can possibly pay to them in your bankruptcy. The amount you must pay to your creditors is determined by the bankruptcy law, not by what you think you should (or would like to) pay to them.

- Scrutinize all of your bankruptcy forms and any other information that you are required to provide. The trustee will be looking for signs that you are trying to abuse the bankruptcy process, such as lying about your income and your assets, claiming unusual expenses, or trying to exempt assets from your bankruptcy that should be included in it. Exempt assets are assets that you keep despite your bankruptcy; nonexempt assets are assets that you may lose in your bankruptcy. The distinction between the two types of assets is explained later in this chapter in the section entitled, "Exempt versus Nonexempt Assets: What's the Difference?"

- Preside over the creditors' meeting in your bankruptcy, which will take place about six weeks after your bankruptcy has started. You'll learn more about this meeting later in this chapter, as well as in chapters 8 and 9.

- File a "motion to dismiss" if the trustee believes that you've abused the bankruptcy system. A hearing will be held on the motion, and during the hearing your attorney will argue why your bankruptcy should not be dismissed. The judge will decide what to do after listening to both sides of the issue. If the judge concludes that you abused the system and dismisses your bankruptcy, you may never be able to file for bankruptcy again or you may have to wait a certain amount of time before you can refile. It will be up to the judge to decide your punishment.

- Maintain responsibility during the bankruptcy process. Some of the trustee's other responsibilities will depend on the particular type of bankruptcy that you file. For example, if you file for Chapter 7, the trustee will take control of all of your nonexempt assets (the assets that are a part of your bankruptcy), sell them, and use the proceeds to pay your debts. If you file for Chapter 13, the trustee will distribute the money that you pay to your creditors during your bankruptcy according to the terms of the debt reorganization plan your attorney will prepare for you. The trustee will also make sure that you comply with all of the terms of the plan during the three to five years that you are in bankruptcy.

Your Creditors

After you have begun your bankruptcy, the bankruptcy court will formally notify your creditors about your bankruptcy and your attorney may notify some of them as well—probably your secured creditors. At that point, your creditors will file *proof of claim* forms with the court in order to get in line to be paid during your bankruptcy. (You'll find a sample proof of claim in the Appendix of this book.) They will also review the information on your bankruptcy forms and some of them— most likely your secured creditors—may attend the creditors' meeting in your bankruptcy and question you about the information on the forms. Also, while you are in bankruptcy, your creditors may file motions or objections with the court in order to make something happen or to prevent something from happening related to the money that you owe to them. Chapters 8 and 9 provide more information on the creditors' meeting.

Your Bankruptcy Attorney

After you've hired a bankruptcy attorney to help you with your bankruptcy, one of the very first things the attorney will do is apply a legally required means test to your finances to determine whether you can file for Chapter 7 bankruptcy or whether you must file for Chapter 13. The means test is described in the "Making Sense of the Means Test" section of this chapter. Your attorney also will complete your bankruptcy petition, fill out all of the other required bankruptcy forms, and file them with the court. In addition, your attorney will help you decide which assets to exempt from your bankruptcy (those you will get to keep), will be by your side at the creditors' meeting, will attend any hearings that may be scheduled during your bankruptcy, will deal with your creditors as necessary, and will be available to answer any questions you may have as you move through the bankruptcy process.

Bankruptcy Judge

If everything goes smoothly in your bankruptcy, you will probably never meet the judge. However, if there is a disagreement between you and the trustee or between you and any of your creditors, the judge will preside over a court hearing during which the judge will listen to the attorneys who represent each side of the issue. The judge will then decide how to resolve the dispute. Examples of the kinds of disagreements that may give rise to a hearing include the following:

- One of your creditors doesn't agree with some of the information on your bankruptcy forms.

- One of your secured creditors files a *motion to lift the stay* because it wants the court's permission to take back its collateral—the asset you used to secure the debt that you owe to the creditor.

- The trustee or one of your creditors files a motion to have your bankruptcy dismissed because they believe that you've abused the bankruptcy system.

- One of your unsecured creditors files an objection to the discharge of the debt that you owe because the creditor believes that you defrauded it in some way when you initially obtained the credit—for example, you lied about your income.

BEGINNING YOUR BANKRUPTCY

Every bankruptcy begins the same way: You ask the court to protect you from your creditors by filing a bankruptcy petition in federal

! Hot Tip

If you hire a bankruptcy attorney to help you with your bankruptcy (and you should), you'll also have to pay your attorney's fees and expenses. Chapter 7, "Working with a Consumer Bankruptcy Attorney," discusses how much your attorney is likely to charge. If you are worried about how you can afford to pay everything, one possible strategy is to begin accumulating the money you'll need during the months prior to the start of your bankruptcy by not paying the debts that will be discharged (wiped out) through the bankruptcy. However, don't use this strategy without first consulting with a bankruptcy attorney so that you know exactly which debts not to pay.

bankruptcy court and by paying the court a filing fee. At the time this book was written, the filing fee for a Chapter 7 liquidation bankruptcy was $299 and the fee for a Chapter 13 reorganization bankruptcy was $274. Occasionally, however, the federal government increases the amount of these fees, so if you want to know how much you'll have to pay before you file, go to *www.uscourts.gov/bankruptcycourts/fees.html.*

Red Alert!

If you haven't lived in your current state for at least 90 days, you'll either have to file in the state where you resided during the majority of the previous 180 days or in the state where your primary assets are located.

After your bankruptcy petition has been filed and your filing fee has been paid, the court will issue an *automatic stay,* which will prohibit most, but not all, of your creditors from trying to collect the money that you owe to them while you are in bankruptcy. Also, later in your bankruptcy, you will have to attend a creditors' meeting during which the trustee in your bankruptcy will question you about the information on your bankruptcy forms and about your finances. Any of your creditors who attend the meeting can ask you questions, too. In some cases, however, you may not be able to file for bankruptcy. Figure 6.1 provides information on when you can't file for bankruptcy.

✋ Red Alert!

Ordinarily, the automatic stay will remain in effect throughout your bankruptcy. However, if you filed for bankruptcy within the past year and the judge dismissed the bankruptcy because you failed to comply with some aspect of the bankruptcy law, the automatic stay in your new bankruptcy will last for only 30 days unless your attorney can convince the judge to extend it. Losing the protection of the automatic stay after just 30 days and being vulnerable again to the collection actions of your creditors as a result will be a particular problem if you've filed for Chapter 13. This is because not only will you face the challenge of trying to complete your bankruptcy, but you will also have to cope with the efforts of creditors to collect the money that you owe to them. Also, if you had two bankruptcies dismissed within the past year, the court will not issue an automatic stay at all when you file a new bankruptcy, unless the judge agrees with your attorney that it should be invoked.

FORMS TO FILL OUT AND FILE

In addition to filing your bankruptcy petition, your bankruptcy attorney will fill out and file many other forms at the start of your bankruptcy, including various Schedules of Assets and Schedules of Debts, as well as a Statement of Financial Affairs. These forms will probably be filed at the same time as your bankruptcy petition, but they can be filed up to 15 days after the petition is filed. Your bankruptcy will be dismissed if any of your forms are not filed on time.

❗Hot Tip

When you attend the creditors' meeting, you'll have to prove your identity to the trustee. Be sure to bring to the meeting your driver's license or some other form of photo ID and your Social Security card or some other proof of your Social Security number.

✋ Red Alert!

Never let your secured creditors know that you are about to file for bankruptcy! If you do, they may decide to beat you to the punch by taking back the assets that are collateralizing your debts.

FIGURE 6.1. When You Can't File for Bankruptcy

Under certain circumstances, no matter how dire the state of your finances, you may not be able to file for bankruptcy when you want to, or you may not be able to file the kind of bankruptcy that you want to. For example, you cannot file the following:

■ A Chapter 13 if you received a discharge of debts in a Chapter 7 (or in a Chapter 11 or 12) within the past four years, or if you completed a Chapter 13 bankruptcy within the past two years.

■ A Chapter 7 if your debts were discharged in a Chapter 7 within the past eight years.

■ A Chapter 7 if you received a discharge of debt in a Chapter 13 within the previous six years. However, this restriction doesn't apply if you paid 100 percent of your creditors' claims in the Chapter 13 bankruptcy or if you paid 70 percent of your creditors' claims and the court believes that you could not have paid any more than that.

Also, if your previous bankruptcy was dismissed because the court determined that you deliberately and knowingly abused the bankruptcy process—you hid assets from the court or you misrepresented the state of your finances on your bankruptcy forms—you may have to wait six months to refile or you may not be able to file for bankruptcy ever again. It will be the judge's decision.

In addition, if your previous bankruptcy was dismissed for any of the following reasons, you'll have to wait six months to file for bankruptcy again:

■ You willfully failed to abide by an order of the court or to appear for a hearing in your bankruptcy.

■ One of your secured creditors filed a motion to lift stay, and your bankruptcy was dismissed at your request so that you could stop the motion from moving forward.

■ You did not get a Certificate of Compliance from a federally approved credit counseling agency sometime during the 180 days preceding your bankruptcy, with a few exceptions.

■ You did not complete a debtor education class while you were in bankruptcy.

Figure 6.2, "Forms, Forms, and More Forms," provides a list of all of the forms that must be filed with the court. The Appendix to this book provides a sample of many of these forms for your reference.

❗**Hot Tip**

If you are married, you and your spouse don't have to file bankruptcy together. However, if the two of you are jointly responsible for most of your debts, it's usually cheaper to file together. Ask your bankruptcy attorney if there are any reasons why only one of you should file.

Your bankruptcy attorney will fill out all of the forms in your bankruptcy using information that you provide, including various documents and records the attorney will ask for. These documents and records will include the following:

- Copies of pay stubs for any work you performed during the 60 days prior to the start of your bankruptcy. If you and your spouse are filing for bankruptcy together and your spouse works outside the home, your spouse must also provide pay stubs. If either of you has your paychecks direct-deposited into a bank account, you must provide deposit confirmations from your employer or bank.

- Your IRS tax returns for the previous two years. If you have not filed these returns, you must file them before your creditors' meeting. If you don't, your bankruptcy will be dismissed. In some jurisdictions, the trustee will ask you to provide tax returns for additional years, as well. If you cannot find them in your records, you will have to order them from the IRS.

- Deeds to any real estate you may own. You need to provide these even if you have a very small interest in the property.

 Red Alert!

If any of your creditors ask for copies of your tax returns, you must provide them. If you don't, your bankruptcy may be dismissed.

- Titles to all of your vehicles. This includes your cars as well as any boats, motorcycles, trailers, or RVs that you may own.

- Copies of any life insurance policies you have on your own life, the life of your spouse, and/or on your children's lives. If you have any whole life policies (policies that combine insurance with a savings component) rather than term life policies (polices that are pure insurance), you must provide your attorney with the *cash surrender value* of those policies. The cash surrender value represents the savings portion of the policy. Generally, the longer you've owned a policy, the larger its cash surrender value. You must also provide copies of policies for any other kinds of insurance you may have, such as auto insurance, homeowners' insurance, and disability insurance.

- Any communications you may have received from debt collectors about your debts.

- Copies of any lawsuits your creditors or someone else may have filed against you.

- Any recent written appraisals you may have. This includes appraisals for your home and/or for any fine art, antiques, jewelry, and the like that you may own.

Your attorney may ask you for other documents and records, too. What you may be asked for will depend on the particular details of your finances.

✋ Red Alert!

Be sure that you provide your attorney with complete and accurate information about all of your assets, debts, and recent financial transactions. If you don't, your bankruptcy may be dismissed; or a debt that doesn't get listed on your Schedules of Debts and that would ordinarily be discharged will survive your bankruptcy, which means that you'll have to pay it once the bankruptcy is over. Your attorney also has an incentive to ensure the completeness and accuracy of your bankruptcy forms, because your attorney must certify to the court that they are complete and accurate. If your attorney turns out to be wrong, the bankruptcy court may require your attorney to pay the court costs and legal fees.

Your Schedules of Assets, Schedules of Debts, and Statement of Financial Affairs

The heart of your bankruptcy is the information on your Schedules of Assets, Schedules of Debts, and Statement of Financial Affairs. The trustee and your creditors will study that information very carefully looking for problems. In fact, your Schedules and Statement of Financial Affairs, more than any of the other forms filed in your bankruptcy, are most apt to trigger disagreements between you and your creditors and/or you and the trustee.

Following is an overview of exactly what kinds of information are on the forms.

Statement of Financial Affairs. Your Statement of Financial Affairs provides information about your financial transactions in recent years. Its main purpose is to alert the trustee to transactions that the trustee

🖐 Red Alert!

Auditors hired by the U.S. Trustee's Office—the office that is charged with monitoring the work of the trustees in each federal bankruptcy court and with reviewing individual bankruptcy cases for signs of abuse—conduct random reviews of consumers' Schedules looking for inaccurate and incomplete information. If your forms are audited and the auditor decides that something is not exactly right, a hearing will be scheduled to look into the matter. You'll be punished if the judge decides that there are problems with your forms and that those problems will have (or have had) serious negative consequences for your creditors, or if you do not have a good explanation for why the problems exist. If this happens, your bankruptcy may be dismissed, which means that none of your debts will be discharged and your creditors can try to collect what you owe to them. Also, if the judge concludes that you deliberately created the problems with your forms—that you made a *material misstatement of fact*—your case will be referred to the Office of the U.S. Attorney General for criminal prosecution. If that office finds you guilty of fraud, you will be sent to prison. Your bankruptcy forms can even be audited after you are out of bankruptcy and, depending on what the auditor finds, the judge might revoke your discharge of debt, which would mean that you would have to pay the debts that had been wiped out through your bankruptcy.

may be able to void (cancel) and to assets that the trustee can liquidate to pay as many of your debts as possible.

Schedules of Assets. Your Schedules of Assets provide information about the various assets you own, including their market values—what you would have to pay for them if you bought the assets today in their current conditions. They include a schedule for your real property (your home and other real estate, including raw land, that you may own in whole or in part) and a schedule for your personal property such as the money in your bank accounts, your household goods and furnishings, your clothing, your car, your jewelry, the interests you may have in any insurance policies, and the like.

Schedules of Debts. Your Schedules of Debts list all of your creditors, including their names and addresses, the account number associated with each of your debts, the amount that you owe to each of your creditors, whether a particular debt is secured or unsecured, and the collateral associated with each secured debt, among other things. Also, if you've been on the losing end of any lawsuits recently, your Schedules of Debts must include the amount of money that the court ordered you to pay to the plaintiff (the individual or business that sued you) as a result. As you can see from reviewing the information in Figure 6.2, there are different Schedules depending on whether the bankruptcy law categorizes the debts that you owe as priority, secured, or unsecured debts. The law requires that you treat each type of debt in a very specific way:

- **Priority debts.** These are the most important kinds of debts in a consumer bankruptcy; therefore, you cannot get rid of them by filing. Instead, you'll have to pay the full amount of your

 Red Alert!

Tell your attorney about every single asset that you own, even if you think that some of them are not worth much or are not in good working order—for example, that clunker sitting in your driveway. If the bankruptcy court discovers that you deliberately omitted an asset from one of your Schedules of Assets, your bankruptcy may be dismissed or you may be denied a discharge of debt.

priority debts. Past due taxes, child and/or spousal support, and student loans are examples of priority debts.

- **Secured debts.** These are debts that you collateralized with some of your assets. If you file for Chapter 7 bankruptcy, you may have to give up those assets unless you can afford to hold on to them. For example, if you exempt an asset that is collateralizing one of your debts, in order to keep that asset you'll have to *reaffirm* the debt. Chapter 8 explains how a *reaffirmation of debt* works.

A Chapter 13 bankruptcy makes it easier to hold on to your collateral. That's because it gives you three to five years to pay off the debts that your collateral secures.

- **Unsecured debts.** These kinds of debts include credit card debts and unpaid medical bills. The bankruptcy judge will probably discharge most, if not all, of them regardless of the kind of bankruptcy you file because unsecured debts are the least important kind of debt in bankruptcy, and because after your more important debts have been dealt with, there is usually little or no money left to pay them.

Depending on the specific type of bankruptcy you file, your attorney may have to complete other forms, as well. For example, in a Chapter 7 bankruptcy, your attorney will also file a Statement of Intention, which indicates how you intend to treat each of the assets that collateralize your secured debts, such as your mortgage, car loan, and furniture

---

 Red Alert!

Be sure that the addresses you provide your attorney for each of your creditors are correct. The addresses should be the ones your creditors designated in at least two of the communications you received from them during the 90 days prior to the start of your bankruptcy. If the addresses listed on your Schedules of Debts are not accurate, your creditors may not receive notification from the court that you've filed for bankruptcy, and as a result, they may violate the automatic stay. If any of them do violate the stay in this case, they won't be penalized by the court because it will be your fault, not theirs, that they did not know about it.

FIGURE 6.2. Forms, Forms, and More Forms

Beginning a bankruptcy involves completing many forms and filing them with the court. If the forms are not filed by the required deadlines, your bankruptcy will be dismissed. It may also be dismissed if any of your forms are not 100 percent complete and accurate. Getting the forms completed correctly and filed on time is one of the key reasons why it is so important to hire a bankruptcy attorney to handle your bankruptcy. The attorney will be very familiar with the forms, so it will be a lot easier for the attorney to complete them accurately and on time.

Following are the forms that apply to both a Chapter 7 and a Chapter 13 bankruptcy:

■ Voluntary Petition (the form that you must complete and file with the bankruptcy court to officially begin your bankruptcy)

■ Cover Sheet for Schedules

■ Summary of Schedules

■ Schedule A—Real Property

■ Schedule B—Personal Property

■ Schedule C—Property Claimed as Exempt

■ Schedule D—Creditors Holding Secured Claims

■ Schedule E—Creditors Holding Unsecured Priority Claims

■ Schedule F—Creditors Holding Unsecured Nonpriority Claims

■ Schedule G—Executory Contracts and Unexpired Leases

■ Schedule H—Codebtors

■ Schedule I—Current Income of Individual Debtor(s)

■ Schedule J—Current Expenditures of Individual Debtor(s)

■ Declaration Concerning Debtor's Schedules

Forms, Forms, and More Forms continues on next page.

- Statement of Financial Affairs

- Chapter 7 Statement of Current Monthly Income and Means-Test Calculation

- List of Creditors Holding 20 Largest Unsecured Claims

- Statement of Compliance

- Statement of Completion

loan. This form is filed with your bankruptcy petition, and your attorney must serve the trustee and your creditors with a copy.

If you file a Chapter 13, your attorney must also file a Statement of Current Monthly Income and Calculation of Commitment Period and Disposable Income, as well as the debt reorganization plan you propose. In your plan, you detail exactly what you intend to do about each of your debts in your bankruptcy.

> **▼ Hot Tip**
>
> Let your attorney know about anyone you think *might* sue you in the near future. Sometimes, just listing a possible claim on your Schedules of Debts is enough to get it discharged.

You can find samples of many of these bankruptcy forms in the Appendix to this book.

BANKRUPTCY-RELATED CONCEPTS YOU SHOULD UNDERSTAND

Before you file for bankruptcy, it's helpful to understand some key concepts related to bankruptcy. They include how the federally mandated means test is used to determine what kind of bankruptcy you can file, what the automatic stay will and won't do during your bankruptcy, and what it means to exempt an asset in your bankruptcy.

Making Sense of the Means Test

Before the BAPCPA was passed, you and your attorney decided whether you would file a Chapter 7 or a Chapter 13 bankruptcy. Now, however, whether you can file for Chapter 7 or whether you must file for Chapter 13 instead is determined by a federally mandated means test that your bankruptcy attorney must apply to your finances. The reason for the means test is that one of the BAPCPA's underlying assumptions is that consumers use credit irresponsibly; and when they begin having problems paying their debts, far too many of them take the "easy way out" by wiping out their debts through a Chapter 7 bankruptcy rather than paying what they owe over time through a Chapter 13. Therefore, the goal of the means test is to force more consumers into a Chapter 13 bankruptcy.

You don't need to understand all of the complex ins and outs of the means test (that's what a bankruptcy attorney is for), but it's helpful to have a general idea of what the test may mean to you. Here is a short explanation: Your attorney will apply the means test to your finances by comparing your average household income for the previous six months to the median (average) household income for your state. If your income falls below that median, you can file for Chapter 7 if you want or you can file for Chapter 13. But, if your income is *above* the median, your attorney will compare your living expenses to your income to determine how much you can afford to pay on your debts over a five-year period. If the comparison shows that you can afford to pay at least $10,000 on your debt over that period of time, or at least $166.67 per month, you must file for Chapter 13. If you can't

---

❗ Hot Tip

Bankruptcy attorneys and other consumer advocates disagree with the underlying assumption behind the means test. They know that most consumers who file for Chapter 7 developed serious money troubles because their finances were ruined by high medical bills, job loss, or divorce, not because the consumers were irresponsible overspenders. They also know that most consumers do everything they can think of to avoid having to file for bankruptcy.

afford to pay that much, your attorney must perform a third calculation, which involves comparing the amount of disposable income you anticipate having over the next five years to the total amount of your nonpriority unsecured debts, such as any outstanding credit card and medical bills you may owe. If the amount of your disposable income is less than 25 percent of the total amount of those debts, you can file for Chapter 7; otherwise, you must file for Chapter 13.

One of the problems with the means test is that when your attorney compares your living expenses to your income, your actual expenses cannot be used. Instead, the bankruptcy law requires your attorney to use IRS-defined dollar amounts for each expense. (These amounts are adjusted to reflect the cost of living in your particular area of the country). Because the IRS amounts may be considerably less than what you are actually spending, it's likely that the means test will show that you can afford to pay more to your creditors than you think is realistic.

❗ Hot Tip

If you know that your income is going to drop a lot very soon because you are about to lose your job or because you own a sole proprietorship, or one of your major contracts is about to end and you have no new contract to replace it, you may be able to qualify for a Chapter 7 by waiting to file for bankruptcy until your average income for the previous six months is low enough. Talk to your bankruptcy attorney about whether this strategy or some other strategy makes sense if you want to file for Chapter 7 bankruptcy.

Appreciating the Power and the Limits of the Automatic Stay

After you've initiated your bankruptcy, the bankruptcy court will issue an automatic stay, which is an injunction prohibiting most of your creditors from trying to collect the debts that you owe to them while you are in bankruptcy. For example, once it's in place:

- Your mortgage lender cannot foreclose on your home.

- Your car lender cannot take back (repossess) your vehicle. The same is true for other secured lenders.

- Your creditors cannot sue you for nonpayment of your debts. Also, any lawsuits that may have already been filed against you will be put on hold.

- Any creditors who have been awarded a money judgment against you as a result of a lawsuit that they filed cannot try to collect on the judgment.

- Most creditors cannot put liens on any of your assets. However, your local property taxing authority *can* put a lien on your home if you're behind on your property taxes.

- The IRS and your state's taxing authorities cannot continue trying to collect any past due taxes you may owe.

- Debt collectors cannot call you about a past due debt that you owe or take any other action to collect from you.

❗ Hot Tip

If you signed a contract before your bankruptcy began and you and/or the other parties to the contract still have duties or obligations to one another under it, you can break the contract once the automatic stay is in place. When you do, you won't have to pay any more money on the contract. For example, you can cancel your health club membership if you signed a year-long contract with the club and you are paying for the membership over time. This kind of contract is referred to as an *executory contract*.

As powerful as the automatic stay is, however, there are things that it can't stop. For example, it can't stop the following:

- Any criminal action that may be initiated against you while you are in bankruptcy. For example, if you give a business a hot check—a check that you don't make good on—the business can press charges against you and the district attorney can prosecute you while you are in bankruptcy.

- Your ex-spouse from trying to collect any past due court-ordered child support you may owe by going after the assets that are not part of your *bankruptcy estate*. (In a Chapter 13 bankruptcy, your bankruptcy estate includes all of your assets; in a Chapter 7, it includes just your nonexempt assets.) The same is true if you have a child from an unmarried relationship and you've fallen behind on your court-ordered child support payments to the child's other parent.

- Your ex-spouse from trying to collect any past due court-ordered spousal support you may owe

- A lawsuit filed to determine whether you are the father of a child or to establish a court order for child and/or spousal support

- An eviction, if the local court with jurisdiction over the matter has already issued a court order for your eviction and if the law in your state says that it's too late for your lease to be reinstated. As a result, even though you've filed for bankruptcy, your landlord can proceed with your eviction.

- An IRS tax audit. The IRS can audit your tax returns while you are in bankruptcy. However, if the agency determines that you owe money, it cannot try to collect that money until your bankruptcy is over, although it can (and will) send you a notice telling you how much you owe. The same is true for other taxing authorities, including your state and local taxing authorities.

- The efforts of a government agency to enforce a regulation you may have violated. For example, if your local government sends you a notice directing you to clean up the junk in your yard and you ignore the notice, the agency can fine you while you are in bankruptcy.

- A divorce proceeding. However, if you and your soon-to-be-ex reach an agreement on the division of your property while you're in bankruptcy, the bankruptcy judge must approve the agreement before it can become an official part of your divorce.

- A domestic violence lawsuit that has been filed against you

- An action to withhold, suspend, or restrict your driver's license

- An action to withhold, suspend, or restrict your professional license

Other important limits of the automatic stay include the following:

- If you owe money to a utility company, it cannot terminate your service while the stay is in effect. However, the company can require that you pay it a *reasonable deposit*, assuming you didn't pay one when you initiated the service. Generally, a reasonable deposit is defined as an amount equal to the average cost of two months of utility service. You must pay the deposit within 20 days of filing for bankruptcy.

- If you have fallen behind on an ongoing lease, such as your apartment or auto lease, the automatic stay gives you time to figure out what to do about it—if you want to continue paying on the lease or break it. If you want to continue paying on the lease so that you can stay in your apartment or keep your leased car, you must pay the full amount of the lease that is past due no later than 30 days after the start of your bankruptcy. However, given the state of your finances, coming up with the money you need by the deadline could be difficult if not impossible for you to do, which would mean that you would have no option but to break the lease.

- If there was an existing court order at the time that you filed for bankruptcy requiring you to pay child and/or spousal support through automatic wage deductions, the court order will stay in effect. Also, if you were not already obligated to pay child and/or spousal support at the time that you filed for bankruptcy, a family law court can establish that obligation after your bankruptcy has begun.

Once the automatic stay has been invoked, the bankruptcy court will mail a notice about the stay to you and to each of the creditors listed on your petition so that they know that you've filed for bankruptcy. The notice will also indicate the name of the trustee assigned to your bankruptcy, the date of your creditors' meeting, the date by which the creditors must file their proof of claim forms, and the date by which they must file objections to your bankruptcy if they want. (In most

---

❗ Hot Tip

If you filed for Chapter 13 and some of your secured or priority creditors don't file a proof of claim with the court, your attorney will file the claims for them so that you can be sure that when you are making payments on your debt reorganization plan during your three to five years in bankruptcy, some of that money will go to those creditors. If you file a Chapter 7, however, your attorney will only file a proof of claim form for any of your priority credi- tors who do not file one for themselves. That way, if there is any money to distribute in your bankruptcy, those creditors will be in line to get some. Otherwise, once your bankruptcy is over, you'll have to pay whatever you owe to them and you'll no longer be protected by the automatic stay at that point; this means that if you don't pay those creditors, they can come after you for the money.

---

consumer bankruptcies, no objections are filed.) However, due to bureaucratic paperwork and red tape, the bankruptcy court probably won't mail the notices to your creditors right away. Therefore, your attorney will immediately contact your secured creditors to let them know you've filed so that they won't take steps to take back your collateral and so that they will suspend any collection efforts they may have already begun.

If any of your creditors ignore the automatic stay, contact your attorney right away. The court will fine them if it can be proved that the creditors knew about the automatic stay and tried to collect from you anyway. The

---

Red Alert!

In a Chapter 7 bankruptcy, the IRS almost never files a proof of claim. Therefore, if you owe past due federal taxes, be sure that your attorney files one for the agency if there is going to be money for the trustee to distribute to your creditors. Otherwise, you'll have to pay your past due tax debt once your bank- ruptcy is over, because the automatic stay no longer protects you. As a result, if you can't afford to pay that debt, you'll be subject to the almost unlimited collection powers of the IRS. Chapter 2 explains the various ways that the IRS can collect past due taxes.

Red Alert!

If a creditor tries to collect from you after the automatic stay is in place because you forgot to tell your attorney that you owed money to that creditor (and as a result the debt was not listed on your Schedules of Debts), let your attorney know immediately. Your attorney will amend the appropriate schedule so that the creditor can be formally notified of your bankruptcy.

bankruptcy judge may also order the creditors to pay you for any damages you may have suffered because they violated the automatic stay.

Exempt versus Nonexempt Assets: What's the Difference?

One of the most important concepts in bankruptcy is the difference between *exempt* and *nonexempt assets.* An exempt asset is an asset that is not part of your bankruptcy estate, which means that you get to keep it. A nonexempt asset, on the other hand, is an asset that *is* part of your bankruptcy estate. Therefore, you may lose it in bankruptcy. The thinking behind being able to exempt assets is that you need a basic amount of property to be able to earn a living, take care of your family, and simply live your life.

If you file for Chapter 7, you will lose most of your nonexempt assets because the trustee will take control of them, sell them, and apply the proceeds to your debts. However, there are things you can do to hold on to those assets, which will be discussed in chapter 8.

If you file for Chapter 13, you can keep all of your nonexempt assets. However, the total value of the nonexempt assets that you keep will determine the minimum amount of money you must pay to your creditors during the three to five years that you are in bankruptcy.

To hold on to an exempt secured asset, regardless of whether you file for Chapter 7 or for Chapter 13, you must pay the creditor to whom you owe the debt all of the money that is past due while you are in bankruptcy, and you must make all future payments on that debt as they come due during your bankruptcy. If you don't, you will lose the asset, even though you filed for bankruptcy, and the creditor can take back the asset, sell it, and apply the sale proceeds to your debt. If the asset doesn't sell for enough to pay the outstanding balance on the debt, the remaining balance will become an unsecured debt and it will be discharged at the end of your bankruptcy.

 Red Alert!

The more *equity* you have in the secured assets that you want to exempt, the more quickly you'll use up all of your property exemptions because there is a limit on the total dollar value of assets you can keep in bankruptcy. If you file for Chapter 7 and you use up all of your exemptions, it means that you'll probably lose most of your nonexempt assets. Equity is the difference between what you currently owe on an asset and what is worth. For example, let's assume you borrowed $500 to purchase a piece of art that has grown in value and is now worth $1,000. And let's say that your loan balance is $250. That means that you have $750 worth of equity in the art, or the difference between its $1,000 market value and your $250 loan balance.

Before you file for bankruptcy, your attorney will help you decide which assets to exempt. Your goal will be to keep as much of your property as possible. When you are deciding what to exempt, your state may allow you to choose between the federal exemptions listed in the bankruptcy code and the exemptions provided by your state, or your state may require you to use its exemptions. States that give you the option of choosing the federal exemptions are Arkansas, Connecticut, Hawaii, Massachusetts, Michigan, Minnesota, New Jersey, New Mexico, Pennsylvania, Rhode Island, Texas, Vermont, Washington, and Wisconsin, as well as the District of Columbia. If you have a choice, your attorney will make sure that you choose whichever set of exemptions benefits you the most.

Most state exemption laws permit you to keep, at a minimum, your clothing, household goods (dishes, pots and pans, and bedding), and a car, up to a certain dollar value, as well as the tools and equipment you need to earn a living. Some states also allow you to retain some of the equity in your homestead (the home you reside in), although the total dollar amount that you can keep varies from state to state. However, federal bankruptcy law states that if you acquired your home within 1,215 days of the start of your bankruptcy, you can only exempt $125,000 of the equity—regardless of how much equity you actually have in your home—even if your state's law allows you to exempt more or all of your equity.

 Red Alert!

If you want to exempt some portion of the equity in your home, you can choose the exemption for the state where you currently reside, assuming you've been living in that state for at least 730 days (two years). Otherwise, you must use the exemption for the state where you lived during most of the 180 days immediately preceding the 730 days.

AN OVERVIEW OF THE CHAPTER 7 BANKRUPTCY PROCESS

When you file for Chapter 7 bankruptcy, the trustee takes control of most or all of your nonexempt assets, sells them, and distributes the sales proceeds among your creditors according to the rules of bankruptcy. After all of the proceeds have been used up, the court discharges your remaining debts, except for any debts that you can't wipe out through bankruptcy (referred to as *nondischargeable debts*) and any debts that you may have reaffirmed, that is, debts that you agreed to continue paying according to your original contracts with your creditors. Examples of debts that are most often discharged in a Chapter 7 include credit card debts, medical debts, debts to friends or family members, and most other kinds of unsecured debts. Once your debts are discharged, which will usually happen about 120 days

❗ Hot Tip

Many consumers who file for Chapter 7 have no assets other than the ones that they exempt, which means that there are no assets in their bankruptcy for the trustee to liquidate. As a result, these *no-asset* bankruptcies are mainly about discharging debts.

after your bankruptcy begins, you'll be out of bankruptcy. Figure 6.3 provides a list of nondischargeable debts.

AN OVERVIEW OF THE CHAPTER 13 BANKRUPTCY PROCESS

A Chapter 13 bankruptcy helps you avoid the loss of your assets and lets you reduce the total amount of money that you must pay on certain types of debt, and it helps you pay off your debts over a three- to five-year period according to the terms of your debt reorganization. The automatic stay will protect you while you are paying off your debts.

Your creditors can object to the terms of the debt reorganization plan that you propose. If the judge upholds their objections, you'll have to revise your plan before the judge will confirm it. Your reorganization plan won't be official until it is confirmed. Once it is, you'll have to live up to everything you promise to do in your plan. However, if you begin having problems living up to your plan, let your attorney know. You may be

---

❗ Hot Tip

An advantage of filing for bankruptcy is that if you borrowed money and used some of your *household goods* to secure the loan, you can use bankruptcy to remove the lien on the loan. This means that the loan will become an unsecured debt that can be discharged. Bankruptcy law defines household goods as clothing, furniture, appliances, china, crockery, kitchenware, educational materials and educational equipment primarily used for your minor children, medical equipment and supplies, furniture exclusively used by your minor children or any dependents who are elderly or disabled, your personal effects including your children's toys and hobby equipment as well as your wedding rings, one radio, one television set, one VCR, and one personal computer and related equipment. According to the law, household goods do not include the following: works of art unless they were created by you or any of your relatives, electronic entertainment equipment with an aggregate value of more than $500, antiques and jewelry valued at more than $500 (except for a wedding ring), additional computers, and motorized vehicles including tractors, lawn tractors, boats, motorized recreational devices, watercraft, and aircraft.

able to avoid having your bankruptcy dismissed—which would mean that your creditors could start trying to collect from you again—by modifying your plan or converting your bankruptcy to a Chapter 7. You'll learn about plan modifications and about conversions in chapter 9.

CHAPTER 7 VERSUS CHAPTER 13: BENEFITS AND DRAWBACKS

Both Chapter 7 and Chapter 13 bankruptcies have their own pluses and minuses. For example, although most of your debts get erased in a relatively short period of time when you file for Chapter 7, that kind of bankruptcy will stay in your credit histories for 10 years. During that time, as a result, your credit scores will be lower than if you hadn't filed for Chapter 7, and you won't qualify for new credit with attractive terms. However, the further in the past your Chapter 7 bankruptcy occurred, the less of a negative impact it will have on your life.

Here are the primary benefits of filing for Chapter 13:

- You can keep most, if not all, of your assets.

- Under certain circumstances, you can pay off some types of secured debts (such as a car loan or a furniture loan) by paying the market value of the collateral that secures the debt in payments over the term of the plan keeping the total amount that you still owe on the debt. When you do, it's referred to as a *cram down*. A cram down makes sense if the loan collateral has lost so much value since you got the loan that the asset is now worth less than what you still owe on it.

 Red Alert!

To qualify for a cram down on a car loan, you must have purchased the car at least 910 days before you filed for bankruptcy. If you want to cram down a furniture loan, you must have purchased the furniture within one year of filing. You cannot use a cram down on a mortgage.

- It helps you get rid of a portion of the outstanding balances on certain types of unsecured debts, assuming that the bankruptcy court believes that you can't afford to pay 100 percent of those balances while you're in bankruptcy. This is also assuming your creditors will receive at least as much as they would have if your assets had been liquidated in a Chapter 7.

- It gives you three to five years to pay the amount of your past due mortgage.

- It gives you three to five years to pay debts that would be nondischargeable in a Chapter 7, such as past due taxes and past due child and/or spousal support.

- The three national credit reporting agencies will report your Chapter 13 bankruptcy for 7 years rather than 10.

The main disadvantages of filing for a Chapter 13 are that you'll be involved with the bankruptcy court for three to five years, and you'll have to pay more on your debts than if you filed for Chapter 7.

WHEN IT'S BETTER TO FILE FOR CHAPTER 13

If the means test gives you a choice about the kind of bankruptcy you can file, it's sometimes better to file for Chapter 13, even though you can wipe out most of your debts in a Chapter 7. Here are some examples of when you're better off filing for Chapter 13:

- You're behind on your payments for the secured assets that you want to keep (your secured exempt assets), such as your home and your car. A Chapter 13 gives you three to five years to catch up on those debts under the protection of the bankruptcy court. In contrast, if you file for Chapter 7, you'll have to begin paying what you still owe on the debts as soon as you are out of bankruptcy, and the automatic stay won't protect you.

- You want to keep some of your nonexempt assets. In a Chapter 7, you'll have to give up those assets unless you can come up with enough cash—maybe by borrowing the money you need from a close friend or relative—to buy them back from the trustee.

- You owe past due taxes. If unpaid taxes represent a large portion of your total debt and you can afford to pay the taxes over time, then a Chapter 13 bankruptcy is probably your best choice because it's very difficult to discharge tax debts in a Chapter 7. Furthermore, even if you can use Chapter 7 to discharge the debts, if the IRS or any other taxing authority had a lien on your property at the time that you filed for bankruptcy, the lien will survive your bankruptcy. As a result, once your Chapter 7 bankruptcy is over, the taxing authority will either take the property that has the lien on it or keep trying to collect from you.

- A friend or relative cosigned for one of your debts and you want to protect that individual from the creditor to whom you owe the debt. When someone cosigns on a debt, that person is as obligated as you are to pay the debt, which means that if you fall behind on your payments, the creditor can try to collect from you and from the cosigner. However, the automatic stay in a Chapter 13 bankruptcy protects not just *your* assets, but your cosigner's, as well—as long as you pay the cosigned debt according to the terms of your reorganization plan. However, if you don't pay 100 percent of a cosigned debt through your reorganization plan, the creditor can ask the court for permission to pursue your cosigner for the amount that is still outstanding. In contrast, Chapter 7 provides no protections for a cosigner.

- You owe past due student loan debt. You can't discharge your student loan debt in a Chapter 7 unless you can qualify for a hardship discharge, which is very difficult to do. Therefore, assuming you don't get a hardship discharge, you'll still owe the debt when your bankruptcy is over. However, if you file for Chapter 13, you can include the debt in your reorganization plan and pay it off over time under the protection of the automatic stay. Review Figure 6.3 for the criteria you must satisfy to get a hardship discharge.

FIGURE 6.3. Debts You'll Still Owe When Your Bankruptcy Is Over

If you file for Chapter 7, some kinds of debts will be nondischargeable, which means that they will survive the bankruptcy. You'll have to pay them once your bankruptcy is over. These debts include the following:

- Past due income taxes, with some exceptions, that you owed at the start of your bankruptcy

- Taxes owed due to tax evasion or fraud

- Past due child support

- Past due spousal support

- Obligations under the terms of a divorce division of property agreement

- Student loan debt, unless you are able to get a *hardship discharge*. To get such a hardship discharge, however, you must prove three things: 1) that you will not be able to maintain a "minimal" standard of living for yourself and your dependents, based on your current income and expenses, if you are forced to repay your student loan; 2) that the current state of your finances is likely to persist for a significant portion of your loan repayment period due to additional circumstances; and 3) that you've made a good-faith effort to repay the loan. To date, court records show that most consumers who ask for a hardship discharge do not get one.

- Criminal fines and criminal restitution (*Restitution* is money that a court may order you to pay the victim of your crime.)

- Civil fines and restitution

- Debts that you obtained through fraudulent means, assuming the creditor to whom you owe the money can prove the fraud. For example, you may have used a false name or lied about your income to get a loan.

- Debts that you owe because you caused a motor-vehicle accident while you were intoxicated or under the influence of illegal drugs

- A cash advance from your credit card for more than $750 that you obtained during the 70 days preceding the start of your bankruptcy

- Any debts you may owe because you willfully or maliciously injured someone

Debts You'll Still Owe When Your Bankruptcy Is Over *continues on next page.*

- A consumer debt for more than $500 that is owed to a single creditor and that you incurred to purchase luxury goods or services during the 90 days prior to the start of your bankruptcy. This assumes that the creditor to whom you owe the money files a complaint against you with the bankruptcy court and is able to prove that you used the credit to purchase luxury goods or services within that time frame.

- The balance due on a credit card account or on a bank loan that is the result of your borrowing money to pay a tax debt, depending on how the tax debt would have been treated in your bankruptcy if you still owed it. In other words, if you use a credit card or a bank loan to pay a tax obligation, the new debt becomes the same kind of debt as the tax debt would have been in your bankruptcy. So if you would not have been able to discharge the debt in bankruptcy, then you won't be able to discharge the balance due on the credit card or on the loan.

- Any debts you may owe from a previous bankruptcy

Debts that you will owe when you are out of Chapter 13 bankruptcy if not paid through the Chapter 13 plan include the following:

- Federal and state tax debts that you owe because you never filed a tax return or an extension to file request, because you filed the return or a request for an extension to file after April 15, or because you did not pay your taxes

- Any past due child and/or spousal support you may owe

- Your obligations under the terms of your divorce division of property agreement

- Any fines or restitution you may owe because you were convicted of a crime (civil or criminal)

- Money you owe because you were convicted of drunk driving

- The amount that is outstanding on your mortgage

- The amount that is outstanding on your student loan debts

- Any liens that are attached to your secured assets. For example, if you have a mortgage, then your lender has a lien on your home. After you are out of bankruptcy, that lien will continue to exist as long as you are still paying on your mortgage, giving your lender the right to take your home if you fall too far behind on your mortgage.

ONCE YOUR BANKRUPTCY IS OVER

Your Chapter 7 bankruptcy will be over once the trustee has paid as many of your debts as possible and discharged all of your remaining debts, except those that will survive your bankruptcy. If you filed for Chapter 13, your bankruptcy will be over once you've completed your debt reorganization plan.

After you are out of bankruptcy, your credit histories will be ruined and your credit scores will be in the dumps. It will be impossible for you to obtain new credit at reasonable terms, although your mailbox may be full of credit card offers with low credit limits and high interest rates and fees, and you won't be able to qualify for a home mortgage or a car loan from a reputable lender right away. That's the bad news. The good news is that you can rebuild your credit, which will add positive information to your credit histories, raise your credit scores, and eventually make you more attractive to creditors, employers, insurance companies, and landlords. Chapter 10 provides an overview of the credit rebuilding process.

WHEN YOUR BANKRUPTCY CAN BE DISMISSED

It's possible that the judge will decide to dismiss your bankruptcy. If that happens, you will no longer be protected by the automatic stay, and you'll still owe all of your debts.

Possible reasons for having your bankruptcy dismissed include the following:

- You knowingly omitted some of your assets from your Schedules of Assets.

- You didn't file the required IRS tax returns with the court.

- You converted nonexempt assets into exempt assets when you shouldn't have.

- You lied at the creditors' meeting.

- You failed to complete the required financial education class before the end of your bankruptcy.

- You hid some of your assets from the court by transferring them to someone else sometime during the two years prior to the start of your bankruptcy.

- You ignored a court order issued by the bankruptcy court.

- You didn't cooperate with the trustee. For example, you didn't provide all of the information the trustee asked for.

- You missed some of your court-ordered child and/or spousal support payments while you were in bankruptcy.

- You are convicted of committing a crime of violence or of drug trafficking, and the victim of the crime files a motion with the court to have your bankruptcy dismissed.

- You received a discharge of debts through another Chapter 7 within eight years of the Chapter 7 you just filed.

- You filed a Chapter 13 bankruptcy within six years of the Chapter 7 you just filed, and less than 70 percent of your creditors' claims were paid in that bankruptcy.

This chapter has given you a lot of information to digest. In fact, before you read chapters 8 and 9, both of which provide more detailed information about bankruptcy, you may want to read this chapter again so that you can be sure that you've absorbed everything. Among other things, by reading this chapter you've learned about the two kinds of bankruptcy most consumers file, gained a basic understanding of how they both work, gotten up to speed on their pros and cons, and found out about the many legal forms that must be filed with the bankruptcy court to begin your bankruptcy. You also learned about the different roles that are played by a federally approved credit counseling agency, bankruptcy trustee, bankruptcy judge, your creditors, and your attorney, and you found out about key bankruptcy concepts such as the difference between exempt and nonexempt assets and the power of the automatic stay. In addition, you found out what will happen when your bankruptcy is over, including the kinds of debts that you'll still owe and the reasons why your bankruptcy might be dismissed, as well as the possible consequences of a dismissal.

Now that you have a fuller appreciation for the complexity of the bankruptcy process, it's time to read the next chapter, which explains the importance of hiring a bankruptcy attorney to handle your bankruptcy. It also briefs you about the particular services the attorney will provide and gives specific advice for finding a good bankruptcy attorney.

Working with a Consumer Bankruptcy Attorney

Bankruptcy is a complicated legal process that has become even more complicated since Congress passed the Bankruptcy Abuse Prevention and Consumer Protection Act (BAPCPA) in 2005. As a result, despite what some books on consumer bankruptcy may say, it's foolhardy to try to handle your own bankruptcy. This is because your creditors will be represented by savvy, seasoned attorneys who know bankruptcy law inside and out, and who will use their knowledge to help protect the interests of their clients at your expense. If you represent yourself, you will also be at much greater risk for having your bankruptcy dismissed because you miss an important deadline, don't file all of the required bankruptcy forms, or provide inaccurate or incomplete forms.

This chapter discusses when you should start talking with a bankruptcy attorney about your finances and how to find a good attorney. It also reviews the kinds of assistance a bankruptcy attorney will provide to you and how much the attorney will probably charge.

WHEN TO MEET WITH A BANKRUPTCY ATTORNEY

It pays to meet with a bankruptcy attorney as soon you begin having problems paying your debts, especially your secured and priority unsecured debts, even if you are not sure that you want to or need to file for bankruptcy. The first meeting will probably cost you nothing because most attorneys offer free initial consultations. The bankruptcy attorney may be able to suggest actions you can take to avoid bankruptcy, including referring you to a reputable credit counseling agency, and can also explain the details of how bankruptcy works, such as the kinds of debts that will or won't survive bankruptcy. In addition, the attorney can warn you against taking certain actions in the months immediately prior to filing for bankruptcy so that you can maximize the benefits of bankruptcy. For example, the attorney will tell you:

- Not to legally transfer property that is in your name into the name of someone else in order to avoid having to include the property in your bankruptcy. If you do, the judge may consider what you did to be a fraudulent transfer. That means the transfer will be reversed and your bankruptcy may be dismissed, which will mean that your creditors can resume trying to collect from you. Ordinarily, judges will be concerned about any transfer you may have made during the two years prior to the start of your bankruptcy.

- Not to purchase more than $500 worth of luxury goods or services from a single creditor during the 90 days prior to the start of your bankruptcy using a credit card. If you do, the judge may not allow you to discharge that debt through your bankruptcy. The same is true if you obtain a cash advance for more than $750 during the 70 days prior to the start of your bankruptcy. Your attorney can explain the difference between luxury goods and services and necessities in the eyes of the law.

- Not to give preferential treatment to one of your unsecured creditors during the 90 days prior to filing by paying that creditor at the expense of your other creditors. The bankruptcy system is supposed to treat all creditors equally. If a creditor received all of your money right before the bankruptcy and no one else did, then that creditor would be receiving a "preference" over the other creditors, and the court does not permit that. The bankruptcy judge may cancel the payment and try to recover the money so that the funds can be distributed among your creditors according to the rules of bankruptcy.

■ Not to write a bad check. If you can't make good on the check and you are criminally prosecuted and found guilty, you may not only be sent to jail, but you won't be able to use bankruptcy to get rid of or reduce the amount of the fine you may be ordered to pay.

🤚 Red Alerts!

Before you file for bankruptcy, don't borrow money and secure it with one of your assets, and don't give one of your creditors additional collateral without talking to a bankruptcy attorney first. Also, if you've fallen behind on any of your secured debts and the creditors are threatening to take your collateral, never voluntarily hand over the collateral. Instead, get in touch with a bankruptcy attorney immediately.

Trying to save money by working with a bankruptcy petition preparer instead of an attorney is penny-wise and pound-foolish.

Although a bankruptcy petition preparer will prepare the forms you need to begin your bankruptcy for a fraction of what a bankruptcy attorney charges, the petition preparer does not have a license to practice law, which means that the preparer lacks the training and the knowledge necessary to help you make good decisions about your bankruptcy, to represent you in court, or to help you resolve bankruptcy-related disputes. Furthermore, if a petition preparer makes any mistakes when completing your bankruptcy forms, your bankruptcy could be dismissed.

❗ Hot Tip

Bankruptcy attorneys are familiar with the attitudes of the trustees in the bankruptcy court where they work. They also understand the unstated customs of the court and the way

that the judges in that court tend to rule on certain issues. Such "insider information" is invaluable and can help ensure that you get the maximum benefit from filing.

When you meet with a bankruptcy attorney, find out about the various kinds of financial information you will need to provide the attorney with if you decide to file. Pulling it all together can be very time-consuming, so it pays to get started sooner rather than later, just in case.

HOW AN ATTORNEY WILL HELP IF YOU FILE FOR BANKRUPTCY

If you decide to file for bankruptcy, your attorney will help you throughout the process and will be available to answer any questions you may have. For example, among other things, your attorney will do the following:

- Complete all of the paperwork that has to be filed with the court to begin your bankruptcy.

- Meet all legally required deadlines in your bankruptcy.

- Notify all of your creditors as soon as the automatic stay in your bankruptcy is invoked. The court will notify them, too, but probably not right away because of bureaucratic paperwork and red tape. The sooner your creditors know about the automatic stay, the sooner they will stop trying to collect from you.

- Try to resolve any problems your creditors may have related to your bankruptcy. For example, some of them may disagree with the amounts that you say you owe to them or they may want to get the court's permission to take back their collateral.

- File motions with the court as necessary to protect your interests.

- Represent you at all bankruptcy-related court hearings.

RESOURCES FOR FINDING A GOOD ATTORNEY

The best way to find a skilled and experienced bankruptcy attorney who is truly interested in helping you is to meet with several different attorneys so you can assess for yourself which one you think will do the best job. There are several ways you can obtain the names of attorneys to meet with:

- Get referrals from people you may know who filed for bankruptcy and were happy with their attorneys.

- Search for a consumer bankruptcy attorney who is nationally certified by the American Board of Certification (ABC), the nation's leading bankruptcy certification organization, at *www.abcworld.org/abchome.html.* To become board certified by the ABC, a consumer bankruptcy attorney must pass a detailed, day-long written exam that covers a wide range of bankruptcy-related topics, demonstrate experience practicing bankruptcy law by providing professional references, and agree to participate in a minimum of 60 hours of continuing legal education over a three-year period.

- Look for an attorney who has been certified in bankruptcy law by your state because that attorney has extensive proven experience handling bankruptcy cases, including time in court. States that certify bankruptcy attorneys include Alabama, Arizona, Arkansas, California, Connecticut, Florida, Georgia, Idaho, Louisiana, Maine, Minnesota, New Jersey, New Mexico, North Carolina, Ohio, Pennsylvania, South Carolina, Tennessee, Texas, and Utah. Your state bar association can tell you if an attorney is board certified. However, know that most attorneys who handle bankruptcy cases are not board certified because the certification process is difficult.

- Find an attorney who is a member of the National Association of Consumer Bankruptcy Attorneys (NACBA). The NACBA is the most well-respected consumer bankruptcy organization in the country. To locate an NACBA member, use the association's attorney finder at *www.nacba.org/attorneyfinder.*

Red Alert!

Being referred to a bankruptcy attorney by a bar association or a bankruptcy-related organization is not a 100-percent guarantee that the attorney will do a good job for you. You'll have to make that call for yourself after meeting with the attorney.

- Ask for referrals from other attorneys you may know. For example, you may have worked with a divorce attorney or a real estate attorney in the past, or you may have a friend or neighbor who is an attorney. Most attorneys, regardless of the kind of law that they practice, either know who the good bankruptcy attorneys are in their area or can find out for you.

- Question bankruptcy trustees. Bankruptcy trustees have a unique vantage point from which to observe and evaluate the various bankruptcy attorneys who are handling cases in your area's bankruptcy court, and most will give you the names of a few good ones if you ask for the information. You can obtain the names and phone numbers of the trustees in your area by calling the federal bankruptcy court for your particular district court or by going to *www.usdoj.gov/ust/eo/ust_org*.

- Read the lawyer ads in your local Yellow Pages. Usually, if a bankruptcy attorney is board-certified, the ad will state so.

- Ask your local or state bar association to provide referrals to bankruptcy attorneys in your area.

 Red Alert!

It may take time to find an attorney to work with, so start looking as soon as filing for bankruptcy becomes a real possibility. If you wait to find an attorney until a creditor is about to seize one of your assets, you may feel like you have to hire the first attorney you talk with, and you may end up being unhappy with the attorney.

Within five days of hiring an attorney, the attorney must provide you with a written retainer agreement. The agreement should spell out the services the attorney will provide to you, the cost for these services, and additional services and bankruptcy-related expenses for which you can be billed if necessary.

HOW MUCH AN ATTORNEY'S HELP WILL COST

If you file for Chapter 13, the bankruptcy law allows your attorney to charge you a fixed fee, which is determined by the bankruptcy court in the particular district where your bankruptcy is filed. Presently, however, the average fee is about $3,085. Your attorney will probably expect you to pay a portion of her fee as well as the entire amount of the filing fee up front. Once you begin paying on your Chapter 13 reorganization plan, the rest of your attorney's service fee will be received through the plan. In other words, the trustee in your bankruptcy will give a portion of your monthly plan payments to your attorney.

If you file for Chapter 7, you'll probably be charged between $1,200 and $2,000. However, according to a recent survey, some bankruptcy attorneys in states such as New York and Arizona charge significantly more—as much as $3,500. On the other hand, some attorneys reduce their fees when they represent elderly consumers or consumers who owe money to just a few creditors. Attorneys who are relatively inexperienced or who are practicing law in more rural areas of the country may also charge less.

❗ Hot Tip

If you believe that you will have a difficult time coming up with the money you need to pay a bankruptcy attorney, find out if any of the attorneys you meet with will let you pay their fee over time or if they will agree to lower their fee.

Red Alert!

It's possible that once your bankruptcy begins, you'll have to pay your bankruptcy attorney more than the basic fee. For example, the cost of your bankruptcy will probably increase if there are a lot of hearings in your case or if your attorney has to amend your bankruptcy forms because you failed to share all of your financial information. Figure 7.1 provides a more complete list of all of the reasons why your attorney may charge you more.

PREPARING TO MEET WITH ATTORNEYS

Before you begin meeting with attorneys to find the one you want to work with, spend some time pulling together as much of the financial information your attorney will need to begin your bankruptcy as you can. This information includes a list of all of your assets and their approximate market values, a list of all of your debts (including the outstanding balance on each debt and whether each debt is secured or unsecured), your most recent pay stubs, and a copy of your household budget, if you have one.

If you don't have a budget, write down your total monthly household income. (This should include your actual take-home pay as well as other sources of income you may receive. If you are married, it should include your spouse's income, too, assuming your spouse works outside the home.) Then write down all of your monthly expenses. If you don't know exactly how much you are spending on something, make a good guess, taking into account that most people tend to underestimate what they spend on various items.

Sharing all of this information with the attorneys you meet with will help them get a quick sense of your finances. This will make it easier for them to ask you the right questions and to answer your questions as completely as possible.

You should also prepare a list of questions to ask each of the attorneys you meet with. Your questions should include the following:

> **❗ Hot Tip**
>
> Before you meet with an attorney, call the attorney's office to ask for a copy of the financial worksheet the attorney uses with clients. Using the worksheet will make it easier for you to organize your financial information in a way your prospective attorney can easily follow.

- How long have you been practicing consumer bankruptcy law? Is it the only kind of law that you practice? Ideally, if your case is complicated, the attorney should have been practicing bankruptcy law for at least five years. However, if you are filing a simple, straightforward Chapter 7 bankruptcy, a relatively new bankruptcy attorney with just a couple years of experience could do a good job for you. Generally, however, the longer an attorney has been handling bankruptcy law cases, the more skilled the attorney has probably become at anticipating and resolving problems, and the more familiar the attorney will be with the attitudes of the trustees and bankruptcy judges in your federal district. All of this experience and understanding helps most attorneys hone their legal skills and provides them with insights and knowledge that can be invaluable to your bankruptcy. For the same reasons, it's best to work with an attorney who only handles bankruptcy cases or for whom those cases represent a very substantial portion of the attorney's legal practice.

- Approximately how many consumer bankruptcy cases do you handle each year? As a rule of thumb, an attorney who only handles bankruptcy cases should be doing at least 10 cases a month.

- Are you board certified by any organizations?

- How many bankruptcy-related seminars did you attend last year?

- Based on what you know about my finances right now, do you believe that there is anything I can do to avoid bankruptcy?

■ Based on your current understanding of my finances, do you think I qualify for a Chapter 7 or will I have to file for Chapter 13? To answer this question the attorney will apply a rough means test to your finances.

■ Are you aware of any special issues or problems related to my bankruptcy that may make it more complicated than most consumer bankruptcies?

■ Are there things I should be doing now to prepare for bankruptcy?

■ How much will you charge to handle my bankruptcy? The amount that the attorney's clients are charged must be reported to the bankruptcy court. If the court believes that an attorney is charging too much, it will make the attorney give some of the money back to the client. Bankruptcy is the only area of the law where attorneys' fees must be approved by the court in order to protect consumers from being overcharged.

■ If I file a Chapter 7 bankruptcy, can I pay your fee over time if I can't afford to pay it in a lump sum?

■ Under what circumstances will you charge me extra for your services? Are you willing to negotiate how much extra, and if I can't pay the extra money, will you withdraw from my case?

■ What expenses will I have to pay? About how much do you expect they will be? If I can't pay them as they come due, will you withdraw from my case?

🖐 Red Alert!

Don't hire an attorney just because that attorney charges less than the other attorneys you've met with. There may be a good reason why the attorney's fee is lower. For example, the attorney may not have much experience practicing bankruptcy law or may not be a good attorney. Hiring the cheapest attorney may cost you more in the end.

- If I hire you, how will you keep me up to date regarding the progress of my case?

- Can I read a copy of the contract you will expect me to sign if I hire you?

Don't work with an attorney who does not use a contract. (It may be called a *letter of engagement*.) The contract should spell out the services the attorney will provide and how much you will be charged for those services, the terms of payment, all other fees and expenses you will be liable for, what services are not covered by the attorney's basic fee that you may also have to pay for, and the contract's duration.

Bring your list of questions to each of your attorney meetings so that you won't forget what you want to ask. Also, bring along a pad of paper and a pen so that you can jot down notes regarding an attorney's answers, demeanor, and your general impressions of each attorney. For example, pay close attention to whether an attorney does any of the following:

- Sets you straight regarding how bankruptcy can and can't help you

- Provides you with a clear explanation of what the bankruptcy process will be like

- Gives you a general overview of the approach the attorney will take in handling your bankruptcy

- Looks you in the eye when you speak and appears to really listen to what you are saying

- Answers your questions using words you can understand, not legalese

- Asks you questions about your finances

- Acts offended by the questions you are asking and/or becomes defensive

A good attorney will understand you are trying to make a difficult decision and will be happy to answer all of your questions.

❗ Hot Tips

When you meet with an attorney, ask to meet the attorney's paralegals because they are the people who will handle much of the paperwork in your bankruptcy. Furthermore, if you have any questions as your bankruptcy moves forward, it will usually be easier to reach one of the paralegals than it will be to reach your attorney. If the paralegal you speak with does not know the answer to one of your questions, the paralegal should either get an answer from your attorney or make sure that the attorney calls you.

If you want to speak with your attorney rather than with a paralegal, say so when you call. You have the right to expect a return call from your attorney within 24 hours of leaving a message.

In this chapter you learned why it's a good idea to talk with a bankruptcy attorney before you file for bankruptcy and about the value of working with one from start to finish if you decide to file. You also found out how to find a good bankruptcy attorney and how much you'll probably have to pay for an attorney's assistance. The next chapter provides you with detailed information about the Chapter 7 process.

FIGURE 7.1. When You Will Be Charged Extra

Although your attorney will charge you a basic fee for handling your bankruptcy, it's very likely that you'll be charged more money if any of the following are true:

■ You don't attend your creditors' meeting.

■ You don't answer all of the questions you are asked by one of your creditors and, as a result, the creditor requests a *Rule 2004 examination*. You'll have to answer more questions at this legal proceeding, which is similar to a deposition. Preparing for the Rule 2004 examination will take more of your attorney's time.

■ Your attorney has to make major revisions to your bankruptcy forms because you didn't provide complete information about your debts and/or assets; the information that you provided was inaccurate; or because after your bankruptcy begins, you change jobs, you're sued, you get divorced, or you sell one of your assets without getting the court's permission first.

■ Your attorney has to file your bankruptcy on an emergency basis because your home is about to be foreclosed on, you are about to lose your car, or some other asset is about to be taken away from you.

■ You want your attorney to oppose an action to evict you or to take your home through a foreclosure while you are in bankruptcy.

■ One of your creditors or the trustee in your bankruptcy formally disputes or contests something in your bankruptcy.

Using a Chapter 7 Liquidation Bankruptcy to Get Rid of Debt

8

As you learned in chapter 6, when you file a Chapter 7 liquidation bankruptcy, the trustee takes control of your nonexempt assets, auctions them off, and uses the proceeds to pay as many of your debts as possible. In this chapter, you'll learn a lot more about exactly how a Chapter 7 bankruptcy works. For example, I'll go into more detail about the various forms your attorney must file at the start of the bankruptcy and about the kinds of information your attorney will need from you to fill out those forms. You'll also find out what will happen after your Chapter 7 bankruptcy begins and about the different options you have for trying to keep assets that the trustee would ordinarily take from you.

This chapter also prepares you for your creditors' meeting by briefing you about the different questions you may be asked. I'll also explain the kinds of actions some of your creditors may take after the meeting, as well as what will happen at the very end of your Chapter 7 bankruptcy.

STARTING YOUR CHAPTER 7 BANKRUPTCY

To begin your bankruptcy, you must file a bankruptcy petition with the court and pay the filing fee. The court will then invoke the automatic stay to stop your creditors from trying to collect from you. Prior to initiating your bankruptcy, you and your attorney will have decided which of your assets you will exempt from your bankruptcy, that is, which ones you will be able to keep. The rest of your assets will become nonexempt assets, which means that after your bankruptcy begins, the trustee will take control of them. In other words, the trustee becomes the legal owner of those assets, although the trustee may not actually take physical possession of them. The trustee will determine what value your nonexempt assets will probably bring at auction, which is the amount of money for which they will sell. If the trustee decides that some of the assets have little or no value, the trustee will *abandon* them, and the assets will be yours again. However, all of the rest of the assets will be sold so that the trustee can apply the sales proceeds to your debts.

 Red Alert!

The trustee in your bankruptcy will receive a small percentage of the proceeds from the sale of your nonexempt assets. Therefore, the trustee has a strong financial incentive to identify every possible nonexempt asset you own that can be included in your bankruptcy estate—the more assets that are included, the more money the trustee makes.

As you found out in chapter 6, your attorney will have to complete a lot of forms at the start of bankruptcy. These forms include Schedules of Assets, Schedules of Debts, and a Statement of Financial Affairs. The next several sections review the kinds of information that your attorney will need from you to fill out the forms. (You attorney will also compete these forms if you file for Chapter 13.)

FILLING OUT YOUR SCHEDULES OF ASSETS

To fill out your Schedules of Assets, your attorney will need to know about all of the real estate (*real property*) you own, including your residence and any other homes, buildings, or undeveloped land you may own in whole or in part, as well as where each piece of real estate is located and their market values. According to bankruptcy law, market value is what you would have to pay for the real estate in its current condition if you bought it today. Your attorney will also need to know about all of your *personal property* and the market value of each of those assets. Your personal property includes such things as the following:

- The money in your bank accounts

- Your certificates of deposit (CDs)

- Your interest in any retirement accounts

- Your stocks, bonds, and annuities

- Any deposits you have paid to public utility companies, phone companies, and your landlord

- Your clothing, furs, and jewelry

- Your furniture, household goods, television sets, computers, etc.

- Your vehicles, boats, motorcycles, and trailers

- Your antiques, artwork, coin and stamp collections, collectibles, and the like

- Your books, CDs, and records

- Your interest in any insurance policies

- Any alimony, child support, or property settlements you may be entitled to

- Farm animals, if you have any

- Farming equipment and implements, if you have any

Be sure to tell your attorney about *all* of your assets. Don't assume that your attorney does not need to know about one of them because the asset is old and not in the greatest of shape or because you don't think that it's worth very much. If the judge learns that one of your assets isn't listed on your Schedules, and if you don't have a very good explanation for why it's missing, the judge may conclude that you are trying to hide the asset from the court so that you can keep it, rather than having it sold to help pay off your debts. If the judge concludes that you were trying to hide an asset, the judge will either dismiss your bankruptcy or prevent you from receiving a discharge of debts, which would mean that you would still have to pay your debts. If what you did was especially serious, you also may be criminally prosecuted for bankruptcy fraud.

FILLING OUT YOUR SCHEDULES OF DEBTS

It is very important that your Schedules of Debts be complete and accurate, too. Mainly that's because any debts that are not listed on the Schedules won't be included in your bankruptcy, which means that you'll have to pay those debts once your bankruptcy is over.

When your attorney is filling out your Schedules of Debts, be prepared to provide the following information:

- The name and address of each of your creditors

- The account numbers for each of your debts

- The amount that you owe on each debt

- The date that you initially incurred each of your debts

- Whether a debt is secured or unsecured

- The collateral associated with each secured debt

If you've been sued and the outcome of the lawsuit hasn't been decided yet, be sure to give your attorney the name and address of the plaintiff

✋ Red Alert!

If you provide your attorney with an incorrect address for one of your creditors, the money that you owe to that creditor may not be discharged because the creditor may not receive notification that you've filed for bankruptcy. If that's the case, you'll still owe the debt once your bankruptcy is over, and if it's a large debt, having to pay it could make it difficult, if not impossible, for you to begin rebuilding your financial life.

in the lawsuit (the individual or business that sued you) and the name and address of the plaintiff's attorney. Better yet, give your attorney a copy of the lawsuit that was filed against you. The automatic stay in your bankruptcy will stop the creditor from getting a judgment against you. Also, if you've already been ordered to pay a money judgment in another lawsuit, give your attorney a copy of the lawsuit and all other papers filed so that your attorney can tell you if there is a chance that the judgment creditor (the person or business that won the lawsuit) will challenge the dischargeability of that debt for some reason—maybe by claiming that you defrauded (cheated) it in some way.

❗ Hot Tip

To be on the safe side, include on your Schedules of Debts anyone you think might sue you in the near future, even if they haven't said that you owe them money. Sometimes just listing a possible debt on your Schedules of Debts is enough to get it discharged in a Chapter 7 bankruptcy.

Your attorney will organize your debts on the various Schedules of Debts forms according to the type of debt, which include the following:

- Priority debts. These kinds of debts include your obligation to pay spousal and/or child support, most unpaid taxes, and any student loan debt you may owe, among other debts. If there is not enough money to pay your priority debts while you are in bankruptcy, these debts will survive your Chapter 7 bankruptcy. Although you won't have to pay the debts while you are in bankruptcy, you will have to pay them as soon as your bankruptcy is over.

■ Secured debts. These are debts that you collateralized with one of your assets. Your attorney must list the specific asset (collateral) that secures each of your debts together with the asset's market value. The market value is important for two reasons:

1. When you exempt your secured assets, the more equity you have in those assets, the more likely it is that you will use up all of your exemptions because there is a maximum dollar amount of exemptions that you can claim in bankruptcy. If you reach the maximum, you're more likely to have to give up some of your assets so they can be liquidated.

2. Whenever you exempt a secured asset, the creditor maintains its lien on that asset. Therefore, to keep the asset, you must get rid of the lien by paying off the debt that the asset secures. In a Chapter 7, one way to do that is to redeem the asset. Another way is to reaffirm the debt. For more information about how redemptions and reaffirmations work, read "Using Redemptions and Reaffirmations to Keep Your Exempt Secured Assets" later in this chapter.

■ Unsecured debts. If you're like most Chapter 7 filers, once your priority debts have been paid, there won't be enough money left to pay your unsecured debts. Therefore, most, if not all, of those debts will be discharged at the end of your bankruptcy.

FILLING OUT YOUR STATEMENT OF FINANCIAL AFFAIRS

The primary purpose of the Statement of Financial Affairs is to help the trustee determine whether you've been totally honest about your finances and about your financial transactions in the recent past. To complete this form, your attorney will need to know, among other things:

- The amounts and sources of your income during the two years prior to the start of your bankruptcy. You must also indicate the amount of employment or business income you've received from the start of the current calendar year to the start of your bankruptcy.

- The amounts and sources of any other income you may receive, such as rental income, income from other investments, spousal support, and the like.

- Any payments you may have made on your unsecured and secured debts during the 90 days preceding the start of your bankruptcy.

- All lawsuits that you may have been a party to in the year prior to the start of your bankruptcy.

- Any gifts or charitable contributions you may have made during the year before your bankruptcy began.

- The cash, securities, or other valuables you may have stored in a safe deposit box or elsewhere sometime during the year prior to the commencement of your bankruptcy.

After reviewing the information on your Statement of Financial Affairs, the trustee may ask for additional information about your finances. That information may include, for example, copies of your bank account records, copies of contracts you may have signed, records related to any investment accounts that are in your name, and copies of tax returns that are older than your most recent returns.

The trustee will review all of this information to answer the following questions:

- Are you being honest about the amount of income you received during the two calendar years preceding your bankruptcy? The trustee will compare what your Statement of Financial Affairs says to the information in your income tax returns for those years and to the information on your Schedules of Assets and Schedules of Debts, looking for discrepancies. For example, if your Statement of Financial Affairs indicates that your total income was relatively high during the two years prior to your bankruptcy, but you don't list many assets on your Schedules of Assets or the assets that are listed aren't worth much, the trustee will wonder if you are hiding any assets.

 Red Alert!

If you think there is anything about your finances that may raise the trustee's suspicions, be sure to share your concerns with your attorney so that your attorney can decide what to do. It you are not totally up front with your attorney about every aspect of your finances, you are likely to create some serious problems for yourself. For example, the bankruptcy judge may dismiss your bankruptcy, refuse to discharge your debts, and/or you may be criminally prosecuted for bankruptcy fraud.

- Did you pay any of your creditors during the previous 90 days at the expense of other creditors? If you did, the trustee will try to reverse those payments so the money can be distributed among your creditors according to the requirements of the bankruptcy law. Most likely, however, if the amount of the payment was small (less than $500), the trustee will do nothing.

- Have you initiated any lawsuits that are not settled yet? If so, the trustee may settle them on your behalf and apply the settlement amounts to your debts. However, if you can exempt the settlement amounts, you can keep the money.

 Red Alert!

If you don't list a lawsuit you have already filed and then you're awarded a money judgment in the lawsuit, you won't be able to keep that money if the court finds out about it.

- During the 120 days leading up to your bankruptcy, did you allow any of your creditors to put a lien on one of your assets or did you settle any of your debts? If you did, the trustee may conclude that you gave those creditors preferential treatment and will try to get back the money that you paid to them so that the funds can be distributed to your creditors according to the requirements of the bankruptcy law.

- Did you give a friend or relative any of your assets during the two years prior to the start of your bankruptcy? If the trustee believes that your motivation for the transfer was to try to hide the asset(s) from the court, the trustee will try to reverse the transfer.

- Have you hidden any of your assets in a safe deposit box, and have you accounted for any certificates of deposit or investment accounts you may have?

Using Redemptions and Reaffirmations to Keep Your Exempt Secured Assets

At the start of your Chapter 7 bankruptcy, your attorney must file a Statement of Intention with the court to indicate to the court and to your creditors what you intend to do with each of your exempt secured assets. For example, the statement may show that you want to keep some of those assets by *redeeming* them or by *reaffirming* the debts that they secure. What to do is an important financial decision that you will make in consultation with your attorney. To help you decide, here is an explanation of what it will mean to reaffirm a debt or redeem an asset:

Reaffirming a debt. When you reaffirm a debt that is secured by one of your exempt secured assets, you agree to continue paying on the debt according to your original agreement with the creditor. However, as a condition of the reaffirmation, you must pay any amount of the debt that is past due. Your attorney will try to get the creditor to agree to let you pay that amount over time, but the creditor is entitled to insist that you pay it in a lump sum. The terms of any agreement you reach with the creditor will be formalized in a Reaffirmation Agreement that your attorney will file with the court for its approval.

You will have 60 days from the date that you sign the agreement or until the discharge of your debts—whichever is longer—to change your mind about reaffirming the debt. If you have a change of heart, you must inform the creditor in writing. Otherwise, you must begin paying the secured debt according to the terms of your reaffirmation agreement. If you default on the agreement, the creditor can take back the asset you're trying to keep, and it will be sold so that the sale proceeds can be applied to your debt. If the proceeds are not enough to pay the total amount that you owe on the debt, you'll have to pay the deficiency once your bankruptcy is over.

Red Alert!

When you reaffirm a secured debt, you forfeit your right to give collateral back to the creditor and to have the debt discharged. Therefore, before you reaffirm a debt, consider whether you really need the asset that secures the debt, and be sure that you can afford to live up to the terms of the reaffirmation agreement. Don't try to hold on to an asset out of pride, stubbornness, or sentimentality.

Redeeming an asset. When you redeem an exempt secured asset, you pay the creditor the asset's market value in a lump sum; the creditor then releases its lien on the asset, and the unpaid balance on the debt is discharged. This means that when your bankruptcy is over, you'll own the asset free and clear. Redeeming it is a good option if the asset has lost value since you purchased it, and it is now worth less than what you still owe on the debt that the asset secures.

If you decide to redeem an exempt secured asset, your attorney will contact your creditor to try to reach an agreement regarding its market value. If they don't reach an agreement, your attorney will file a *motion to redeem the asset,* and a hearing on the motion will be scheduled so that the bankruptcy judge can listen to both sides and then render a decision regarding how much you'll have to pay to keep the asset.

If you decide to reaffirm a debt or redeem an asset, you must do so no later than 45 days after you've filed your Statement of Intention. Otherwise, you'll have to give back to your creditors the assets you had hoped to keep. When you give them back, the debts they are securing will be discharged.

Holding On to Other Assets in a Chapter 7

If you have other assets besides your exempt secured assets that you would like to keep and you can't exempt them because you've used up all of your exemptions, you may be able to buy the assets back from the trustee. The trustee may agree to sell them to you if the trustee feels that the amount that you want to pay is reasonable and if the trustee does not believe that it can get more money for the assets by liquidating them. However, you'll have to pay the purchase price in one lump sum.

Also, if you are purchasing an asset that you would like to keep through a rent-to-own contract—a contract that allows you to lease an item and eventually own it through your lease payments—you can hold on to the asset by assuming the lease. If you do, you agree to make all of the payments that are still due on the contract. Furniture and televisions are commonly purchased through rent-to-own contracts.

HOW YOUR CREDITORS MAY RESPOND TO YOUR CHAPTER 7 BANKRUPTCY

Once they learn about your bankruptcy, most of your unsecured creditors will accept the fact that you've filed because they'll know that it's not worth their time or money to do anything else other than file their proof of claim with the court.

Some of your secured creditors, however, may respond to the news by filing motions to lift the stay, especially if you owe them a lot of money. There will be at least one hearing on each motion during which the judge will hear from all sides in the matter and then will issue a decision on the motion. If the court grants your creditors' motions, they will be entitled to try to take back their collateral. However, their motions won't be granted unless the creditors can prove that you are behind on your payments to them and that you have no equity in your collateral.

Some of your secured creditors may also file *objections to disallow the discharge,* which means that they are asking the court to prevent the debt that you owe to them from being wiped out. (They will have up to 60 days after the meeting to file their objections.) They may file this kind of complaint because they have proof that you tried to defraud them by lying on your loan application or by doing something else equally dishonest related to your debt prior to the start of your bankruptcy. Your attorney will file a formal response to the objections and will contact the creditors to try to resolve things outside of court; but if your attorney's efforts don't succeed, a trial for each objection will be scheduled. First, however, the objections will be referred to mediation in another effort to settle the disputes outside of court. If the mediation doesn't work, the trials will take place.

THE CREDITORS' MEETING

Your creditors' meeting will take place within 45 days of the start of your bankruptcy. The trustee will preside over the meeting, which will occur in a private office or in a public meeting room at the federal courthouse. Your attorney will attend the meeting, and you must show up, too. If you don't, your bankruptcy can be dismissed.

The main purpose of the creditors' meeting is to give the trustee and your creditors an opportunity to ask you questions about the information on your bankruptcy forms. The trustee will keep things low key and nonconfrontational so the meeting won't feel like an inquisition. If your bankruptcy is very simple and straightforward—that is, you own few assets, few if any of your creditors attend, and the trustee does not ask you a lot of questions—your creditors' meeting may last

---

❗ Hot Tip

Before the day of your creditors' meeting, find out exactly where the federal courthouse is located, how to get there, and where to park. It's important to show up on time. Getting lost or not being able to find a parking space is not a good excuse for being late!

If your creditors' meeting will take place in a public meeting room and you arrive before your meeting is scheduled to begin, take a seat inside the room. Try to get a feel for how a creditors' meeting is run and listen to the kinds of questions the trustee is asking. Observing the proceedings will not only provide you with information that may be helpful when it's time for your creditors' meeting, but also knowing what to expect can calm your nerves if you're feeling anxious about what's to come.

---

for as little as five minutes. If any of your creditors do attend, they are likely to be some of your secured creditors because they will be worried about their collateral.

Sometime before the start of your creditors' meeting, your attorney should review the questions the trustee is likely to ask you at the meeting so that you will be prepared to answer them. If the date of the meeting draws near and your attorney has not talked with you about the questions, ask your attorney about them.

The Kinds of Questions You May Be Asked

During your creditors' meeting, the trustee will ask you questions about the information on your various bankruptcy forms, paying special attention to your Schedules of Assets, Schedules of Debts, and Statement of Financial Affairs. You will be under oath during the meeting, so be sure to tell the truth. If you lie and are found out, your bankruptcy will be dismissed, and you will have to pay the debts that would have been discharged if you had completed the bankruptcy.

Here are examples of the kinds of questions the trustee is likely to ask you:

■ Why did you file for bankruptcy? The trustee's main reason for asking this question is to find out if you owned a business that you ran as a sole proprietorship and if its failure caused or contributed to your bankruptcy. If that's the case, the trustee will ask you questions to make sure that you listed all of your business's assets on your Schedules of Assets. If you didn't, the trustee will want to know what happened to them.

■ Are all of your assets and debts listed on your Schedules? If you realize that you've left something off, let the trustee know. The trustee will give you an opportunity to amend your Schedules. If you lie about their completeness and the trustee later finds out, your bankruptcy will be dismissed.

■ How did you determine the market value of the assets listed on your Schedules of Assets? The trustee wants to make certain that you've valued them realistically. If the trustee believes that the market value on any of the assets is too low, the trustee may have them appraised. Also, if the trustee believes that you've placed too high a market value on any of your exempt assets, the trustee may try to turn them into nonexempt assets so they can be sold and the proceeds can be applied to your debts.

■ Did you transfer any of your assets to friends, relatives, or anyone else during the two years prior to the start of your bankruptcy? The trustee is concerned that by transferring the assets out of your name and into someone else's name, you are trying to hold on to them rather than letting the trustee have them so the assets can be sold and the sales proceeds can be applied to your debts. If you made such a transfer, the trustee will try to reverse the transfer and take control of the assets so that they can be sold, and the trustee can use the funds to pay your debts.

■ Are you waiting to receive a federal and/or state income tax refund? If you are, the amount of the refund must be listed on your Schedules of Assets. The trustee will take the refund once it is paid unless you can exempt it.

> ## ! Hot Tips
>
> ■ If you learn that you have received an inheritance during the six months following the start of your bankruptcy, you must notify the trustee. You will be given a chance to exempt it, but if you can't because you've used up all of your exemptions, then the trustee will take whatever part of the inheritance you cannot exempt, sell it, and use the money to pay your debts.
>
> ■ During the creditors' meeting, if the trustee or one of your creditors asks you a question that you don't know how to answer, don't make up an answer. Instead, tell the trustee that you don't know. You won't be punished. Also, never admit to anything that you are not sure about because you feel intimidated or don't want to look difficult or stupid. If you are not totally honest in your answers, you may create problems for yourself.

■ Were you harmed in any accidents during the past year, and do you anticipate receiving any money in compensation for the harm as a result of a lawsuit that you filed? The amount of the claim must be listed on your Schedules of Assets. Unless you can exempt it, the trustee will settle the claim on your behalf—probably for less than what you sued for—and use the settlement money to pay your debts.

■ Are you about to receive an inheritance, or do you think that you may receive one sometime during the six months following the start of your bankruptcy? You must treat an inheritance like any other kind of asset, so it must be listed on your Schedules of Assets. The only way to keep an inheritance is to exempt it.

The trustee may also ask you questions about any financial documents and records you were directed to provide the trustee with prior to the start of the creditors' meeting. For example, you may have been asked to provide the following:

■ Copies of your cancelled checks and bank statements for a specific time period

■ Copies of your insurance policies

- Income tax returns in addition to the returns for the two years prior to the start of your bankruptcy that you normally have to provide the trustee. You could be asked to provide tax returns for several years back.

- Deeds and titles to the real estate you may own

- Titles to your vehicles

- Stock certificates

- Information about any other investments you may own, such as mutual funds and bonds, and the value of those investments

- Copies of any asset appraisals you may have had done

Depending on what the trustee learned from reviewing this information, you may be asked about the following:

- Assets that you may have listed on your tax returns but that you did not list on your Schedules of Assets

- Season tickets you may have purchased to watch your favorite sports team play, to attend the ballet, the opera, or the theater that you did not exempt

- Information about the fact that your bank records may show that you had more money in your checking and/or savings accounts when you filed for bankruptcy than what's reflected on your Schedules of Assets. If you do not have a good explanation for the discrepancy, the trustee will take the extra money in the accounts and use it to pay your debts unless you can exempt those funds.

You may be asked other questions, as well. It will depend on your circumstances, the information on your bankruptcy forms, and on the trustee, among other things.

Before the end of your creditors' meeting, the trustee will make sure that you understand all of the following:

- The potential consequences of filing for Chapter 7 bankruptcy, including the fact that it will damage your credit histories

- That you are entitled to file a Chapter 13 bankruptcy instead of a Chapter 7

- The effects of having your debts discharged through a Chapter 7 bankruptcy

- What it means if you've agreed to reaffirm a debt

After the Creditors' Meeting

Ten days after your creditors' meeting, the trustee will file a form with the court indicating whether you've passed the means test. If you haven't, then you should have filed for Chapter 13 rather than for Chapter 7. If the trustee believes that you filed for Chapter 7 as a result of an innocent mistake—you forgot to tell your attorney about some of your income or you overstated an expense, for example—then you'll probably be allowed to convert your bankruptcy to a Chapter 13. However, if the trustee concludes that you tried to abuse the bankruptcy process by filing for Chapter 7—that you knowingly lied about some aspect of your finances—then the trustee will file a motion with the court to have your bankruptcy dismissed, and the judge will decide whether you can convert your bankruptcy. If the judge dismisses your bankruptcy, you'll have to file a Chapter 13 bankruptcy. The next chapter tells you how a Chapter 13 bankruptcy works.

 Red Alert!

The trustee in your bankruptcy and your creditors will have 30 days after the creditors' meeting to file objections to your exemptions. The judge will decide on the objections after a hearing. Also, your creditors will have 60 days after the meeting to formally object to the discharge of the debts that you owe to them. The "How Your Creditors May Respond to Your Chapter 7 Bankruptcy" section of this chapter explains the process for resolving their objections.

If you pass the means test, your Chapter 7 bankruptcy will move forward, and the trustee will pay as many of your debts as possible after liquidating all of your nonexempt assets. Your debts will be paid according to the requirements of the bankruptcy law, which means that any past due court-ordered spousal and/or child support payments you may owe will be paid first. Next, the trustee's administrative expenses will be paid. In most Chapter 7s, once these debts and expenses are paid, there is no money left to pay anything else. However, if there is money left, the trustee will pay other priority claims next, such as your past due taxes and any wages and salaries you may owe to the employees of your sole proprietorship. Most likely, your unsecured creditors won't receive a dime of what you owe to them. Those debts will be discharged instead.

It may take the trustee a relatively brief amount of time to liquidate all of your nonexempt assets, or it may take years. How long it takes will depend on the number of assets in your bankruptcy and their complexity. However, if none of your creditors objects to the discharge of your debts, you should receive notification of the discharge little more than 60 days after your creditors' meeting, even if the trustee has not yet finished liquidating everything.

❗ Hot Tip

While you are waiting for your bankruptcy to be over, review all of your Schedules. If you realize that one of your assets or debts is not listed, you still have time to amend them, so tell your attorney immediately. Your attorney will notify the trustee, and the missing information will be listed on the appropriate forms.

Once the trustee has paid as many of your debts as possible, you'll receive a discharge notice in the mail, which marks the official end of your Chapter 7 bankruptcy. Store the notice in a safe place in case one of your creditors tries to collect a debt that was discharged.

In this chapter you learned a lot about many of the specifics of the Chapter 7 liquidation bankruptcy process, including the legal forms that have to filed at the start of your bankruptcy and how you can use redemptions and reaffirmations to hold on to assets you would other-wise lose in your bankruptcy. This chapter also explained how your creditors may respond to the fact that you've filed for bankruptcy, the kinds of questions you will be asked at your creditors' meeting, and what to expect after that meeting. Finally, you learned what will happen at the end of your bankruptcy. The next chapter provides detailed information about the Chapter 13 bankruptcy process.

Moving Through the Chapter 13 Bankruptcy Process

As you learned in chapter 6, a federally mandated financial means test will determine whether you will have the choice of filing for either a Chapter 7 or a Chapter 13 bankruptcy, or whether you will have to use Chapter 13 to deal with your debts. If the means test entitles you to choose, you may decide to file for Chapter 13 bankruptcy even though you can use Chapter 7 to wipe out most of your debts. Why? Because in a Chapter 7, you must give up most of your assets, but in a Chapter 13, you get to hold on to most of your assets in exchange for agreeing to pay most of your debts over a three- to five-year period.

In this chapter, you'll learn how the Chapter 13 bankruptcy process works. The chapter focuses most of its attention on the centerpiece of that process—your debt reorganization plan. Among other things, you'll find out how you have to treat certain types of debt in your plan, what your responsibilities will be once your plan is approved (confirmed) by the court, and what options you will have if you begin having trouble living up to the terms of your plan.

BEGINNING YOUR CHAPTER 13 BANKRUPTCY

Chapter 6 explained that many aspects of a Chapter 13 and a Chapter 7 bankruptcy are exactly the same. For example, you begin both kinds of bankruptcy by filing a bankruptcy petition with the court (and then a lot of other forms, too) and by paying a filing fee. Next, the court invokes the automatic stay to stop your creditors from trying to collect what you owe to them; and no more than 45 days later, you'll have to attend the creditors' meeting for your bankruptcy, where you'll answer questions from the trustee and maybe from your creditors.

However, one of the key distinctions between a Chapter 13 bankruptcy and a Chapter 7 bankruptcy is the debt reorganization plan that your attorney must prepare for you and file with the court for the judge's approval. This plan must spell out exactly how you will use your monthly disposable income to repay most of your debts over the three- to five-year period that you'll be in Chapter 13. (The plan must last for five years if your income is above the median income for your area, unless you intend to pay all your creditors 100 percent of what you owe to them through your reorganization plan.) Your monthly disposable income is the amount of money that your bankruptcy attorney determines you can afford to pay on your debts each month after taxes, Social Security, and your essential living expenses have been deducted from your total monthly income. Your attorney will use the federally required means test to make this calculation. The next several sections of this chapter explain the details of your reorganization plan, including its goals, how the plan must deal with certain

 Red Alert!

Your actual monthly expenses may be higher than the amounts that are allowable under the means test. Also, the test may not treat some of your regular monthly expenses as essential expenses, which means that they won't be included in your attorney's means test calculations. As a result, according to the test, you may have more disposable income to apply to your debts each month than you believe you can comfortably manage, given your actual expenses. That means that to be able to complete your Chapter 13 bankruptcy, you'll have to reduce your spending.

kinds of debts that you may owe, what will happen after your plan has been filed, and your responsibilities once it's been approved.

PREPARING YOUR DEBT REORGANIZATION PLAN

When preparing your plan, your bankruptcy attorney will have the following goals:

- To help you keep as many of your assets as possible

- To get rid of as much of your debt as possible

- To modify the rights of your secured creditors, if possible

The plan must treat certain kinds of debts in very specific ways. For example, it must show how you will pay the full amount of your priority debts during your bankruptcy. Priority debts include the following:

- Any past due court-ordered spousal and/or child support you may owe. In addition, while you are in Chapter 13, you must also keep up with all of your current spousal and/or child support payments. For example, let's assume that you owe $2,000 in past due child support, that your regular monthly support payments are $500, and that the term of your plan is five years. This means, that while your plan is in effect, you'll pay a total of $533.35 per month in child support—$33.35 per month in past due support and your regular $500 monthly payment.

- Any past due wages you may owe. For example, wages you may owe to the employees of your sole proprietorship.

- All past due taxes. This includes any past federal and state income taxes and/or property taxes you may owe. Past due taxes are the most common type of priority debt in a consumer bankruptcy.

- Unpaid criminal fines. This is for any crime you may have committed.

- Unpaid student loan debt. This is the amount that is past due on your student loans.

- Money that you may owe because you injured or killed someone. For example, an accident that you caused while you were under the influence of alcohol or illegal drugs.

The plan must also show what you intend to do about your secured debts, such as your mortgage and car loan, and how you intend to treat your unsecured debts, such as your credit card and medical debts. The next few sections discuss your plan and these debts.

DEALING WITH YOUR MORTGAGE, CAR LOAN, AND OTHER SECURED DEBTS IN YOUR PLAN

Your plan must deal with certain kinds of secured debts in very specific ways, assuming that you want to keep the collateral that secures them. Secured debts include the following:

- Your home mortgage. If you've fallen behind on your mortgage payments, you must pay the full amount of the arrearage over the term of your plan, and at the same time, you must make each current mortgage payment when it comes due while you are in bankruptcy. (The same is true if you owe money on a home equity loan.) Also, if your mortgage agreement requires

! Hot Tip

If you got your mortgage after October 22, 1994, while you are in bankruptcy, you won't have to pay interest on any past due loan amount unless your mortgage agreement or a nonbankruptcy law in your state requires you to pay it. But if you got the loan before October 22, 1994, you'll have to pay interest on the past due amount, although you can pay it in installments over the term of your plan.

you to make a balloon payment sometime during the five years following the start of your bankruptcy, you can pay the amount of the balloon payment in installments, too, over the term of your plan rather than in one lump sum.

❢ Hot Tip

While you are in bankruptcy, if you realize that you can't keep up with your mortgage payments and, at the same time, pay any mortgage arrearage you may owe, your attorney will ask the court to let you try to sell it (assuming you have a lot of equity in your home). You then can use the sale proceeds to pay the outstanding balance on your mortgage, including all interest and fees, rather than giving your home back to the lender or to the loan servicer. This is because you're likely to get more money by selling your home than if the lender or loan servicer sells it at auction. If you have little or no equity in your home, though, your attorney will advise you to give it back so that the lender or loan servicer can sell it. However it is sold, if your home doesn't sell for enough to pay what you owe on your mortgage, the deficiency will become an unsecured debt, which will be wiped out at the end of your bankruptcy.

- Your car loan. If you purchased the vehicle for your personal use (not for use in a business that you operate as a sole proprietorship) within 910 days of the start of your bankruptcy, while you're in bankruptcy, you'll have to pay the full balance due on your car loan, including all interest and late fees. However, if you purchased it earlier than 910 days prior to the start of your bankruptcy, you'll only have to pay the current value of the vehicle plus interest over the term of your reorganization plan, and because vehicles depreciate rapidly as soon as they leave the car lot, that amount will probably be less than the outstanding balance on the loan.

- Other secured debts that you incurred more than one year before your bankruptcy began. You can try to cram down these debts. When you cram down a debt, you can pay it off for less than what you owe on it. If the creditor to whom you owe the money objects to the cram down, the judge decides what will happen.

One of the main reasons why consumers file for Chapter 13 is to keep as many of their secured assets as possible by paying off the debts those assets collateralize through their reorganization plan. However, if you can't afford to pay everything, you'll have to return some of the assets to your creditors. Even so, giving back some assets in order to keep other more important assets is a worthwhile trade-off.

You can use your reorganization plan to cancel (or void) a *nonpurchase money security lien.* When you do, the debt that is associated with the lien becomes an unsecured debt. A nonpurchase money security lien exists when you secure a loan (usually a loan from a finance company) with some of your household goods. The word *nonpurchase* refers to the fact that you are not collateralizing the loan with the asset that the loan is helping you to buy—rather, you are using assets you already own as collateral. Bankruptcy law defines *household goods* to include clothing, furniture, appliances, one television, one VCR, one radio, china, kitchenware, medical equipment and supplies, and one personal computer, among other items. Household goods do not include works of art, unless you or a relative created them, nor do they include electronic equipment, jewelry and antiques valued at more than $500, or a boat, among other assets.

If you are leasing personal property, such as a car or furniture, when your plan is being prepared, you must decide whether you will *assume* or *reject* the lease. If you assume it, you'll have to pay the full amount of any past due lease payments you owe right away, and you'll also have to continue paying on the lease.

If you reject the lease, you must give the personal property that you are leasing back to the lessor. Then, the lessor will file a proof of claim in your bankruptcy for the balance due on the lease. However, because the remaining debt will be unsecured, whatever is left on the lease will be discharged at the end of your bankruptcy.

Red Alert!

Within 60 days of filing for Chapter 13, you must give each of your secured creditors a notice showing that you have insured their collateral. This requirement also applies to any property you are leasing if you have assumed the lease.

DEALING WITH UNSECURED DEBTS IN YOUR PLAN

When preparing your reorganization plan, your attorney will tackle your unsecured debts last because bankruptcy law considers them to be the least important kind of debt that you owe. At a minimum, your plan must show that during your bankruptcy you will pay your unsecured creditors at least as much as you would if you had filed for Chapter 7 (where your nonexempt assets are liquidated and the money would be used to pay your debts). However, if your attorney determines that you can afford to pay more than this minimum, then your plan must show exactly how much you will pay. After you've completed your reorganization plan, whatever you still owe on your unsecured debts will be discharged.

 Red Alert!

The trustee will carefully scrutinize the income and expense information that you provided to the court when you filed for bankruptcy, and any other financial information, to make sure that you pay as much as you possibly can on your unsecured debts. If the trustee decides that you can pay more than your plan says you will, the trustee will require that you revise your plan before you ask the judge to approve it.

AFTER YOUR PLAN HAS BEEN FILED

Once your reorganization plan has been drafted and reviewed with you, your attorney will file it with the court, along with your bankruptcy petition and your other required forms. Your attorney will also mail either a copy of the plan or a plan summary to each of your creditors. Although the plan won't be official until the judge confirms it, you'll have to begin paying your debts according to the plan no later than 30 days after the start of your bankruptcy. Your payments will either be automatically deducted from your paychecks and sent to the trustee in your bankruptcy, or you'll be required to send them directly to the trustee by a certain date each month. The payment method you'll have to use will depend on the policy of the court where you've filed your bankruptcy and on the particular types of debts you are paying off. Regardless of the method, the trustee will distribute your payment money to your creditors according to the terms of your plan.

❗Hot Tip

If the bankruptcy court requires that your plan payments be deducted from your paychecks and the automatic deductions will create a financial hardship for you, you can ask for permission to pay the trustee directly instead. The benefit of doing so would be if you are hit with an unexpected expense that you feel you have to pay—for example, your child breaks his leg and you have to take him to the emergency room—you could pay that expense rather than paying the trustee. However, you risk having your bankruptcy dismissed as a result. In reality, it's unlikely that the court will give you permission to pay the trustee directly.

Between the start of your bankruptcy and the date of your creditors' meeting, your attorney will contact your secured creditors to find out if they have any problems with the way your plan shows that you intend to treat the debts that you owe. For example, some creditors:

- May disagree with the amount that you say you owe to them.

- May want you to pay them more money than you are proposing.

- May not want you to keep your collateral. If that's the case, the creditors will file motions to lift the stay and the court will decide whether you can keep the assets. These kinds of motions are rare in consumer bankruptcies because usually the only collateral involved is a consumer's home, car, and/or furniture, and creditors know that the court won't make the consumer give up those assets as long as the consumer can pay for them. However, they will file those motions if the consumer stops making payments.

- May not believe that you prepared your plan "in good faith" or may believe that you can afford to pay more of what you owe to them. As a result, the creditors may decide to formally object to the confirmation of your plan.

Your attorney will try to resolve any problems prior to the date of your creditors' meeting. If all of the problems are not able to be resolved, your attorney can try again at the meeting.

Also prior to the creditors' meeting, you must file any pre-petition tax returns you may not have filed that were due during the four years preceding the start of your bankruptcy. If you don't file them before the meeting, the trustee in your bankruptcy or the taxing authority may ask the court to convert your bankruptcy to a Chapter 7. However, if circumstances beyond your control make it impossible for you to file all of your returns before the meeting, the trustee may give you extra time to file them.

 Red Alert!

You will probably have to hire a tax accountant to help you get your past due tax returns filed on time, which will increase the total cost of your bankruptcy.

AT THE CREDITORS' MEETING

At your Chapter 13 creditors' meeting, the trustee will ask you many of the same questions you would have had to answer if you'd filed for Chapter 7. (These questions were reviewed in the previous chapter.) However, the trustee also will ask you specific questions about your debt reorganization plan, and depending on your answers, you may have to make changes to the plan.

Any creditors who attend the meeting can also ask you questions about your finances and the details of your plan. Don't be surprised, however, if the only creditors who show up are your secured creditors.

If all of the concerns that your secured creditors had with your plan prior to the meeting were not resolved, your attorney will try again to resolve them during the meeting. If your attorney strikes out again, the creditors may formally object to the confirmation of your plan and/or they may file motions to lift the stay in your bankruptcy. If they do, the judge will hear their objections at the confirmation hearing and will hear their motions on another day. Depending on what the judge decides at the end of the hearing, you may have to revise your plan before it can be approved and/or you may have to give some of your secured assets back to the creditors who filed motions to lift the stay.

After the creditors' meeting, the trustee and your secured creditors will have 30 days to file objections to any of the assets that you've exempted. If they do, hearings will be held so that the judge can decide how to rule on the objections. Also, all of your creditors, other than governmental entities, will have 90 days after the creditors' meeting to file their proof of claim forms.

THE CONFIRMATION HEARING

Your debt reorganization plan won't be official until it has been approved by the bankruptcy judge at a confirmation hearing, which will take place no later than 45 days after the date of your creditors' meeting. At the hearing, your attorney will formally present your plan to the judge and will answer any questions the judge may have about it.

To decide if your plan should be confirmed, the judge will take into account a number of different criteria:

- Whether you've met all of the technical requirements of a Chapter 13 bankruptcy. For example, are your bankruptcy forms complete and accurate; did you pay your Chapter 13 filing fee; did you file all of your tax returns—federal and state—for the previous four years; and have you been paying all of your legally required post-petition spousal and/or child support payments?

- Whether your plan treats your creditors according to the rules of bankruptcy. That is, are they being treated in their best interest?

- If you've proposed your plan in good faith. Although there is no official definition of *in good faith*, when it is felt that a consumer is trying to abuse the bankruptcy process in some way, a bankruptcy judge often uses a lack of good faith as a reason to dismiss the bankruptcy.

- Whether your plan shows that you are making your best effort to pay all of your debts. For example, if you will be paying your creditors less than the full amount that you owe to them while you are in bankruptcy, and your income is below your state's median, then the judge will expect you to pay on your plan for at least 36 months; if your income is higher than your state's median, you will be expected to pay on it for at least 60 months. However, if you will be paying 100 percent of your debts plus interest while you are in bankruptcy, you can then pay on your plan for less than the minimum 36 months, assuming that you can afford to pay everything you've promised in a shorter amount of time.

- Whether you can afford to live up to your plan. The trustee will have already reviewed your income and the budget that you filed at the start of your bankruptcy to determine if your plan is financially realistic and will have made a recommendation regarding whether the plan should be confirmed. The judge will review this same information, but typically the judge goes along with whatever the trustee recommends.

Red Alert!

It's possible that some of your creditors will file their proof of claim forms after your reorganization plan has been confirmed because they can submit those forms up to 90 days after your creditors' meeting, and your plan confirmation hearing will happen no later than 45 days after that meeting. If any of your creditors submit proof of claim forms after your plan has been confirmed, depending on the amount of each creditor's claim, the trustee will either change your plan so that the claims can be paid while you are in bankruptcy, or your attorney will file objections to their claims. If that happens, a hearing on each objection will be held, and the judge will decide how you will have to treat each claim.

AFTER YOUR PLAN HAS BEEN CONFIRMED

Once your plan has been confirmed, your creditors must live with it, and you must pay your debts exactly as you've notated. If you don't, your bankruptcy may be dismissed, which means that your dischargeable debts won't be wiped out, and you'll be at the mercy of your creditors once again unless you file another bankruptcy right away. However, if you file for Chapter 13 immediately, the automatic stay in your new bankruptcy will only last for 30 days unless your attorney can convince the judge during a hearing on the matter that the automatic stay should be extended. Also, if you refile and that bankruptcy is also dismissed, although you can file for Chapter 13 a third time, you won't be protected by the automatic stay at all in the third bankruptcy unless the judge agrees to invoke it after a hearing.

 Red Alert!

Your secured creditors can file motions related to your bankruptcy after your plan has been confirmed. For example, your mortgage lender may file a motion to lift the stay to try to foreclose on your home if you fall behind on your loan payments during your bankruptcy.

While you are paying on your plan, you must also do the following:

- Maintain the appropriate amount of insurance on your loan collateral.

- Not incur any significant amounts of new debt without the court's approval. If you do, you may be required to pay the full amount of that debt while you're in bankruptcy, even though ordinarily in a Chapter 13 you would be able to pay less on the debt.

- Get the bankruptcy court's approval to refinance or sell your home.

- Get the court's approval to incorporate a business that you are operating as a sole proprietorship if you included the business in your bankruptcy estate.

▼ Hot Tip

If you are not sure whether you need the court's permission to take a specific action, talk to your attorney. Otherwise, you may unknowingly do something that could cause your bankruptcy to be dismissed.

- File a statement of your income and expenses with the bankruptcy court each year within 45 days of the anniversary of your plan's confirmation. If you don't, your bankruptcy may be dismissed. Your bankruptcy attorney will prepare the forms for you.

🖐 Red Alert!

While you are in Chapter 13, the trustee and your creditors can ask for copies of your income tax returns for previous years, and if you don't comply with their requests, your bankruptcy may be dismissed.

Red Alert!

If you are considering completing your Chapter 13 bankruptcy sooner than your plan indicates—for example, your plan shows that you will pay your debts over a five-year period, but you now think that you can complete it in three years—the court may require you to revise your plan and pay all of your creditors 100 percent of what you owe to them before you can get out of bankruptcy.

THE DISCHARGE OF DEBT

Once you've completed your reorganization plan, the judge will discharge all of your remaining debts, not including any debts that can't be wiped out according to bankruptcy law. You will have to start paying those debts as soon as you are out of bankruptcy. The discharge marks the official end of your bankruptcy.

You will probably receive your discharge notice in the mail rather than at a discharge hearing because most courts don't have discharge hearings. However, even if there is a discharge hearing in your bankruptcy, you may or may not have to attend the hearing; it will depend on how the bankruptcy court in your district works. If you must attend, your attorney will accompany you and you'll either receive your notice of discharge at the end of the hearing or through the mail.

 Red Alert!

Before you can get out of bankruptcy, you must complete a debtor financial education class offered by a federally approved credit counseling agency. Read chapter 6 for more information about this class and for a link to the agencies that have been approved to offer it.

IF YOU HAVE PROBLEMS LIVING UP TO THE TERMS OF YOUR PLAN

As much as you may try, you can't plan out your life exactly. Therefore, despite your best efforts to comply with all of the requirements of your debt reorganization plan, you may experience a setback that makes it difficult, if not impossible, for you to live up to the terms of the plan. For example, you may go through a divorce, experience a serious illness, or lose your job. Get in touch with your bankruptcy attorney as soon as you realize that you are in trouble. Otherwise, if you get behind on your plan payments, some of your secured creditors may file a motion to lift the stay so that they can take back their collateral—although they probably won't take that step right away. Also, if you ignore the fact that you're no longer complying with the terms of your reorganization plan, the court may eventually decide to dismiss your bankruptcy, which would mean that you'd be fair game for your creditors again.

Your attorney will help you evaluate your situation and advise you about your best courses of action, some of which are explained in the following sections.

A Moratorium

If you're experiencing a temporary financial setback and you've only missed a few of your plan payments, the judge may give you permission to get caught up. You can also ask for a moratorium if you haven't missed any payments yet, but you have reason to believe that you will.

A Modification

You can ask the court for permission to lower the amount of your payments so that you can continue paying off your debts. For example, you may ask the judge for permission to do the following:

- Extend the term of your plan, assuming your plan lasts for three years. You cannot extend a five-year plan.

- Reduce the amount that you must pay to your unsecured creditors each month. However, you can't pay them less than they would receive if you had filed for Chapter 7.

- Give up an asset that you are currently paying on in order to reduce your monthly expenses.

When your attorney files a request for a modification with the court, your attorney will notify all of your creditors about the request so that they can formally object to it if they want. If there are no objections, the judge will approve your request assuming that the revised plan meets all of the requirements of a Chapter 13.

If any of your creditors file objections, the judge will hear the objections and then decide whether you can modify your plan as you requested, whether you'll have to change the plan in some way in response to the concerns of your creditors, or whether your request for a modification will be denied.

A Conversion

When you can't figure out a way to meet all of your plan obligations, you can convert your Chapter 13 to a Chapter 7 bankruptcy. Your attorney will file a request for the conversion with the court, and the judge will automatically grant it without a hearing. After the conversion, a Chapter 7 trustee will be assigned to your bankruptcy, and you will have to attend a Chapter 7 creditors' meeting.

All of the assets that you owned at the time that you began your Chapter 13 bankruptcy and that you still own when you initiate the conversion will be included in your Chapter 7 bankruptcy, but not any assets that you acquired after you filed for Chapter 13. Also, if you incurred any new debt while you were in Chapter 13, you'll be able to discharge that debt through your Chapter 7 bankruptcy, depending on the kind of debt. However, if the judge decides that you converted

to a Chapter 7 to defraud some of
your creditors, or that you did not
cooperate with the trustee while
you were in Chapter 13, then all of
the assets that you owned when you
began the conversion, as well as all
of the assets you acquired after you
filed for Chapter 13, will be included
in your new bankruptcy.

 Red Alert!

If you received a discharge of debt in
a Chapter 7 within eight years of filing
for Chapter 13 and you convert your 13
bankruptcy to another Chapter 7, you
won't be eligible to receive a discharge
of debt.

A Hardship Discharge

Your attorney may suggest that you ask the bankruptcy judge for a
hardship discharge. If your request is granted, your Chapter 13 bankruptcy will end before you have completed your plan, and you will
receive a discharge of debt. However, you will still owe the unpaid
balance on your priority debts and you will either have to continue
paying on your secured debts or give the collateral for those debts
back to your creditors. You also may have to pay any consumer debts
that you incurred while you were in bankruptcy.

To get a hardship discharge, each of the following three criteria must
apply to you:

1. You can't afford to continue paying on your plan because of
   circumstances that are beyond your control—for example, a
   debilitating injury or disability.
2. You've already paid your unsecured creditors through your
   reorganization plan as much as they would have received if
   you had filed for Chapter 7.
3. Modifying your reorganization plan in order to remain in
   Chapter 13 is impractical for you.

This chapter stepped you through the Chapter 13 bankruptcy process.
It explained the role of your debt reorganization plan in your bankruptcy and how your creditors may respond to the plan. It also discussed your options if you start having problems paying your debts

according to the terms of the plan and told you what will happen after you've completed your plan.

The next chapter is the first of two that looks to the future. It tells you how to rebuild your credit histories and why having good credit histories and high credit scores is important to your life. It also provides advice for buying a home and a car after you've filed for bankruptcy.

Rebuilding Your Life and Your Finances After Bankruptcy

Rebuilding Your Credit After Bankruptcy

10

Once you are out of bankruptcy, your credit histories will be ruined and your FICO (Fair Isaac Corporation) scores will be low, low, low. This will make it difficult for you to qualify for new credit with attractive terms and to purchase insurance you need at a reasonable price. Also, some employers may be reluctant to hire you, especially if you apply for a job that involves handling or managing money, and landlords may hesitate about renting to you. Therefore, rebuilding your credit is your next challenge.

This chapter tells you how to meet that challenge. It begins by providing you with some basic information about your credit histories: I'll explain the kinds of information they contain, introduce you to the three national credit reporting agencies, and highlight your key credit reporting rights under the federal Fair Credit Reporting Act (FCRA). In addition, I'll fill you in on the various credit rebuilding preliminaries you should pursue as soon as you are out of bankruptcy to lay the groundwork for rebuilding, tell you how to order copies of your credit histories and find out your FICO scores, and then guide you through the credit rebuilding process. This chapter also warns you about credit rebuilding scams, and ends by offering some advice on how to buy a car or a home after bankruptcy.

WHY YOUR CREDIT HISTORIES AND YOUR FICO SCORES ARE IMPORTANT

Your *credit history* (also referred to as a *credit report, a credit record,* or a *credit file*) is a detailed record of how you have managed your credit over time. Among other information, it lists your credit accounts and their current outstanding balances, how often you were late paying an account, whether any of your accounts were turned over to debt collectors, whether the IRS put a tax lien on any of your assets, and whether any of your creditors obtained a money judgment against you as a result of a lawsuit, among other things. Your credit history will also show that you filed for bankruptcy.

Each of the credit reporting agencies (CRAs) collects information about you from creditors and from public records and maintains it in a computerized database. They then sell that information to anyone who the federal FCRA says is entitled to use it, such as creditors, employers, insurance companies, landlords, and public agencies. The

> **! Hot Tip**
>
> You have a credit history with each of the three national credit reporting agencies—Equifax, Experian, and TransUnion—and the information in each individual history is likely to be slightly different from the other two.

FCRA governs what the CRAs can and cannot do with the information in your credit histories, and it also regulates what the users of that information can do with it. In addition, the law gives you specific rights with regard to your credit record information, including the right to receive copies of your credit histories and the right to dispute the accuracy of information in those records and to have inaccuracies corrected.

Your FICO scores (your FICO Classic score, in particular, which is the specific type of FICO score that is most widely used by creditors)—the three-digit credit scores that a growing number of creditors, insurance companies, and other organizations are using to make decisions about you rather than reviewing your actual credit histories—are derived from the information in your credit records. You actually have three different FICO scores: one score based on your Equifax credit history, another on your Experian credit file, and the third on your TransUnion score. If the information in your credit files is positive, then your FICO scores will be high, or in the 700s (for the very best terms of credit, your FICO scores should be at least 720). Unfortunately, because you've filed for bankruptcy, your FICO scores will be low. To order your FICO Classic scores, go to *www.myfico.com.*

Whenever you apply for new credit, a job, insurance, a place to rent, a government license, and the like, it's likely that one of your credit histories and/or at least one of your FICO scores will be reviewed. If there is a lot of negative information in your credit history or if your FICO score is low, your application may be denied. If you are approved for credit, however, you'll be charged a very high interest rate because of your bad credit history and low FICO score. For the same reason, if an insurance company agrees to sell you insurance, you can expect the amount of your premium to be higher than normal.

As you've already learned in this book, most of the negative information in your credit histories will disappear after 7 years, although the FCRA says that a bankruptcy can stick around for 10 years. (The three CRAs report completed Chapter 13 bankruptcies for just 7 years.) Therefore, over time, as the negative information disappears and

> **▼ Hot Tip**
>
> Periodically during the credit rebuilding process, you should measure the impact of your rebuilding efforts by ordering your FICO scores.

as you add positive information to those records through the credit rebuilding process, your credit histories will start to improve, your FICO scores will rise, and you'll become more attractive to creditors, employers, insurance companies, landlords, and others.

GETTING READY TO REBUILD YOUR CREDIT HISTORIES

As soon as you are out of bankruptcy, you should begin preparing to rebuild your credit by:

- Examining how you contributed to the financial problems that pushed you into bankruptcy.

- Increasing the amount of money in your savings account.

- Correcting problems in your credit histories.

- Adding information to your credit histories about credit accounts with positive payment histories that are not being reported to the CRAs.

The next several sections of this chapter discuss how to lay this groundwork.

Take a Look at Yourself

Take time to assess the role that you may have played in creating the financial problems that pushed you into bankruptcy. For example, you may not have strong money management skills; as a result, once you began having financial problems, you did not know how to address them, and the problems grew worse and created more problems. Or maybe you spent money for emotional reasons, even when you couldn't afford to spend it. If you realize that you contributed to the problems that led you into bankruptcy, then it's important to address them. Otherwise, they may sabotage your rebuilding efforts and could even push you into bankruptcy again.

If you believe that a lack of money know-how contributed to your financial troubles, then enroll in a class on basic money management offered at your local community college, or sign up for a money management workshop offered by a nonprofit credit counseling agency close to where you live or work. Also, there are many excellent books and websites that provide easy-to-understand information about managing your money. (Check out the Resources section at the end of this book for some of them.) In addition, the last chapter of this book discusses money management basics that can help you avoid financial problems in the future.

If your money problems developed because you have emotional problems with money—for example, you spend when you are bored, when you feel bad about yourself, or when you are depressed—begin attending Debtors Anonymous meetings in your area and/or work with a mental health counselor. Chapter 1 provides contact information for Debtors Anonymous as well as resources for finding a good mental health counselor.

Build Up Your Savings Account

Start putting money into your savings account as soon as you can. Having a healthy balance in savings is essential to your credit rebuilding efforts, because at the start of the process you probably won't be able to qualify for unsecured credit from most banks or most major credit card companies. Instead, they will want you to collateralize any credit they may extend to you with the money in your savings account or with a certificate of deposit (CD) that you purchase with that money.

Another reason for having money in savings is that if you lose your job or are hit with a big expense that you can't afford to pay, you can draw on the funds in your savings account instead of using credit. In other words, having money in a savings account is like having a financial safety net.

Financial experts advise that you save at least 10 percent of your income each month. However, if you can't afford to save that much right away, use your budget to determine how much you can afford, and then commit to putting that amount of money into your account each month. Even if it's only a small sum, your money will grow over time, and as your finances improve, you'll be able to increase the amount that you are saving.

❗ Hot Tips

Consider taking a second job to build up your savings faster.

The best way to save is to have your employer direct-deposit a set amount of money into your savings account each month.

If your employer doesn't offer direct deposits or you are self-employed, arrange to have your bank regularly transfer funds from your checking account into your savings account.

Clear Up Problems in Your Credit Histories

It's not unusual for consumers to find damaging (and erroneous) problems in their credit histories. Here are some of the most common kinds of problems:

- Accounts that don't belong to you are on your report.

- There is inaccurate account information. For example, one of your credit reports shows an outstanding balance on an account that is more than the actual balance, or it indicates that you've frequently been late with your account payments when you've always paid the account on time.

- Accounts that you've closed are being reported as open.

- Debts that your spouse acquired prior to your marriage are in your credit history. Those debts are your spouse's separate debts, not yours, so they don't belong in your credit history.

- There are inaccuracies in the identifying section of your credit history, which is the section where your name, address, and Social Security number appear.

- Negative information that the FCRA says is too old to be reported is in one of your credit reports.

- Your credit history doesn't tell the whole story about some of the negative information it's reporting. For example, although the IRS removed the tax lien it had on your home, your credit history shows that the lien is still intact.

Order copies of your Equifax, Experian, and TransUnion credit histories, and review them for problems. If you find any, the FCRA entitles you to get the problems corrected. If you don't correct them, the problems may interfere with your credit rebuilding efforts.

How to Order Your Credit Histories

You can order your credit histories online, by phone, or through the mail. Ordinarily, you'll have to pay $10 for each copy. However, under certain circumstances, you are entitled to free credit reports. Figure 10.1 discusses getting your credit reports for free. Figure 10.2 provides a sample letter for ordering your credit histories by mail.

Ordering Your Equifax Credit Report

- To order online, go to *www.equifax.com*, and select "Equifax Credit Report" under "Products" in the pull-down menu at the top of the page. Once you are on the ordering page, click on the circle next to the words "Get only your Equifax Credit Report for $10.00," and unclick the box on the right-hand side of the page next to "Add Equifax Credit Ranking for only $8.95."

- To order by phone, call 800-685-1111.

- To order by mail, write a request letter and send it to:

    Equifax Information Services
    LLC Disclosure Department
    P.O. Box 740241
    Atlanta, GA 30374

Ordering Your Experian Credit Report

- To order online, go to *www.experian.com/consumer_online_products/index.html*, and click on the yellow "Order Now" button at the bottom of the column labeled "Experian credit report."

- To order by phone, call 888-397-3742.

- To order by mail, write to:

> Experian
> National Consumers Assistance Center
> P.O. Box 2104
> Allen, TX 75013-2104

Ordering Your TransUnion Credit Report

- To order online, go to *www.transunion.com,* and click on "FACT ACT" at bottom of your screen under "More for Consumers." Click on the highlighted area at the bottom of the page to order one copy of your credit report.

- To order by phone, call 800-916-8800.

- To order by mail, send your request letter to:

> TransUnion
> Consumer Disclosure Center
> P.O. Box 2000
> Chester, PA 19022-2000

Correcting a Problem in Your Credit History

If you find a problem in one of your credit histories, the FCRA entitles you to initiate an investigation into the problem with the CRA that is reporting the information or with the provider of the problem information. You can initiate an investigation with a CRA by phone, by mail, or online.

To begin an investigation by phone, call the CRA's toll-free number for disputes/investigations. The number will either be on the credit report that contains the information you want investigated or on the dispute form that may have come with the credit report if you ordered the report by phone or by mail.

FIGURE 10.1. Obtaining Your Credit Reports for Free

The FCRA entitles you to one free copy of each of your credit reports every 12 months. To order them, go to *www.annualcreditreport.com* or call 877-322-8228. Avoid other websites that claim to offer free credit reports. Their "free" offers always come with a catch that will cost you money. The *only* site for ordering free copies of your credit reports, no strings attached, is *www.annualcreditreport.com*.

The law also entitles you to one or more additional free credit reports under the following circumstances:

- You are denied credit, employment, insurance, or the opportunity to rent an apartment because of information in one of your credit histories. (You are entitled to a free copy of the credit history containing the information.)

- A creditor, insurer, or employer takes some other adverse action against you, such as raising the interest rate on credit you already have, increasing the amount of your premium, or demoting you because of information in one of your credit histories. (You are entitled to a free copy of the credit history that the creditor, insurer, or employer reviewed prior to taking the adverse action.)

- You add fraud alerts to your credit histories because you believe that your identity has been stolen. (You are entitled to free copies of all three of your credit histories.)

- You're unemployed and intend to apply for work in the next 60 days. (You are entitled to free copies of all three of your credit histories.)

FIGURE 10.2. Sample Letter for Ordering Your Credit Report

When you order your credit reports by mail, unless you include specific information in your letter, your request won't be processed. Here is a model letter to use so that you will not miss any relevant information:

[Date]
[Name of CRA]
[Address of CRA]

To Whom It May Concern:

Please send me a copy of my credit report. The following information is provided to help you process this request:

- [Your full name, including Sr., Jr., III, etc.]

- [Your Social Security number]

- [Your date of birth]

- [Your spouse's full name, if you are married]

- [Your spouse's Social Security number]

- [Your current address, and your previous address(es) if you haven't lived at your present address for at least two years. Include your apartment number or private mailbox number, if appropriate.]

- [Your evening and daytime phone numbers, including area codes]

I have enclosed a _____ [check or money order] in the amount of $10.00 to pay for my credit report. [Depending on your circumstances or state, you may not need to include the previous sentence, or the amount of your check or money order may be for a different amount.]

Please mail my credit report to: [Provide your name and mailing address].

Thank you in advance for your prompt attention to this request.

Sincerely,
[Your signature]

To initiate an investigation through the mail, type a letter in which you clearly and specifically spell out the exact information you want investigated and what you want the CRA to do about the information: delete it, correct it, or add something to make the information more accurate and complete. Attach to your letter a copy of the page from your

> **❗ Hot Tip**
>
> If there is a confirmation number, account number, or file number on the first page of your credit report, include that number in your letter to expedite the processing of your request.

credit history where the problem information is located, and circle or highlight the information. If you have any receipts, cancelled checks, letters, account statements, or any other written documentation that helps prove the problem, make copies and attach them to your letter, too. Mail everything to the CRA's address for disputes, which will either be listed on the credit report containing the problem you are asking to have investigated or on the investigation/dispute form that may have come with the report. Send everything via certified mail with a return receipt requested so that you will have proof of when your letter was received and who signed for it. Model your investigation request letter after the one in Figure 10.3.

To start an investigation online, use the CRA's dispute form. You can access the appropriate forms at the following websites:

—**Equifax.** *www.equifax.com.* Click on "Online Dispute" at top of page.

—**Experian.** *www.experian.com.* Click on "Disputes" at bottom of page.

—**TransUnion.** *www.transunion.com.* Click on "Dispute an item on your report" at bottom of page.

FIGURE 10.3. Sample Investigation Request Letter

When you initiate an investigation with a CRA using the mail, model your letter after the one below so you can be sure that you provide the CRA with all of the information it needs. If you omit any of the information from your letter, the CRA's investigation won't begin until you provide the missing information.

[*Date*]

[*Your name*]
[*Your address*]
[*Your city, state, and zip code*]
[*Your Social Security number*]
[*Credit report confirmation number*]

Dispute Department
[*Name of CRA*]
[*Address*]
[*City, state, and zip code*]

To Whom It May Concern:

I am disputing the following information in my credit report. *[Explain exactly what you are disputing. If you are disputing more than one thing, list each item as a separate bullet. Whenever you are disputing information related to one of your credit accounts, indicate the name of the creditor as it appears on your credit history and your account number. Also, for each item that you list, clearly explain why the information is wrong, incomplete, or outdated. For example: this is not my account; this debt was discharged in bankruptcy on (date); and so on. Also, whenever you list information on your credit history that you are disputing, indicate what you want the credit reporting agency to do about it. For example, you want an account deleted, information added, an error corrected, and so on. Be as specific as possible.]*

■ _____

■ _____

■ _____

Sample Investigation Request Letter continues on next page.

I have attached copies of the following documents in support of my dispute. Also, enclosed is a copy of the page from my credit history with the information I am disputing highlighted.

Please get in touch with me if you have any questions about this letter. I can be reached at [*your daytime area code and phone number*].

Sincerely,

Signature [*Sign your name as it appears on your credit history.*]

Enclosures: [*List each document you are attaching to your letter.*]

If the CRA's Investigation Corrects Your Problem

Once the CRA receives your investigation request, the FCRA says that it must contact the provider of the information you're disputing. If the information provider confirms that the information you disputed is correct, then the information will remain in your credit history and will continue to be reported to creditors, employers, and others. However, if the information provider agrees with you that the information you're disputing is indeed inaccurate, incomplete, or outdated, the CRA must correct your credit history immediately, and it must also inform the other two CRAs about the correction so that they can correct their own databases. The provider of the information must immediately correct its database, too. The CRA must complete its investigation within 30 days of receiving your request, unless you provide it with additional information after its investigation has begun. If you do, then the CRA will have 45 days to complete its investigation.

Once the CRA's investigation is over, it must send you a written notice of its findings as well as a copy of your corrected credit report, assuming that its investigation confirmed the problem that you disputed. The CRA must also inform you of your right to have it send a copy of your corrected credit history to any employers who may have reviewed it over the past two years and to anyone else who may have looked at it over the past six months.

Sometimes, information that is corrected is mistakenly reinserted into a consumer's credit history because of a computer glitch or human error. Therefore, a month or two after a problem in your credit history has been corrected, order another copy to confirm that this has not happened. You should do the same with your other two credit histories if either or both of them were also corrected.

If you find that the problem information is back in any of your credit histories, contact the CRAs reporting the information to ask that they correct your credit record again. Attach to your letter a copy of the notice you received from the CRA that conducted the investigation informing you that the problem had been resolved.

What to Do When an Investigation Doesn't Resolve Your Problem

If a CRA's investigation doesn't resolve a problem in your credit history, you have several options:

- Try to locate additional information to help prove the problem. If you do, send it to the CRA together with a cover letter referencing the outcome of its first investigation and asking that, in light of the new information, it correct your credit history.

- Contact the provider of the information that you want corrected. It's possible that the CRA did not share with the information provider all of the documents you may have provided when you initially requested the investigation, even though the FCRA says that the CRA must share everything. It's also possible that in response to the CRA, the information provider did not do a thorough job of reviewing its own records on your account. Contact the information provider in writing, and then follow up by phone to ensure that the provider is clear about exactly what you are asking it to do and to request that it notify you in writing of its conclusion.

If the information provider sends you a notice confirming that the credit history information you questioned is incorrect, outdated, or incomplete and that it has corrected the information in its own database, make copies of that notice and send a copy to the CRAs together with a letter demanding that they correct your credit history. Although the information provider is legally obligated to notify the CRAs about the correction, when it comes to resolving problems in your credit histories, it's best to leave nothing to chance.

- Prepare a written statement of no more than 100 words explaining why the information in your credit history is wrong, outdated, or incomplete, and send a copy of the statement to the CRA that conducted the investigation. The FCRA says that it must make the statement a part of your credit history so that anyone who reviews your credit file can read it.

 Red Alert!

Creditors, employers, or anyone else who uses your FICO scores to make decisions about you instead of reviewing your credit histories won't ever see your written statement.

- Contact a consumer law attorney. It's possible that you may have grounds for a lawsuit against the CRA, the information provider, or both.

Initiating an Investigation with an Information Provider

The FCRA entitles you to begin an investigation into a problem in your credit history with the provider of the information. Each provider has its own process for beginning an investigation, so call it to find out how to initiate the investigation process. All of the same FCRA requirements that apply to an investigation that is conducted by a CRA also apply to investigations conducted by information providers.

Adding Missing Accounts with Positive Information to Your Credit Files

When you review your credit histories, you may notice that some of your credit accounts—probably accounts that you have with regional and/or local retailers and banks—are not being reported. That's because some creditors only report information about consumer accounts when the accounts are in default or when they write off debts as *uncollectible;* still other creditors never report consumer account information to the CRAs.

 Red Alerts!

Don't give up if one of the CRAs doesn't respond to you the first time you ask to have missing account information added to your credit file. It may take a couple letters before you get a yes or no.

If you have a positive payment history for an account that is not in your credit files, write to each of the CRAs to ask that they add the missing information. Attach to the letters a copy of your most recent billing statement for the missing account, and send everything certified mail with a return receipt requested. Although the FCRA does not require the CRAs to comply with your request, they may agree to add the missing account information once they've verified its accuracy. However, they may charge you a fee for the addition.

If none of these approaches is successful, prepare a written statement about the missing information. Then, whenever you apply for important credit, insurance, employment, and the like, attach the statement to your application along with proof that the information is accurate. Examples of proof include a letter from your creditor stating that you've always paid your account on time or documentation showing that you paid a loan in full.

Red Alert!

Having positive information in your credit histories related to any accounts you may have with regional or local retailers and banks won't be as helpful to your credit rebuilding efforts as positive payment history informa- tion on a MasterCard, Visa card, or mortgage. However, when you are trying to rebuild your credit after bankruptcy, having any kind of positive account payment information in your credit histories is better than none at all.

MOVING THROUGH THE CREDIT REBUILDING PROCESS

Once you've gotten the preliminaries out of the way, it's time to begin the credit rebuilding process. The process involves slowly adding positive information to your credit histories by obtaining small amounts of new credit and managing it responsibly.

At first, the terms of the new credit that you qualify for won't be as attractive as if you had not had money troubles and bankruptcy. For example, the interest rates on the new credit will be relatively high, you won't qualify for unsecured credit, and your credit limits will be low. Gradually, however, as your credit histories improve, the terms of the credit you can qualify for will improve.

There is no one right way to rebuild your credit histories. However, the next several sections of this chapter guide you through the method that has worked well for countless consumers and should work equally well for you. There are several steps you can take to begin rebuilding your credit:

- Apply for a MasterCard or Visa.

- Get a small bank loan.

- Get a second bank loan once you've paid off the first loan.

- Monitor your credit histories and your FICO scores.

- Make all of your credit payments on time.

Red Alert!

Applying for a lot of new credit will harm your rebuilding efforts because creditors will worry that you are trying to get too much credit and that you may develop money troubles again. Also, each time that you apply for credit, your application will show up as an "inquiry" in the Inquiries section of your credit histories; having a lot of inquiries will damage your credit histories. When it comes to credit rebuilding, slow and steady wins the race.

Apply for a MasterCard or Visa

At the start of the rebuilding process, you won't be able to qualify for a regular, unsecured MasterCard or Visa card; you'll have to apply for a secured card instead. However, if you manage that responsibly, you'll eventually qualify for an unsecured MasterCard or Visa.

A secured MasterCard or Visa looks just like a regular MasterCard or Visa. However, there are several important differences between the two types of cards:

- When you're approved for a secured card, you must secure the purchases you make with the card. One way to do this is to deposit a certain amount of money in a savings account located at the bank that issued you the card. The amount will vary, but it will probably be between a couple hundred dollars and a couple thousand dollars. Or, the bank may require that you purchase from it a certificate of deposit (CD) of a certain amount. While your credit card account is open, you won't have access to the money in the savings account or to the CD.

- Secured MasterCards and Visas have much lower credit limits than regular cards. The credit limit on the secured card you get will be a percentage of the value of your collateral. Also, secured cards tend to have higher interest rates and higher fees.

Just like regular MasterCards and Visas, some secured cards have more attractive terms than others. For example, some require less collateral,

> **❢ Hot Tip**
>
> If you had a MasterCard or Visa with a zero balance on it at the time that you filed for bankruptcy, then the bank that issued you the card was not a part of your bankruptcy. Therefore, you probably still have the card, assuming the creditor didn't learn about the bankruptcy and cancel your account. If you still have the card, you don't need to apply for a new card in order to begin rebuilding your credit. You can do that using the card you already have.

have bigger credit limits, lower interest rates, and fewer and lower fees. Therefore, when you are shopping for a secured card, apply for the one with the very best terms of credit. If you are turned down for that card, then apply for the one with the second most attractive terms of credit, and so on.

When you are comparing card offers, pay close attention to the following in order to identify the best deal on a secured card:

- Whether you must pay an application fee when you apply for the card and the amount of the fee. Also, note whether the fee is refundable if you are turned down for the card. It should be.

- The kind and amounts of any other fees associated with the card. The fewer the fees and the lower the fees, the better.

- The cards' credit limits. Is it enough to meet your needs?

- The interest rates associated with the cards and whether the rates are fixed or variable. Apply for the card with the lowest fixed fee you can find.

- The amount of collateral you must put up. The lower the better.

- The interest your collateral will earn. The higher the better.

- The grace period on the card. This is the amount of time you have to pay a card's outstanding balance before you will be charged interest on the balance. A longer grace period is better than a short grace period or no grace period at all if you will be carrying a balance on your card. Watch out for cards with no grace period.

■ Whether you can increase your credit limit and under what conditions. For example, some secured credit card issuers require you to put up more collateral to get a higher credit limit, while others will increase your credit limit after you've built up a record of on-time payments on your secured card over a certain number of months.

■ The circumstances that entitle the card issuer to take your collateral.

■ Whether you can get whatever is left of your collateral if the card issuer closes your account. If you can get that money, be clear about the timing.

■ Whether you can covert the card to a regular MasterCard or Visa after a certain number of months. Ideally, this is no more than 18 months—if you make all of your payments on time. If you can convert, pay attention to the interest rate, fees, credit limit, and other terms associated with the unsecured card. You may be better off applying for an unsecured card from a different creditor.

 Red Alert!

Before you apply for a secured card, confirm that your account payments will be reported to all three of the credit reporting agencies. Otherwise, there is no reason to have the card because it won't help you rebuild your credit.

Once You Have a Secured MasterCard or Visa

To add positive information to your credit histories, use your card in one of two following ways:

1. Every month, purchase essentials such as gasoline and groceries using your card, making sure to pay the card's full outstanding balance by the due date.

2. Use the card to finance the purchase of a more expensive product or service that you need, and then pay for that purchase over time. Try to pay more than the minimum due each month and don't use the card to purchase anything else until the balance is paid in full. Then use the card again to buy something else and pay off that balance over time.

Get a Bank Loan

Apply for a small, secured loan before, after, or at the same time that you apply for a MasterCard or Visa. The timing will depend on whether you have enough money to secure a credit card *and* a bank loan at the same time. At first, the most you'll probably be able to borrow is $1,000.

If you have a good relationship with your current bank, set up a meeting with a loan officer there to discuss a loan. At the meeting, explain that you recently got out of bankruptcy, that you want to begin rebuilding your

🖑 Red Alerts!

Maxing out your credit card will damage your credit histories and lower your FICO scores. It's best to use no more than 30 percent of your card's total credit limit.

Once your bankruptcy is over, you'll probably begin receiving preapproved offers for MasterCards and Visas. Credit card issuers send these offers to consumers who meet certain criteria based on the information in their credit histories. Although a credit card company that sends you a preapproved offer is signaling that it's willing to give you credit despite your bankruptcy, scrutinize the terms of the credit carefully by reading all of the fine print in the card offer. When you do, you may discover that the low, low interest rate touted in the large print is going to last for just a short period of time—maybe only six months—and that the interest rate will increase dramatically after the time is up, or that the interest rate on the card will shoot up if you are just one day late with a payment. Look for a better deal on a secured MasterCard or Visa at websites such as *www.cardweb.com, www.cardtrak.com,* and *www.bankrate.com.*

FIGURE 10.4. Steer Clear of Credit Card Scams!

Some consumers with damaged credit histories who are overly anxious to obtain new credit and who don't want to go through the credit rebuilding process fall for credit card scams. As a result, they spend money that they shouldn't, get little or nothing for that money, and do nothing to rebuild their credit histories. Here are some examples of credit card scams:

■ TV and newspaper ads that tell you to call a "900" number to get a credit card. A "900" number is not the same as an "800" number, which is toll-free, so when you call a "900" number, you will either be charged a high per-minute fee for as long as you stay on the line (and the person you speak with will try to keep you on the line as long as possible) or a flat fee that may be $50 or more. Also, at some point during your conversation, you may be transferred to another "900" number, at which point you will be charged an additional fee.

If you call a "900" number to get a credit card, all you may receive in return is an application for a credit card and instructions to return the application together with a substantial application fee. If you follow these instructions, all you may get for your money is a list of banks that offer MasterCards or Visas—information that you could get for yourself for free on the Internet—or a credit card (but not a MasterCard or Visa) that has a very high interest rate and high fees and that you can only use to purchase overpriced products from a catalog provided by the card issuer. In addition, the card issuer will not report your card payments to any of the CRAs, so the card won't help you rebuild your credit.

■ Unsolicited offers for preapproved, unsecured credit cards. Some companies regularly review court records, looking for the names and addresses of consumers who have filed for bankruptcy, and then they send those consumers information that tells them that they've been approved for a major credit card with a substantial credit limit despite their recent financial problems. If you receive such an offer, it may feature a logo much like the ones that you see on MasterCards and Visas, so you may assume that if you pay the card issuer the fee that it's asking for, you'll receive a national bank card in return. In reality, you'll receive some other kind of credit card together with a catalog of products, and you'll be told that once you purchase a certain dollar amount of products from the catalog using the card—in many cases, $500 or more worth of products—you'll receive a MasterCard or Visa application. Again, this kind of card won't help you rebuild your credit, so it's a total waste of money.

■ Emails offering you a credit card, no questions asked. The emails may tell you that an "offshore bank" will issue you a MasterCard or Visa if you send the bank an up-front fee. Don't bite!

> ### ❗ Hot Tip
>
> You cannot discharge a home mortgage, car loan, or student loan in bankruptcy, so you can use your post-bankruptcy payments on such loans to rebuild your credit. As a result, you don't need to apply for another loan. Just pay the loans you already have on time each month.

credit, and that as part of that effort you would like a small bank loan. If you have a good explanation for why you ended up in bankruptcy, such as a job loss or high medical bills, as opposed to overspending, share it with the loan officer. Also, regardless of the reasons for your financial problems, let the loan officer know what you're doing to help minimize the likelihood that you'll develop problems again in the future. For example, you're now working at a better paying job, your spouse has begun working outside the home, or you are living on a budget and saving money every month.

If the loan officer refuses to give you a loan, politely ask why. You may be told that you need more money in savings, more time needs to pass since the end of your bankruptcy, or your income must be higher or more stable. Use whatever feedback you receive to make yourself more creditworthy. Then, after following the loan officer's advice, set up a second meeting with the same loan officer or schedule a meeting with a loan officer at a different bank in your area.

If you can't find a bank that is willing to give you a loan right away, bide your time and continue to save, to responsibly manage any credit you may already have, and to pay all of your bills on time. Sooner or later, you will qualify for a loan.

Apply for a Second Loan

After you've paid off your first loan, ask the same lender for a second loan; this time, however, ask for one that is unsecured. If the lender won't give you an unsecured loan, either ask for a second secured loan that is larger than the one you just paid off, or apply for an unsecured loan from a different bank.

❗ Hot Tips

After you've paid off your first loan, order a copy of your credit report from whichever CRAs the bank reports to so that you can be sure all of the information about the loan is complete and accurate. If it's not, before you apply for additional credit, get the information corrected using the advice provided earlier in this chapter in the section entitled, "Correcting a Problem in Your Credit History."

If you can't qualify for a loan on your own, you may be able to get one if someone you know, maybe a close friend or relative, will cosign for the loan. There is a downside to this arrangement, however, because your cosigner will be as responsible as you are for repaying the debt, which means that if you miss some payments or if you can't repay the loan at all for some reason, the lender will look to your cosigner for the money that you owe. Having to pay the debt for you could not only create a financial hardship for your cosigner, but it could also ruin your relationship with one another.

Make on-time payments on the second loan. Once you've paid it off, check your credit histories again to confirm that all of the information associated with the loan is complete and accurate. Then, if the second loan was secured, try again to qualify for an unsecured loan. Assuming you have been managing your finances responsibly, you should be able to qualify for one this time.

Other Ways to Add Positive Information to Your Credit Histories

Following the previous advice is the best way to rebuild your credit histories. However, you may also want to consider doing the following:

- Get a credit card from a major retailer and/or from an oil and gasoline company, such as Chevron or Texaco. These kinds of cards are quite easy to qualify for.

- Ask someone with good credit to make you an authorized user on his or her credit card. When you are an authorized user on someone else's account, your name is added to the account and the cardholder's account payment information ends up in your credit histories. How ever, being an authorized user on an account won't carry as much weight with creditors as if you had qualified for the credit yourself and were responsible for making the account payments.

 Red Alert!

If the person who makes you an authorized user on one of his or her accounts pays the account late or defaults on the account, the information will harm your credit rebuilding efforts.

ADVICE FOR BUYING A CAR OR A HOME SOON AFTER BANKRUPTCY

Some of you may need to purchase a car once your bankruptcy is over and/or you may begin thinking about buying a home, but achieving these goals will be more difficult because of your damaged credit histories and low FICO scores.

Buying a Car After Bankruptcy

If the car you are driving breaks down not long after you've completed your bankruptcy and the cost of repairing it is too high, you may need to buy another car. Before you do, however, explore alternatives to getting where you need to go, including using public transportation, riding your bike, walking, and carpooling. If you conclude that you can't do without a car, minimize the amount of money you must spend on one by finding a reliable used car that meets your needs. There are many ways to find a good used car:

- Use the Internet or local newspapers. Review the classifieds section of your local newspaper, visit Craigslist at *www.craigslist.org*, read cars-for-sale publications that are distributed in your area, and check out used car websites such as *www.usedcars.com* and *www.cars.com*, among others.

❗ Hot Tip

For detailed tips and advice about buying a used car, visit websites such as *www.carbuy ingtips.com/used* and *www.samarins.com,* and read the Federal Trade Commission's "Buying a Used Car" publication at *www.ftc.gov/bcp/* *conline/pubs/alerts/ucaralrt.shtm*. Also, for a detailed and very helpful step-by-step guide to buying a used car, go to *www.edmunds. com/advice/buying/articles/45310/article*.

- Talk to your friends and relatives. One of them may have a car that they will sell to you. Someone also may be willing to let you pay for the car over time.

- Visit reputable car dealerships in your community that sell used cars. Most of them have a "high-risk loan" department that makes loans to consumers with bad credit. However, you'll need a stable work history and a steady income to qualify for the loan. Be prepared to share a copy of your bankruptcy discharge paperwork with the dealership.

Once you find a used car that you'd like to buy, go to *www.edmunds.com* to find out what it's worth, and then use that information to negotiate a good purchase price. Also, have a mechanic you trust check out the car before you pay the seller any money or sign any purchase paperwork. Never just accept the seller's assurance that the car "runs great."

Buying a Home After Bankruptcy

Ordinarily, you won't be able to qualify for a mortgage until you've been out of bankruptcy for at least 18 months to two years. During this time, therefore, focus on rebuilding your credit and saving for a down payment. Once you are ready to buy a home, explore the home buying programs sponsored by the federal government. For example, the Federal Housing Administration (FHA)

❗ Hot Tip

Ordinarily, you'll get a better deal on a used car if you purchase it from an individual rather than from a dealership.

has a loan program for first-time home buyers. If you qualify for an FHA loan, you'll only have to make a very small down payment on the home you are buying, and your closing costs will be minimal. To learn more about FHA loans, go to *www.hud.gov/fha/loans.cfm*. Another option is to purchase a home foreclosed by the Department of Housing and Urban Development (HUD). If you buy one of these homes, you won't have to put down any money. To learn about HUD-foreclosed homes, go to *www.hud.gov/homes/index.cfm*.

Your state, county, or local government may also sponsor home buying programs that require no down payments or very small down payments. However, to qualify for the programs, your income may have to be below a certain amount for your family size. To learn more about government-sponsored loan programs in your area, go to *www.hud.gov/buying/localbuying.cfm*.

If you don't want to wait 18 months to two years to buy a home, or if you wait that long and have trouble qualifying for a mortgage, there are some alternatives:

- Enter into a lease-to-buy agreement. This is a good option when you want to be a homeowner but you don't have a down payment. When you purchase a home this way, you initially rent the home you are living in and a portion of your rent payments go toward a down payment. As a result, your monthly

❗ Hot Tips

For information about different kinds of mortgages, choosing the right mortgage, and predatory lending, or for mortgage calculator and worksheets, visit Fannie Mae's website at *www.fanniemae.com/index.jhtml*. You also can speak to a Fannie Mae counselor by calling 800-732-6643. Fannie Mae is a private company that helps increase the number of people who can afford to purchase their own homes by working with mortgage lenders to ensure that there is an adequate supply of money to finance home buying.

For free help thinking through your home buying options, schedule an appointment with a HUD-approved housing counseling agency. To find an agency near you, go to *www.hud.gov/offices/hsg/sfh/hcc/hcs.cfm*.

Red Alert!

Sometimes, as much as you may want to own your own home, being a renter is a better option, especially when you consider that as a homeowner you will not only have to make regular mortgage payments, but you'll also have to purchase homeowners' insurance and pay property taxes every year; this will increase the overall cost of home ownership. Remember, too, that you'll inevitably have to spend money—maybe lots of it—on essential home repairs and maintenance, for instance, dealing with a leaky roof, treating your home for termites, replacing a water heater or air conditioner, fixing plumbing problems, and so on. Not taking care of problems like these will cause your home to lose value and may lead to other costly problems.

rent payments will probably be a little higher than they would be if you were not going to buy the home. Before you move in, you and the homeowner should agree on a purchase price for the home and on the amount of your down payment, and everything you agree on should be included in a written lease-to-buy agreement. The agreement may require you to make a small initial down payment before you move in. If you later decide that you don't want to buy the home after all, you can cancel the deal. However, depending on the terms of your agreement, you may have to forfeit any money you have already paid toward your down payment.

■ Buy a home with owner financing. Most sellers don't offer owner financing, but you may get lucky and find one who will. Get the details of the financing in writing and have the agreement reviewed by a real estate attorney before you sign it.

 Red Alert!

Now that the subprime mortgage lending industry has collapsed, it is harder for consumers who have recently completed a bankruptcy to get a mortgage. It used to be that these consumers could get no-money-down mortgages, mortgages without having their incomes verified, and interest-only mortgages from subprime lenders. Not anymore.

Red Alerts!

Never enter into a lease-to-buy arrangement unless all of the terms of your agreement with the owner of the home are in writing and unless you have a real estate attorney review the agreement before you sign it to be sure that you're adequately protected by the agreement.

One of the potential risks of a lease-to-buy arrangement is that before you become the owner of the property, the seller will default on the mortgage and lose the home.

This chapter provided you with a lot of information that is essential to rebuilding your life after bankruptcy. You learned about the whys and hows of rebuilding your credit histories and raising your FICO scores after your bankruptcy is over, the steps you should take before you begin the rebuilding process, and about your credit history rights according the to federal Fair Credit Reporting Act. In addition, the chapter warned you about credit rebuilding scams and provided you with basic advice about how to buy a car and/or a home after bankruptcy.

The next, and final, chapter will provide you with information to help ensure that you don't have to reread this book because you've mismanaged your finances or are not prepared for the loss of your job, a serious and costly illness in your family, or any other event that would force you to file another bankruptcy. It also will discuss financial goal setting.

Red Alert!

Beware of predatory lenders who take advantage of consumers who have bad credit and who are desperate to own a home. These lenders charge a lot of up-front fees and pack unneeded insurance charges onto the amount of a loan in order to increase their profit margins. For information about predatory lending, check out this Freddie Mac website, www.dontborrowtrouble.com. Freddie Mac is a private company that was chartered by Congress to provide mortgage financing to lower- and middle-class families.

Managing Your Finances to Avoid Future Money Troubles

11

Once your bankruptcy is behind you and you've begun rebuilding your credit histories and raising your FICO scores, the last thing you want is to develop serious money troubles again and maybe even have to file for bankruptcy another time. Although there is nothing you can do to make yourself totally bulletproof against the impact of problems that are beyond your control, such as a job loss or an expensive illness, there are things you can do to help minimize the likelihood that such problems will seriously derail your finances. There are also actions you can take to help ensure that your finances are not damaged due to your own mismanagement.

This chapter provides you with basic information and advice about how to avoid being financially blindsided by unexpected problems and setbacks. It also reviews the actions you can take to ensure that your money management skills are up to speed. Among other things, you'll learn about the importance of living on a budget even when you are not in a financial crisis, establishing and working toward financial goals, and working with the right financial professionals.

MANAGE YOUR MONEY WITH A BUDGET

One of the most important—if not *the* most important—things that you can do to keep your finances on an even keel is to plan your spending by using a household budget. You learned how to create a get-out-of-debt budget in chapter 1, but now that your debt problems are behind you, you'll need to modify that budget to reflect the current state of your finances. Your new budget should also reflect your financial goals, including the amount of money you intend to contribute to savings every month. The next section of this chapter discusses financial goal setting.

Once you have a new, updated budget, take time each month to compare what you actually spent in the previous month to what you budgeted. Reconciling your spending to what you budgeted for is important for two reasons. First, it will help you spot early signs of financial trouble so that you can address those problems when they are

 Red Alert!

Once your financial crisis is over, don't get sloppy about managing your finances by discarding your budget and just "winging it." If you do, you risk overspending and missing early signs of trouble in your financial life.

still relatively easy to deal with. Second, using a budget makes it more likely that you will be able to achieve your financial goals. Be sure to address and modify your budget as necessary to reflect changes in your life, such as a salary increase or decrease.

❗ Hot Tips

- Treat your budget as a dynamic document. In other words, you should amend it as your income goes up or down, when your expenses increase or decrease, and as your financial priorities change.

- If you need help budgeting, work with a nonprofit credit counseling agency that is affiliated with the National Foundation for Credit Counseling (NFCC) or with the Association of Independent Consumer Credit Counseling Agencies (AICCCA). To find an NFCC affiliate in your area, go to *www.nfcc.org* or call 800-388-2227. To locate a credit counseling agency that is affiliated with the AICCCA, visit *www.aiccca.org* or call 703-934-6118.

SET FINANCIAL GOALS

Now that you're out of the financial woods and have begun to rebuild your credit, it's time to dream a little! What are your financial goals? What would you like to do with your money? Do you want to buy a home? Do you want to add on to the home you already have? Do you want to take your family on a vacation? Do you need to begin saving for your retirement?

When you are setting your financial goals, be realistic about the amount of money you will need to achieve each of them and about how long each will take. If your goals are unattainable, pie-in-the sky dreams, you're setting yourself up for failure and disappointment.

You should also decide which goals are most important to you now, because you probably can't work toward all of them right away. When you are thinking about how to prioritize them, it's helpful to place your goals in one of three categories:

1. **Short-term goals.** These are goals that you think you can reach within a year, such as having X amount of money in your savings account or having enough money to take a family vacation.
2. **Intermediate-term goals.** These are goals that you believe are attainable within the next five years. They may include paying off your car loan or having enough money for a down payment on a home.

! Hot Tip

Our credit-oriented society has conditioned us to think in terms of gratifying our desires instantly by using credit cards, convenience checks, and home equity loans, rather than saving up for the things we want. It's easy to get caught up and resist the idea of goal setting and delayed gratification. However, if your financial problems developed because you went into debt in order to have everything you wanted *now,* you've learned how dangerous that can be. It's not that using credit is a bad thing—credit can be a great means to an end when used judiciously. However, the less you use credit, the better off you will be.

3. **Long-term goals.** These are goals that you anticipate will take you longer than five years to attain, such as having enough money to retire.

After you've identified your goals and assigned a realistic total dollar amount to each one, figure out how much you can afford to save every month to achieve them. Then reflect these amounts in your budget. If achieving a particular goal is really important to you and you want to accelerate the rate at which you will achieve it, reduce your spending and put the money that you free up toward that goal. Another option is to somehow increase your income.

> **❗ Hot Tips**
>
> If you have children who are nearing college age and you have little or nothing put away for their educations or for your retirement, focus on saving for your retirement. You can't borrow money to finance your retirement, but your children can obtain low-interest college loans and other forms of financial assistance to pay for their educations.
>
> Use Bankrate.com's online calculator to figure out the true cost of paying only the minimum due on your credit cards (*www.bankrate.com/msn/calc/minpayment.asp*).

MANAGE YOUR MONEY WISELY

Managing your money wisely is essential to achieving your financial goals and avoiding a reoccurrence of the problems that contributed to your bankruptcy. Therefore, in addition to living on a budget, observe these basic money management rules of thumb:

- Minimize your credit card balances. Always try to pay your balances in full each month. If you can't, don't charge anything more until you've reduced the balances to zero by paying more than the minimum due each month.

- Don't have a lot of credit cards. Just one or two MasterCard or Visa cards are plenty. The more credit cards you have, the more apt you are to use them—unless you are extremely disciplined.

Furthermore, applying for a lot of credit cards and having a lot of open accounts, especially if you are close to your credit limits on those cards, will harm your FICO scores.

- Record in your check register all of the checks you write and all of the debit and ATM transactions you make. If you don't, you may lose track of exactly how much money is in your checking account. As a result, you may end up with an overdrawn account and not enough money to pay your bills.

- Never pay your bills late. When you do, you risk damaging your credit histories and FICO scores, and you'll have to pay hefty late fees, too—money that you could have put toward paying down your account balances and/or achieving your financial goals.

 Red Alert!

When you pay a credit card account late, the card issuer may raise the interest rate on the account. Also, if one of your credit cards includes a *universal default* clause, even if you are not late paying on that account, the clause entitles the card issuer to raise the interest rate you are paying if you pay any of your other credit cards late.

- Monitor the state of your finances by reviewing your Equifax, Experian, and TransUnion credit histories every six months and by checking out your FICO Classic scores, too. If there are problems in any of your credit histories, get them corrected. If your FICO scores have gone down, figure out why and what you need to do to raise them.

- Never ignore signs of financial trouble. It's easy for small financial problems to snowball and become big ones when they are ignored. Furthermore, the sooner you address a problem, the more options you have for resolving it, and the less expensive those options will be.

- Invest in your employer's 401(k) plan at least up to the amount of your employer's match. You are throwing free money away otherwise.

SEEK THE ADVICE OF FINANCIAL PROFESSIONALS

Most of you don't have the time, the education, or the inclination to become experts about all aspects of your financial life. Even if you did, it might be difficult for you to think objectively about every issue and problem you may face. Therefore, as your finances improve and you have more money to spend and invest and more assets to protect, the more important it is for you to assemble a cadre of financial professionals who can answer your questions, give you advice, and generally help you keep your financial boat floating in the right direction. Among other things, these professionals can help you minimize the amount of taxes you owe, develop a plan for achieving your financial goals, make certain that you have the right mix and amount of insurance, and advise you about the kind of estate planning you should do.

Following are the kinds of professionals you may need on your team.

A Financial Planner

A financial planner can prepare an overall plan that will map out where you want to go financially and how to get there. Your financial planner will point out potential future problems that you need to begin planning for, and will be an invaluable sounding board who helps you make certain that you've thought through the ins and outs of important financial steps you want to take, such as buying a home or retiring early.

It's best to work with a financial planner who either charges by the hour or takes a percentage of the value of the assets being managed, which may include stocks, mutual funds, and bonds. Avoid financial planners who are commission-based. They get paid by receiving a commission on the financial products that they sell to you. Therefore, they have an incentive to sell you as many products as possible, regardless of whether you really need

> **▼ Hot Tip**
>
> Many banks as well as major brokerage firms offer financial planning services.

them. To find an independent financial planner in your area, go to *www.fpanet.org/plannersearch/search.cfm*. At this site, you'll also find valuable information about financial planning in general and working with a financial planner.

A Certified Public Accountant (CPA)

A CPA can help you plan how to save more, invest more, and minimize your spending. Also, a tax CPA can prepare your tax return and provide advice about what you can do to reduce the amount of taxes you'll have to pay in future years. To find a qualified CPA in your area, check out the website of

> **❗ Hot Tip**
>
> If your finances are very simple and you don't itemize deductions, you probably can do your own taxes and don't need the assistance of a tax CPA.

the American Institute of Certified Public Accountants at *www.aicpa. org/consumer+information/find+a+cpa*.

An Insurance Broker or Agent

Insurance of any kind protects you from possible financial loss. Also, life insurance can be an integral part of your estate planning. An insurance broker or agent can advise you about the insurance you should have, help you find the best policies (good coverage at a reasonable price), and help you resolve any problems you may have with a claim that you file. An insurance agent represents a specific insurance company (e.g., State Farm or GEICO), while a broker represents a variety of companies. Therefore, you have more insurance options when you work with an insurance broker. Visit the website of the Independent Insurance Agents & Brokers of America at *www.iiaba.net* to find a broker or agent near you.

An Estate Planning Attorney

Don't let the word "estate" throw you. You don't need to be worth as much as Donald Trump to benefit from the advice of an estate planning attorney. The attorney's advice is essential if you have assets that you want to protect in the event that you become too ill or incapacitated to make your own financial decisions, and if you want to be sure that when you die, your assets go to the people you want to have them. An estate planning attorney will help you preserve what you have and transfer your assets upon your death, using the appropriate estate planning tools such as durable powers of attorney, health care directives, insurance, wills, and trusts.

 Red Alert!

As your wealth grows, whenever your marital status changes, you expand your family, or you experience other significant changes in your life, be sure to review your estate plan and update it as appropriate.

In addition to checking out association websites to get the names of financial professionals you may want to hire, you can also get referrals from your friends and relatives, your loan officer, or a financial professional you may be working with already. Before you hire anyone, however, meet with each professional to gain a clear understanding of the services that individual can offer you and to find out how each one charges. The meetings will also give you an opportunity to decide whether you like a particular financial professional on a personal level and would feel comfortable working with that person.

It's a good idea to identify the financial professionals you want on your team now, before you have a problem, need a question answered, or would just like some up-front financial advice. Also, it's a good idea to have an annual meeting with each of the professionals you decide to work with. During each meeting, you can review your financial status and discuss any significant changes that may mean that you should purchase new or additional insurance, revise your estate planning, change your investment plan, and so on. Meeting with your financial team members is especially important when the following life-changing events are imminent:

- You are about to get married or divorced, or if you have just become widowed.

- You are ready to begin a family.

- You are going to receive an inheritance.

- You are thinking about retiring in the next few years.

Each of these life events will have important implications for many aspects of your financial life. It's important to plan ahead for them.

In this chapter, you learned about what you can do to help avoid having to file for bankruptcy again in the future. For example, you learned about the importance of managing your money with a budget even when you are not having money troubles, about the value of financial goal setting. You also learned about specific actions you can take to be a good money manager, such as minimizing your use of credit and not ignoring the early signs of money trouble. This chapter also told you about the various financial professionals who can help you plan and manage your finances so that you can look forward to a lifetime of good credit and financial stability.

Acknowledgments

Thanks to my writing partner, Mary Reed, who is also my best friend. Also thanks to my editor, Sheryl Gordon. Her enthusiasm and wise suggestions made the editing process a pleasure. This book is better for her involvement.

Appendix

Glossary

automatic stay. A court injunction that stops all creditor collection actions including lawsuits, foreclosures, and wage garnishments, after you file a petition to begin your bankruptcy.

bankruptcy estate. The assets that you own at the time that you file for bankruptcy, except for the property that you've claimed as exempt.

bankruptcy petition. The document you file to begin your bankruptcy. It asks the court to give you relief from your creditors.

Chapter 7. A kind of bankruptcy that involves the liquidation (sale) of your nonexempt assets to pay your debts.

Chapter 13. A kind of bankruptcy that involves the preparation of a debt reorganization plan and the payment of your debts according to the plan over a three- to five-year period.

confirmation. The bankruptcy judge's approval of your Chapter 13 reorganization plan.

cram down. When your debt reorganization plan provides that you'll pay less than the full amount that you owe on a secured debt, and the plan is confirmed over the objections of the creditor to whom you owe the debt.

creditors' meeting. (Also called a *341 meeting*.) The meeting of your creditors that takes place after your bankruptcy has begun. During the meeting, you will be under oath, and you'll have to answer questions from the trustee. Any of your creditors who attend the meeting may also ask you questions.

discharge of debt. When you are released from any responsibility to pay certain debts at the end of your bankruptcy. Once the debts are discharged, the creditors to whom you owed them cannot take any actions to collect from you.

dischargeable debt. A debt that you can wipe out through bankruptcy. Some kinds of debts are nondischargeable, which means that you must pay them.

equity. The value of your interest in an asset after the amount that you owe on it is subtracted from the asset's current market value.

executory contract or lease. Contracts and leases that you signed and under which you and the other parties to the agreement still have duties to perform. When you file for bankruptcy, you are entitled to reject an executory contract or lease. You can also affirm the contract or lease by agreeing to continue paying on it.

exemptions, exempt property. Specific assets that you can keep when you file for bankruptcy according to the federal bankruptcy law or your state's law.

lien. A legal claim on an asset that you own that turns that asset into collateral for one of your debts. When there is a lien on the asset and you default on the debt that it collateralizes, the creditor is entitled to take the asset as payment.

liquidation. The sale of your assets by the trustee so that the proceeds can be applied to your debts after all administrative expenses associated with your bankruptcy are paid.

means test. A calculation performed by your attorney that takes into account your income and your expenses as well as your family size to determine whether you can file for Chapter 7 or whether you must file for Chapter 13 bankruptcy instead.

motion to lift the automatic stay. A request by one of your creditors for permission to take the collateral that secures one of your debts, such as your home or car, when you can't afford to pay the debt.

no-asset case. When you file for bankruptcy and you own no assets that can be liquidated so that the money can be applied to your debts.

nondischargeable debt. A debt that cannot be eliminated in bankruptcy, such as your mortgage, debts for alimony or child support, certain kinds of taxes, or debts that you owe because you were driving while intoxicated or under the influence of drugs and you killed or injured someone as a result.

objection to dischargeability. When a creditor formally asks the court not to discharge (eliminate) a debt that you owe to it.

petition preparer. A business that prepares bankruptcy petitions for consumers, but that is not licensed to practice law.

plaintiff. A business or individual who files a lawsuit with the court.

preference payment. A debt payment made to one creditor at the expense of your other creditors during the 90 days prior to the start of your bankruptcy. The trustee will try to undo the payment so the money can be paid to your creditors according to the rules of bankruptcy.

priority claim. An unsecured creditor who is entitled to be paid in your bankruptcy before other types of unsecured creditors.

proof of claim. A special form that your creditors must file with the court to indicate how much they believe that you owe to them. Once a creditor files the form, the creditor will be in line to get paid through your bankruptcy.

reaffirmation agreement. An agreement in a Chapter 7 bankruptcy that entitles you to hold on to an asset that secures one of your dischargeable debts in exchange for your agreeing to pay the debt in full after you are out of bankruptcy.

redeeming a debt. When you pay a secured creditor the market value of an asset that secures a debt that you owe to the creditor in one lump sum; you do this rather than paying the creditor the outstanding balance that is due on the debt. When you redeem a debt, the creditor releases its lien on the asset, the unpaid balance on the asset gets discharged, and you own the asset free and clear.

reorganization plan. A written plan in a Chapter 13 bankruptcy that is prepared by your attorney and that details how you intend to pay your creditors over a three- to five-year period.

schedules. Forms that you must file at the start of your bankruptcy to provide the trustee, your creditors, and the judge with detailed information about each of your debts and each of your assets.

secured creditor. A creditor who has a lien on one of your assets. The lien entitles the creditor to take the asset if you fail to pay the money you owe to the creditor according to the terms of your agreement.

secured debt. A debt that is secured (collateralized) by an asset that you own. Common examples of secured debts include your mortgage and your car loan.

Statement of Financial Affairs. A form that you must file at the start of your bankruptcy to provide the trustee, your creditors, and the judge with information about the sources of your income, any transfers of assets you may have made, and any lawsuits that may have been filed against you by your creditors, among other information.

Statement of Intention. A form that you must complete at the start of your Chapter 7 bankruptcy to indicate what you intend to do about your secured debts—whether you intend to keep the assets that secure them, and if you do, how you plan on paying for them or if you intend to give the assets back to your creditors.

trustee. The individual assigned to your bankruptcy by the court who is charged with reviewing the information on all of your bankruptcy forms and with making sure that you pay as much of your debts as possible. In a Chapter 7, the trustee takes control of your nonexempt property, liquidates those assets, and uses the proceeds to pay your debts. In a Chapter 13, the trustee oversees your reorganization plan, receives your plan payments, and disburses that money to your creditors.

unsecured debt. A debt that you owe for which you did not guarantee payment by giving the creditor a lien on one of your assets. You just gave your word that you would repay the debt instead. The most common example of an unsecured debt is a credit card debt.

U.S. trustee. An officer of the Department of Justice who is responsible for supervising the administration of all bankruptcy cases.

Resources

Check out this list of resources for more information and advice about bankruptcy and credit rebuilding. The list includes websites and books, as well as nonprofit organizations and federal government agencies.

BOOKS ABOUT DEBT, BANKRUPTCY, AND CREDIT REBUILDING

Elias, Stephen R. *The New Bankruptcy: Will It Work for You?* Nolo Press, 2005. A guide to filing for bankruptcy since the new federal bankruptcy law was passed in 2005. Solid information but too much emphasis on do-it-yourself bankruptcy.

Lawrence, Judy. *The Budget Kit: The Common Cents Money Management Workbook.* 4th ed. Kaplan Publishing 2004. This budgeting classic has helped countless consumers control and monitor their spending and even helps readers monitor their money in an era of debit cards, online banking, and automatic deposits and drafts. The book is loaded with practical worksheets and forms and also comes with its own budgeting software.

Taylor-Hough, Deborah. *Frugal Living for Dummies.* Wiley 2003. This book shows you how to spend less and "live the good life" at the same time.

Ventura, John. *The Credit Repair Handbook.* Kaplan Publishing, 2007. A friendly and comprehensive guide to rebuilding your credit after money troubles and to preventing and dealing with identity theft.

Ventura, John, and Mary Reed. *Managing Debt for Dummies.* Wiley, 2007. This book tells you everything you need to know when you owe too much to your creditors and are trying to avoid bankruptcy.

WEBSITES

American Bankruptcy Institute, *www.abiworld.org.* The Consumer Education Center located at this site offers basic information about the bankruptcy process along with a set of informative frequently asked questions about bankruptcy.

AnnualCreditReport.com. Here you can order your three annual credit reports. The site was set up by Equifax, Experian, and TransUnion at the direction of Congress. It is the *only* website that provides free copies of credit reports with *no strings attached*.

Bankrate.com. This site offers a wealth of information about dealing with debt, bankruptcy, credit rebuilding, credit reporting, and applying for and using credit.

CardRatings.com. Established by U.S. Citizens for Fair Credit Card Terms, Inc., this site provides detailed information about more than 1,000 different credit cards, including cards for consumers with no credit or poor credit, cards with low introductory rates, cards that offer points or rewards when you use them, and so on. The site also features consumer reviews of various credit cards with new reviews added daily, along with information about credit reports, credit scores, and rebuilding credit, sample letters to write when you are trying to resolve credit-related problems.

CardWeb.com. Go to this site to search for a credit card that meets your needs when you are rebuilding your credit. If you're not sure what type of credit card might be best for you, fill out the site's online questionnaire, and you'll receive recommendations for specific cards.

DebtAdvice.org. The information at this site is provided by various nonprofit credit counseling agencies that are members of the National Foundation for Consumer Credit (NFCC). You'll find tips for selecting the right credit counseling agency, information about credit and credit reporting, a budgeting calculator, and an online directory for finding an NFCC-affiliated agency near you or one that offers credit counseling by phone.

DebtSmart.com. This site is a great resource for anyone who wants to get smarter about managing debt, using credit cards, and rebuilding credit, among other topics. You can also find out about good deals on credit cards at this site and sign up to have a free *DebtSmart* newsletter sent directly to your computer two times every month.

Equifax.com. Equifax is one of the three national credit reporting agencies. You can download a copy of your Equifax credit report at this site.

Experian.com. Experian is another one of the three national credit reporting agencies. Go to this site to download a copy of your Experian credit report.

Myfico.com. Order your three Classic FICO scores at this site. There, you can also learn about the different factors that will go into calculating your scores and how to raise your scores.

PersonalBankruptcyInformation.com. This comprehensive site includes information about alternatives to bankruptcy, state-by-state information about property exemptions, links to the websites for each of the federal bankruptcy district courts, explanations of the Chapter 7 and Chapter 13 bankruptcy processes, a series of frequently asked questions, and links to useful resources.

StopDebtCollectorsCold.com. If you're having problems with debt collectors, or if you just want to become more informed about your federal debt collection rights, this is the site for you.

TransUnion.com. Another one of the three national credit reporting agencies; you can download your TransUnion credit report at this site.

USCourts.gov/bankruptcycourts. Visit this site to locate the federal district bankruptcy court for your area and to download information about bankruptcy and copies of the official bankruptcy forms.

NONPROFIT ORGANIZATIONS AND FEDERAL AGENCIES

Administrative Office of the U.S. Courts, Bankruptcy Judges Division. This office offers information about the bankruptcy process in general and about the Chapter 7 and Chapter 13 processes in particular. It also discusses the discharge of debt in bankruptcy and features a detailed glossary of bankruptcy terms. *www.uscourts.gov/bankruptcycourts/bankruptcybasics.html*

The Federal Trade Commission (FTC). The FTC publishes a wide variety of free publications including "Fiscal Fitness: Choosing a Credit Counselor," "Before You File for Personal Bankruptcy: Information About Credit Counseling and Debtor Education," and "Credit Repair: Self-Help May Be Best." You can view these and other FTC publications at *www.ftc.gov/bcp/consumer.shtm*, or you can order them by writing to Consumer Response Center, Federal Trade Commission, 600 Pennsylvania Avenue, NW, H-130, Washington, DC 20580.

National Association of Consumer Bankruptcy Attorneys (NACBA). This is the only national organization dedicated to serving the needs of consumer bankruptcy attorneys and to protecting the rights of consumers who file for bankruptcy. Visit NACBA's website at *www.nacba.com* to stay up to date about bankruptcy-related news and developments that may affect you and for helpful advice about bankruptcy-related topics, such as how to find a bankruptcy attorney and what not to do when you're contemplating bankruptcy. Also, you can use the site's "Attorney Finder" at *www.nacba.org/attorneyfinder* to locate an NACBA-member bankruptcy attorney in your area.

National Consumer Law Center (NCLC). A national organization that helps low-income consumers and their advocates effectively use consumer laws, NCLC publishes several brochures on bankruptcy, including "Bankruptcy Client Brochure," "Your Legal Rights During and After Bankruptcy," and "Using Credit Wisely After Bankruptcy." Visit *www.consumerlaw.org/issues/bankruptcy/index.shtml* to download the brochures or to read them online. You can also order them by calling 617-542-8010.

U.S. Trustee Program. This office is charged with approving the credit counseling agencies that are entitled to provide prebankruptcy counseling and a post-filing financial education to consumers, among its other responsibilities. To locate an approved agency near you, go to *www.usdoj.gov/ust/eo/bapcpa/ccde/cc_approved.htm*.

Forms

Form B6A
(10/05)

In re _____ ,   Case No. _____
         Debtor   **(If known)**

SCHEDULE A - REAL PROPERTY

Except as directed below, list all real property in which the debtor has any legal, equitable, or future interest, including all property owned as a co-tenant, community property, or in which the debtor has a life estate. Include any property in which the debtor holds rights and powers exercisable for the debtor's own benefit. If the debtor is married, state whether husband, wife, or both own the property by placing an "H," "W," "J," or "C" in the column labeled "Husband, Wife, Joint, or Community." If the debtor holds no interest in real property, write "None" under "Description and Location of Property."

Do not include interests in executory contracts and unexpired leases on this schedule. List them in Schedule G - Executory Contracts and Unexpired Leases.

If an entity claims to have a lien or hold a secured interest in any property, state the amount of the secured claim. See Schedule D. If no entity claims to hold a secured interest in the property, write "None" in the column labeled "Amount of Secured Claim."

If the debtor is an individual or if a joint petition is filed, state the amount of any exemption claimed in the property only in Schedule C - Property Claimed as Exempt.

DESCRIPTION AND LOCATION OF PROPERTY	NATURE OF DEBTOR'S INTEREST IN PROPERTY	HUSBAND, WIFE, JOINT, OR COMMUNITY	CURRENT VALUE OF DEBTOR'S INTEREST IN PROPERTY, WITHOUT DEDUCTING ANY SECURED CLAIM OR EXEMPTION	AMOUNT OF SECURED CLAIM

Total▶

(Report also on Summary of Schedules.)

Form B6B
(10/05)

In re _____ ,   Case No. _____
        Debtor   **(If known)**

SCHEDULE B - PERSONAL PROPERTY

    Except as directed below, list all personal property of the debtor of whatever kind. If the debtor has no property in one or more of the categories, place an "x" in the appropriate position in the column labeled "None." If additional space is needed in any category, attach a separate sheet properly identified with the case name, case number, and the number of the category. If the debtor is married, state whether husband, wife, or both own the property by placing an "H," "W," "J," or "C" in the column labeled "Husband, Wife, Joint, or Community." If the debtor is an individual or a joint petition is filed, state the amount of any exemptions claimed only in Schedule C - Property Claimed as Exempt.

    Do not list interests in executory contracts and unexpired leases on this schedule. List them in Schedule G   Executory Contracts and Unexpired Leases.

If the property is being held for the debtor by someone else, state that person's name and address under "Description and Location of Property." In providing the information requested in this schedule, do not include the name or address of a minor child. Simply state "a minor child."

TYPE OF PROPERTY	N O N E	DESCRIPTION AND LOCATION OF PROPERTY	HUSBAND, WIFE, JOINT, OR COMMUNITY	CURRENT VALUE OF DEBTOR'S INTEREST IN PROPERTY, WITH-OUT DEDUCTING ANY SECURED CLAIM OR EXEMPTION
1. Cash on hand.				
2. Checking, savings or other financial accounts, certificates of deposit, or shares in banks, savings and loan, thrift, building and loan, and homestead associations, or credit unions, brokerage houses, or cooperatives.				
3. Security deposits with public utilities, telephone companies, landlords, and others.				
4. Household goods and furnishings, including audio, video, and computer equipment.				
5. Books; pictures and other art objects; antiques; stamp, coin, record, tape, compact disc, and other collections or collectibles.				
6. Wearing apparel.				
7. Furs and jewelry.				
8. Firearms and sports, photographic, and other hobby equipment.				
9. Interests in insurance policies. Name insurance company of each policy and itemize surrender or refund value of each.				
10. Annuities. Itemize and name each issuer.				
11. Interests in an education IRA as defined in 26 U.S.C. § 530(b)(1) or under a qualified State tuition plan as defined in 26 U.S.C. § 529(b)(1). Give particulars. (File separately the record(s) of any such interest(s). 11 U.S.C. § 521(c); Rule 1007(b)).				

Form B6B-Cont.
(10/05)

In re _____,   Case No. _____
                    Debtor   **(If known)**

SCHEDULE B - PERSONAL PROPERTY
(Continuation Sheet)

TYPE OF PROPERTY	N O N E	DESCRIPTION AND LOCATION OF PROPERTY	HUSBAND, WIFE, JOINT, OR COMMUNITY	CURRENT VALUE OF DEBTOR'S INTEREST IN PROPERTY, WITH-OUT DEDUCTING ANY SECURED CLAIM OR EXEMPTION
12. Interests in IRA, ERISA, Keogh, or other pension or profit sharing plans. Give particulars.				
13. Stock and interests in incorporated and unincorporated businesses. Itemize.				
14. Interests in partnerships or joint ventures. Itemize.				
15. Government and corporate bonds and other negotiable and non-negotiable instruments.				
16. Accounts receivable.				
17. Alimony, maintenance, support, and property settlements to which the debtor is or may be entitled. Give particulars.				
18. Other liquidated debts owed to debtor including tax refunds. Give particulars.				
19. Equitable or future interests, life estates, and rights or powers exercisable for the benefit of the debtor other than those listed in Schedule A – Real Property.				
20. Contingent and noncontingent interests in estate of a decedent, death benefit plan, life insurance policy, or trust.				
21. Other contingent and unliquidated claims of every nature, including tax refunds, counterclaims of the debtor, and rights to setoff claims. Give estimated value of each.				

Form B6B cont.
(10/05)

In re _____ ,   Case No. _____
        Debtor   **(If known)**

SCHEDULE B -PERSONAL PROPERTY
(Continuation Sheet)

TYPE OF PROPERTY	N O N E	DESCRIPTION AND LOCATION OF PROPERTY	HUSBAND, WIFE, JOINT, OR COMMUNITY	CURRENT VALUE OF DEBTOR'S INTEREST IN PROPERTY, WITH-OUT DEDUCTING ANY SECURED CLAIM OR EXEMPTION
22. Patents, copyrights, and other intellectual property. Give particulars.				
23. Licenses, franchises, and other general intangibles. Give particulars.				
24. Customer lists or other compilations containing personally identifiable information (as defined in 11 U.S.C. § 101(41A)) provided to the debtor by individuals in connection with obtaining a product or service from the debtor primarily for personal, family, or household purposes.				
25. Automobiles, trucks, trailers, and other vehicles and accessories.				
26. Boats, motors, and accessories.				
27. Aircraft and accessories.				
28. Office equipment, furnishings, and supplies.				
29. Machinery, fixtures, equipment, and supplies used in business.				
30. Inventory.				
31. Animals.				
32. Crops - growing or harvested. Give particulars.				
33. Farming equipment and implements.				
34. Farm supplies, chemicals, and feed.				
35. Other personal property of any kind not already listed. Itemize.				

_____ continuation sheets attached   Total ▶ $ _____

(Include amounts from any continuation
sheets attached. Report total also on
Summary of Schedules.)

Official Form 6C (04/07)

In re _____,   Case No._____
Debtor   (if known)

SCHEDULE C - PROPERTY CLAIMED AS EXEMPT

Debtor claims the exemptions to which debtor is entitled under: ☐ Check if debtor claims a homestead exemption that exceeds
(Check one box) $136,875
☐ 11 U.S.C. § 522(b)(2)
☐ 11 U.S.C. § 522(b)(3)

DESCRIPTION OF PROPERTY	SPECIFY LAW PROVIDING EACH EXEMPTION	VALUE OF CLAIMED EXEMPTION	CURRENT VALUE OF PROPERTY WITHOUT DEDUCTING EXEMPTION

Official Form 6D (10/06)

In re _____ ,   Case No. _____
                    Debtor   **(if known)**

SCHEDULE D - CREDITORS HOLDING SECURED CLAIMS

State the name, mailing address, including zip code, and last four digits of any account number of all entities holding claims secured by property of the debtor as of the date of filing of the petition. The complete account number of any account the debtor has with the creditor is useful to the trustee and the creditor and may be provided if the debtor chooses to do so. List creditors holding all types of secured interests such as judgment liens, garnishments, statutory liens, mortgages, deeds of trust, and other security interests.

List creditors in alphabetical order to the extent practicable. If a minor child is a creditor, indicate that by stating "a minor child" and do not disclose the child's name. See 11 U.S.C. § 112. If "a minor child" is stated, also include the name, address, and legal relationship to the minor child of a person described in Fed. R. Bankr. P. 1007(m). If all secured creditors will not fit on this page, use the continuation sheet provided.

If any entity other than a spouse in a joint case may be jointly liable on a claim, place an "X" in the column labeled "Codebtor," include the entity on the appropriate schedule of creditors, and complete Schedule H – Codebtors. If a joint petition is filed, state whether the husband, wife, both of them, or the marital community may be liable on each claim by placing an "H," "W," "J," or "C" in the column labeled "Husband, Wife, Joint, or Community."

If the claim is contingent, place an "X" in the column labeled "Contingent." If the claim is unliquidated, place an "X" in the column labeled "Unliquidated." If the claim is disputed, place an "X" in the column labeled "Disputed." (You may need to place an "X" in more than one of these three columns.)

Total the columns labeled "Amount of Claim Without Deducting Value of Collateral" and "Unsecured Portion, if Any" in the boxes labeled "Total(s)" on the last sheet of the completed schedule. Report the total from the column labeled "Amount of Claim Without Deducting Value of Collateral" also on the Summary of Schedules and, if the debtor is an individual with primarily consumer debts, report the total from the column labeled "Unsecured Portion, if Any" on the Statistical Summary of Certain Liabilities and Related Data.

☐   Check this box if debtor has no creditors holding secured claims to report on this Schedule D.

CREDITOR'S NAME AND MAILING ADDRESS INCLUDING ZIP CODE AND AN ACCOUNT NUMBER *(See Instructions Above.)*	CODEBTOR	HUSBAND, WIFE, JOINT, OR COMMUNITY	DATE CLAIM WAS INCURRED, NATURE OF LIEN , AND DESCRIPTION AND VALUE OF PROPERTY SUBJECT TO LIEN	CONTINGENT	UNLIQUIDATED	DISPUTED	AMOUNT OF CLAIM WITHOUT DEDUCTING VALUE OF COLLATERAL	UNSECURED PORTION, IF ANY
ACCOUNT NO.								
			VALUE $					
ACCOUNT NO.								
			VALUE $					
ACCOUNT NO.								
			VALUE $					
_____ continuation sheets attached			Subtotal ▶ (Total of this page)				$	$
			Total ▶ (Use only on last page)				$	$
							(Report also on Summary of Schedules.)	(If applicable, report also on Statistical Summary of Certain Liabilities and Related Data.)

Official Form 6E (04/07)

In re _____ ,   Case No._____
                              Debtor   **(if known)**

SCHEDULE E - CREDITORS HOLDING UNSECURED PRIORITY CLAIMS

A complete list of claims entitled to priority, listed separately by type of priority, is to be set forth on the sheets provided. Only holders of unsecured claims entitled to priority should be listed in this schedule. In the boxes provided on the attached sheets, state the name, mailing address, including zip code, and last four digits of the account number, if any, of all entities holding priority claims against the debtor or the property of the debtor, as of the date of the filing of the petition. Use a separate continuation sheet for each type of priority and label each with the type of priority.

The complete account number of any account the debtor has with the creditor is useful to the trustee and the creditor and may be provided if the debtor chooses to do so. If a minor child is a creditor, indicate that by stating "a minor child" and do not disclose the child's name. See 11 U.S.C. § 112. If "a minor child" is stated, also include the name, address, and legal relationship to the minor child of a person described in Fed. R. Bankr. P. 1007(m).

If any entity other than a spouse in a joint case may be jointly liable on a claim, place an "X" in the column labeled "Codebtor," include the entity on the appropriate schedule of creditors, and complete Schedule H-Codebtors. If a joint petition is filed, state whether the husband, wife, both of them, or the marital community may be liable on each claim by placing an "H," "W," "J," or "C" in the column labeled "Husband, Wife, Joint, or Community."   If the claim is contingent, place an "X" in the column labeled "Contingent." If the claim is unliquidated, place an "X" in the column labeled "Unliquidated." If the claim is disputed, place an "X" in the column labeled "Disputed." (You may need to place an "X" in more than one of these three columns.)

Report the total of claims listed on each sheet in the box labeled "Subtotals" on each sheet. Report the total of all claims listed on this Schedule E in the box labeled "Total" on the last sheet of the completed schedule. Report this total also on the Summary of Schedules.

Report the total of amounts entitled to priority listed on each sheet in the box labeled "Subtotals" on each sheet. Report the total of all amounts entitled to priority listed on this Schedule E in the box labeled "Totals" on the last sheet of the completed schedule. Individual debtors with primarily consumer debts who file a case under chapter 7 or 13 report this total also on the Statistical Summary of Certain Liabilities and Related Data.

Report the total of amounts <u>not</u> entitled to priority listed on each sheet in the box labeled "Subtotals" on each sheet. Report the total of all amounts not entitled to priority listed on this Schedule E in the box labeled "Totals" on the last sheet of the completed schedule. Individual debtors with primarily consumer debts who file a case under chapter 7 report this total also on the Statistical Summary of Certain Liabilities and Related Data.

☐ Check this box if debtor has no creditors holding unsecured priority claims to report on this Schedule E.

TYPES OF PRIORITY CLAIMS (Check the appropriate box(es) below if claims in that category are listed on the attached sheets)

☐ **Domestic Support Obligations**

Claims for domestic support that are owed to or recoverable by a spouse, former spouse, or child of the debtor, or the parent, legal guardian, or responsible relative of such a child, or a governmental unit to whom such a domestic support claim has been assigned to the extent provided in 11 U.S.C. § 507(a)(1).

☐ **Extensions of credit in an involuntary case**

Claims arising in the ordinary course of the debtor's business or financial affairs after the commencement of the case but before the earlier of the appointment of a trustee or the order for relief. 11 U.S.C. § 507(a)(3).

☐ **Wages, salaries, and commissions**

Wages, salaries, and commissions, including vacation, severance, and sick leave pay owing to employees and commissions owing to qualifying independent sales representatives up to $10,950* per person earned within 180 days immediately preceding the filing of the original petition, or the cessation of business, whichever occurred first, to the extent provided in 11 U.S.C. § 507(a)(4).

☐ **Contributions to employee benefit plans**

Money owed to employee benefit plans for services rendered within 180 days immediately preceding the filing of the original petition, or the cessation of business, whichever occurred first, to the extent provided in 11 U.S.C. § 507(a)(5).

Official Form 6E (04/07) - Cont.

In re _____ ,   Case No._____
  Debtor   **(if known)**

☐ **Certain farmers and fishermen**

Claims of certain farmers and fishermen, up to $5,400* per farmer or fisherman, against the debtor, as provided in 11 U.S.C. § 507(a)(6).

☐ **Deposits by individuals**

Claims of individuals up to $2,425* for deposits for the purchase, lease, or rental of property or services for personal, family, or household use, that were not delivered or provided. 11 U.S.C. § 507(a)(7).

☐ **Taxes and Certain Other Debts Owed to Governmental Units**

Taxes, customs duties, and penalties owing to federal, state, and local governmental units as set forth in 11 U.S.C. § 507(a)(8).

☐ **Commitments to Maintain the Capital of an Insured Depository Institution**

Claims based on commitments to the FDIC, RTC, Director of the Office of Thrift Supervision, Comptroller of the Currency, or Board of Governors of the Federal Reserve System, or their predecessors or successors, to maintain the capital of an insured depository institution. 11 U.S.C. § 507 (a)(9).

☐ **Claims for Death or Personal Injury While Debtor Was Intoxicated**

Claims for death or personal injury resulting from the operation of a motor vehicle or vessel while the debtor was intoxicated from using alcohol, a drug, or another substance. 11 U.S.C. § 507(a)(10).

* Amounts are subject to adjustment on April 1, 2010, and every three years thereafter with respect to cases commenced on or after the date of adjustment.

_____ continuation sheets attached

Official Form 6E (04/07) - Cont.

In re _____ ,   Case No. _____
                    Debtor   **(If known)**

SCHEDULE E - CREDITORS HOLDING UNSECURED PRIORITY CLAIMS
(Continuation Sheet)

Type of Priority for Claims Listed on This Sheet
_____

CREDITOR'S NAME, MAILING ADDRESS INCLUDING ZIP CODE, AND ACCOUNT NUMBER *(See instructions above.)*	CODEBTOR	HUSBAND, WIFE, JOINT, OR COMMUNITY	DATE CLAIM WAS INCURRED AND CONSIDERATION FOR CLAIM	CONTINGENT	UNLIQUIDATED	DISPUTED	AMOUNT OF CLAIM	AMOUNT ENTITLED TO PRIORITY	AMOUNT NOT ENTITLED TO PRIORITY, IF ANY
Account No.									
Account No.									
Account No.									
Account No.									

Sheet no. ____ of ____ continuation sheets attached to Schedule of Creditors Holding Priority Claims

Subtotals▶ (Totals of this page) $ $

Total▶
(Use only on last page of the completed Schedule E. Report also on the Summary of Schedules.) $

Totals▶
(Use only on last page of the completed Schedule E. If applicable, report also on the Statistical Summary of Certain Liabilities and Related Data.) $ $

Official Form 6F (10/06)

In re _____,   Case No. _____
           Debtor   **(if known)**

SCHEDULE F - CREDITORS HOLDING UNSECURED NONPRIORITY CLAIMS

State the name, mailing address, including zip code, and last four digits of any account number, of all entities holding unsecured claims without priority against the debtor or the property of the debtor, as of the date of filing of the petition. The complete account number of any account the debtor has with the creditor is useful to the trustee and the creditor and may be provided if the debtor chooses to do so. If a minor child is a creditor, indicate that by stating "a minor child" and do not disclose the child's name. See 11 U.S.C. § 112. If "a minor child" is stated, also include the name, address, and legal relationship to the minor child of a person described in Fed. R. Bankr. P. 1007(m). Do not include claims listed in Schedules D and E. If all creditors will not fit on this page, use the continuation sheet provided.

If any entity other than a spouse in a joint case may be jointly liable on a claim, place an "X" in the column labeled "Codebtor," include the entity on the appropriate schedule of creditors, and complete Schedule H - Codebtors. If a joint petition is filed, state whether the husband, wife, both of them, or the marital community may be liable on each claim by placing an "H," "W," "J," or "C" in the column labeled "Husband, Wife, Joint, or Community."

If the claim is contingent, place an "X" in the column labeled "Contingent." If the claim is unliquidated, place an "X" in the column labeled "Unliquidated." If the claim is disputed, place an "X" in the column labeled "Disputed." (You may need to place an "X" in more than one of these three columns.)

Report the total of all claims listed on this schedule in the box labeled "Total" on the last sheet of the completed schedule. Report this total also on the Summary of Schedules and, if the debtor is an individual with primarily consumer debts filing a case under chapter 7, report this total also on the Statistical Summary of Certain Liabilities and Related Data..

☐   Check this box if debtor has no creditors holding unsecured claims to report on this Schedule F.

CREDITOR'S NAME, MAILING ADDRESS INCLUDING ZIP CODE, AND ACCOUNT NUMBER *(See instructions above.)*	CODEBTOR	HUSBAND, WIFE, JOINT, OR COMMUNITY	DATE CLAIM WAS INCURRED AND CONSIDERATION FOR CLAIM. IF CLAIM IS SUBJECT TO SETOFF, SO STATE.	CONTINGENT	UNLIQUIDATED	DISPUTED	AMOUNT OF CLAIM
ACCOUNT NO.							
ACCOUNT NO.							
ACCOUNT NO.							
ACCOUNT NO.							
			Subtotal▶				$

_____ continuation sheets attached

Total▶ $

(Use only on last page of the completed Schedule F.)
(Report also on Summary of Schedules and, if applicable, on the Statistical
Summary of Certain Liabilities and Related Data.)

Form B6G
(10/05)

In re _____ ,   Case No._____
                Debtor   **(if known)**

SCHEDULE G - EXECUTORY CONTRACTS AND UNEXPIRED LEASES

Describe all executory contracts of any nature and all unexpired leases of real or personal property. Include any timeshare
interests. State nature of debtor's interest in contract, i.e., "Purchaser," "Agent," etc. State whether debtor is the lessor or
lessee of a lease. Provide the names and complete mailing addresses of all other parties to each lease or contract described. If
a minor child is a party to one of the leases or contracts, indicate that by stating "a minor child" and do not disclose the child's
name. See 11 U.S.C. § 112; Fed.R. Bankr. P. 1007(m).

☐ Check this box if debtor has no executory contracts or unexpired leases.

NAME AND MAILING ADDRESS, INCLUDING ZIP CODE, OF OTHER PARTIES TO LEASE OR CONTRACT.	DESCRIPTION OF CONTRACT OR LEASE AND NATURE OF DEBTOR'S INTEREST. STATE WHETHER LEASE IS FOR NONRESIDENTIAL REAL PROPERTY. STATE CONTRACT NUMBER OF ANY GOVERNMENT CONTRACT.

B6H
(6/90)

In re _____ ,   Case No. _____
            Debtor   (if known)

SCHEDULE H - CODEBTORS

      Provide the information requested concerning any person or entity, other than a spouse in a joint case, that is also liable on any debts listed by debtor in the schedules of creditors. Include all guarantors and co-signers. In community property states, a married debtor not filing a joint case should report the name and address of the nondebtor spouse on this schedule. Include all names used by the nondebtor spouse during the six years immediately preceding the commencement of this case.

☐   Check this box if debtor has no codebtors.

NAME AND ADDRESS OF CODEBTOR	NAME AND ADDRESS OF CREDITOR

Official Form 6I (10/06)

In re _____ ,   Case No._____
         Debtor   **(if known)**

SCHEDULE I - CURRENT INCOME OF INDIVIDUAL DEBTOR(S)

The column labeled "Spouse" must be completed in all cases filed by joint debtors and by every married debtor, whether or not a joint petition is filed, unless the spouses are separated and a joint petition is not filed. Do not state the name of any minor child.

Debtor's Marital Status:	DEPENDENTS OF DEBTOR AND SPOUSE	
	RELATIONSHIP(S):	AGE(S):

Employment: Occupation	DEBTOR	SPOUSE
Name of Employer		
How long employed		
Address of Employer		

INCOME: (Estimate of average or projected monthly income at time case filed)	DEBTOR	SPOUSE
	$_____	$_____
1. Monthly gross wages, salary, and commissions (Prorate if not paid monthly)	$_____	$_____
2. Estimate monthly overtime		
3. SUBTOTAL	$_____	$_____
4. LESS PAYROLL DEDUCTIONS		
a. Payroll taxes and social security	$_____	$_____
b. Insurance	$_____	$_____
c. Union dues	$_____	$_____
d. Other (Specify): _____	$_____	$_____
5. SUBTOTAL OF PAYROLL DEDUCTIONS	$_____	$_____
6. TOTAL NET MONTHLY TAKE HOME PAY	$_____	$_____
7. Regular income from operation of business or profession or farm (Attach detailed statement)	$_____	$_____
8. Income from real property	$_____	$_____
9. Interest and dividends	$_____	$_____
10. Alimony, maintenance or support payments payable to the debtor for the debtor's use or that of dependents listed above	$_____	$_____
11. Social security or government assistance (Specify):_____	$_____	$_____
12. Pension or retirement income	$_____	$_____
13. Other monthly income (Specify):_____	$_____	$_____
14. SUBTOTAL OF LINES 7 THROUGH 13	$_____	$_____
15. AVERAGE MONTHLY INCOME (Add amounts shown on lines 6 and 14)	$_____	$_____
16. COMBINED AVERAGE MONTHLY INCOME: (Combine column totals from line 15; if there is only one debtor repeat total reported on line 15)	$ _____	

(Report also on Summary of Schedules and, if applicable, on Statistical Summary of Certain Liabilities and Related Data)

17. Describe any increase or decrease in income reasonably anticipated to occur within the year following the filing of this document:

_____

_____

Official Form 6J (10/06)

In re _____ ,   Case No._____
　　　　　　Debtor　　　　　　　　　　　　　　　　　　　　　(if known)

SCHEDULE J - CURRENT EXPENDITURES OF INDIVIDUAL DEBTOR(S)

Complete this schedule by estimating the average or projected monthly expenses of the debtor and the debtor's family at time case filed. Prorate any payments made bi-weekly, quarterly, semi-annually, or annually to show monthly rate.

☐   Check this box if a joint petition is filed and debtor's spouse maintains a separate household. Complete a separate schedule of expenditures labeled "Spouse."

1. Rent or home mortgage payment (include lot rented for mobile home)　　　　　　　$ _____
   a. Are real estate taxes included?　　Yes _____　No _____
   b. Is property insurance included?　　Yes _____　No _____
2. Utilities: a. Electricity and heating fuel　　　　　　　　　　　　　　　　$ _____
       b. Water and sewer　　　　　　　　　　　　　　　　　　　　$ _____
       c. Telephone　　　　　　　　　　　　　　　　　　　　　　$ _____
       d. Other _____　$ _____
3. Home maintenance (repairs and upkeep)　　　　　　　　　　　　　　　　　$ _____
4. Food　　　　　　　　　　　　　　　　　　　　　　　　　　　　　　$ _____
5. Clothing　　　　　　　　　　　　　　　　　　　　　　　　　　　　$ _____
6. Laundry and dry cleaning　　　　　　　　　　　　　　　　　　　　　　$ _____
7. Medical and dental expenses　　　　　　　　　　　　　　　　　　　　　$ _____
8. Transportation (not including car payments)　　　　　　　　　　　　　　　$ _____
9. Recreation, clubs and entertainment, newspapers, magazines, etc.　　　　　　　$ _____
10. Charitable contributions　　　　　　　　　　　　　　　　　　　　　　$ _____
11. Insurance (not deducted from wages or included in home mortgage payments)
    a. Homeowner's or renter's　　　　　　　　　　　　　　　　　　　$ _____
    b. Life　　　　　　　　　　　　　　　　　　　　　　　　　　$ _____
    c. Health　　　　　　　　　　　　　　　　　　　　　　　　　$ _____
    d. Auto　　　　　　　　　　　　　　　　　　　　　　　　　　$ _____
    e. Other _____　$ _____
12. Taxes (not deducted from wages or included in home mortgage payments)
(Specify) _____　　$ _____
13. Installment payments: (In chapter 11, 12, and 13 cases, do not list payments to be included in the plan)
    a. Auto　　　　　　　　　　　　　　　　　　　　　　　　　　$ _____
    b. Other _____　$ _____
    c. Other _____　$ _____
14. Alimony, maintenance, and support paid to others　　　　　　　　　　　　　$ _____
15. Payments for support of additional dependents not living at your home　　　　　$ _____
16. Regular expenses from operation of business, profession, or farm (attach detailed statement)　$ _____
17. Other _____　　　$ _____
18. AVERAGE MONTHLY EXPENSES (Total lines 1-17. Report also on Summary of Schedules and,
    if applicable, on the Statistical Summary of Certain Liabilities and Related Data.)　$ _____
19. Describe any increase or decrease in expenditures reasonably anticipated to occur within the year following the filing of this document:
_____
_____
_____

20. STATEMENT OF MONTHLY NET INCOME
   a. Average monthly income from Line 15 of Schedule I　　　　　　　　　$ _____
   b. Average monthly expenses from Line 18 above　　　　　　　　　　　$ _____
   c. Monthly net income (a. minus b.)　　　　　　　　　　　　　　　　$ _____

Official Form 7
(04/07)

UNITED STATES BANKRUPTCY COURT

_____ **DISTRICT OF** _____

In re: _____ ,   Case No. _____
                  Debtor   (if known)

STATEMENT OF FINANCIAL AFFAIRS

     This statement is to be completed by every debtor. Spouses filing a joint petition may file a single statement on which the information for both spouses is combined. If the case is filed under chapter 12 or chapter 13, a married debtor must furnish information for both spouses whether or not a joint petition is filed, unless the spouses are separated and a joint petition is not filed. An individual debtor engaged in business as a sole proprietor, partner, family farmer, or self-employed professional, should provide the information requested on this statement concerning all such activities as well as the individual's personal affairs. Do not include the name or address of a minor child in this statement. Indicate payments, transfers and the like to minor children by stating "a minor child." See 11 U.S.C. § 112; Fed. R. Bankr. P. 1007(m).

     Questions 1 - 18 are to be completed by all debtors. Debtors that are or have been in business, as defined below, also must complete Questions 19 - 25. **If the answer to an applicable question is "None," mark the box labeled "None."** If additional space is needed for the answer to any question, use and attach a separate sheet properly identified with the case name, case number (if known), and the number of the question.

DEFINITIONS

     "In business." A debtor is "in business" for the purpose of this form if the debtor is a corporation or partnership. An individual debtor is "in business" for the purpose of this form if the debtor is or has been, within six years immediately preceding the filing of this bankruptcy case, any of the following: an officer, director, managing executive, or owner of 5 percent or more of the voting or equity securities of a corporation; a partner, other than a limited partner, of a partnership; a sole proprietor or self-employed full-time or part-time. An individual debtor also may be "in business" for the purpose of this form if the debtor engages in a trade, business, or other activity, other than as an employee, to supplement income from the debtor's primary employment.

     "Insider." The term "insider" includes but is not limited to: relatives of the debtor; general partners of the debtor and their relatives; corporations of which the debtor is an officer, director, or person in control; officers, directors, and any owner of 5 percent or more of the voting or equity securities of a corporate debtor and their relatives; affiliates of the debtor and insiders of such affiliates; any managing agent of the debtor. 11 U.S.C. § 101.

_____

1.   Income from employment or operation of business

None
☐

     State the gross amount of income the debtor has received from employment, trade, or profession, or from operation of the debtor's business, including part-time activities either as an employee or in independent trade or business, from the beginning of this calendar year to the date this case was commenced. State also the gross amounts received during the **two years** immediately preceding this calendar year. (A debtor that maintains, or has maintained, financial records on the basis of a fiscal rather than a calendar year may report fiscal year income. Identify the beginning and ending dates of the debtor's fiscal year.) If a joint petition is filed, state income for each spouse separately. (Married debtors filing under chapter 12 or chapter 13 must state income of both spouses whether or not a joint petition is filed, unless the spouses are separated and a joint petition is not filed.)

          AMOUNT   SOURCE

2

2. Income other than from employment or operation of business

None ☐

State the amount of income received by the debtor other than from employment, trade, profession, operation of the debtor's business during the **two years** immediately preceding the commencement of this case. Give particulars. If a joint petition is filed, state income for each spouse separately. (Married debtors filing under chapter 12 or chapter 13 must state income for each spouse whether or not a joint petition is filed, unless the spouses are separated and a joint petition is not filed.)

AMOUNT   SOURCE

---

3. Payments to creditors

Complete a. or b., as appropriate, and c.

None ☐

a. *Individual or joint debtor(s) with primarily consumer debts:* List all payments on loans, installment purchases of goods or services, and other debts to any creditor made within **90 days** immediately preceding the commencement of this case if the aggregate value of all property that constitutes or is affected by such transfer is not less than $600. Indicate with an asterisk (*) any payments that were made to a creditor on account of a domestic support obligation or as part of an alternative repayment schedule under a plan by an approved nonprofit budgeting and creditor counseling agency. (Married debtors filing under chapter 12 or chapter 13 must include payments by either or both spouses whether or not a joint petition is filed, unless the spouses are separated and a joint petition is not filed.)

NAME AND ADDRESS OF CREDITOR	DATES OF PAYMENTS	AMOUNT PAID	AMOUNT STILL OWING

None ☐

b. *Debtor whose debts are not primarily consumer debts:* List each payment or other transfer to any creditor made within **90** days immediately preceding the commencement of the case if the aggregate value of all property that constitutes or is affected by such transfer is not less than $5,475. (Married debtors filing under chapter 12 or chapter 13 must include payments and other transfers by either or both spouses whether or not a joint petition is filed, unless the spouses are separated and a joint petition is not filed.)

NAME AND ADDRESS OF CREDITOR	DATES OF PAYMENTS/ TRANSFERS	AMOUNT PAID OR VALUE OF TRANSFERS	AMOUNT STILL OWING

None ☐

c. *All debtors:* List all payments made within **one year** immediately preceding the commencement of this case to or for the benefit of creditors who are or were insiders. (Married debtors filing under chapter 12 or chapter 13 must include payments by either or both spouses whether or not a joint petition is filed, unless the spouses are separated and a joint petition is not filed.)

NAME AND ADDRESS OF CREDITOR AND RELATIONSHIP TO DEBTOR	DATE OF PAYMENT	AMOUNT PAID	AMOUNT STILL OWING

---

4. Suits and administrative proceedings, executions, garnishments and attachments

None ☐ a. List all suits and administrative proceedings to which the debtor is or was a party within **one year** immediately preceding the filing of this bankruptcy case. (Married debtors filing under chapter 12 or chapter 13 must include information concerning either or both spouses whether or not a joint petition is filed, unless the spouses are separated and a joint petition is not filed.)

CAPTION OF SUIT AND CASE NUMBER	NATURE OF PROCEEDING	COURT OR AGENCY AND LOCATION	STATUS OR DISPOSITION

None ☐ b. Describe all property that has been attached, garnished or seized under any legal or equitable process within **one year** immediately preceding the commencement of this case. (Married debtors filing under chapter 12 or chapter 13 must include information concerning property of either or both spouses whether or not a joint petition is filed, unless the spouses are separated and a joint petition is not filed.)

NAME AND ADDRESS OF PERSON FOR WHOSE BENEFIT PROPERTY WAS SEIZED	DATE OF SEIZURE	DESCRIPTION AND VALUE OF PROPERTY

5. Repossessions, foreclosures and returns

None ☐ List all property that has been repossessed by a creditor, sold at a foreclosure sale, transferred through a deed in lieu of foreclosure or returned to the seller, within **one year** immediately preceding the commencement of this case. (Married debtors filing under chapter 12 or chapter 13 must include information concerning property of either or both spouses whether or not a joint petition is filed, unless the spouses are separated and a joint petition is not filed.)

NAME AND ADDRESS OF CREDITOR OR SELLER	DATE OF REPOSSESSION, FORECLOSURE SALE, TRANSFER OR RETURN	DESCRIPTION AND VALUE OF PROPERTY

6. Assignments and receiverships

None ☐ a. Describe any assignment of property for the benefit of creditors made within **120 days** immediately preceding the commencement of this case. (Married debtors filing under chapter 12 or chapter 13 must include any assignment by either or both spouses whether or not a joint petition is filed, unless the spouses are separated and a joint petition is not filed.)

NAME AND ADDRESS OF ASSIGNEE	DATE OF ASSIGNMENT	TERMS OF ASSIGNMENT OR SETTLEMENT

4

None ☐ b. List all property which has been in the hands of a custodian, receiver, or court-appointed official within **one year** immediately preceding the commencement of this case. (Married debtors filing under chapter 12 or chapter 13 must include information concerning property of either or both spouses whether or not a joint petition is filed, unless the spouses are separated and a joint petition is not filed.)

NAME AND ADDRESS OF CUSTODIAN	NAME AND LOCATION OF COURT CASE TITLE & NUMBER	DATE OF ORDER	DESCRIPTION AND VALUE Of PROPERTY

7. Gifts

None ☐ List all gifts or charitable contributions made within **one year** immediately preceding the commencement of this case except ordinary and usual gifts to family members aggregating less than $200 in value per individual family member and charitable contributions aggregating less than $100 per recipient. (Married debtors filing under chapter 12 or chapter 13 must include gifts or contributions by either or both spouses whether or not a joint petition is filed, unless the spouses are separated and a joint petition is not filed.)

NAME AND ADDRESS OF PERSON OR ORGANIZATION	RELATIONSHIP TO DEBTOR, IF ANY	DATE OF GIFT	DESCRIPTION AND VALUE OF GIFT

8. Losses

None ☐ List all losses from fire, theft, other casualty or gambling within **one year** immediately preceding the commencement of this case **or since the commencement of this case**. (Married debtors filing under chapter 12 or chapter 13 must include losses by either or both spouses whether or not a joint petition is filed, unless the spouses are separated and a joint petition is not filed.)

DESCRIPTION AND VALUE OF PROPERTY	DESCRIPTION OF CIRCUMSTANCES AND, IF LOSS WAS COVERED IN WHOLE OR IN PART BY INSURANCE, GIVE PARTICULARS	DATE OF LOSS

9. Payments related to debt counseling or bankruptcy

None ☐ List all payments made or property transferred by or on behalf of the debtor to any persons, including attorneys, for consultation concerning debt consolidation, relief under the bankruptcy law or preparation of a petition in bankruptcy within **one year** immediately preceding the commencement of this case.

NAME AND ADDRESS OF PAYEE	DATE OF PAYMENT, NAME OF PAYER IF OTHER THAN DEBTOR	AMOUNT OF MONEY OR DESCRIPTION AND VALUE OF PROPERTY

10. Other transfers

5

None
□
a. List all other property, other than property transferred in the ordinary course of the business or financial affairs of the debtor, transferred either absolutely or as security within **two years** immediately preceding the commencement of this case. (Married debtors filing under chapter 12 or chapter 13 must include transfers by either or both spouses whether or not a joint petition is filed, unless the spouses are separated and a joint petition is not filed.)

		DESCRIBE PROPERTY
NAME AND ADDRESS OF TRANSFEREE,		TRANSFERRED AND
RELATIONSHIP TO DEBTOR	DATE	VALUE RECEIVED

None
□
b. List all property transferred by the debtor within **ten years** immediately preceding the commencement of this case to a self-settled trust or similar device of which the debtor is a beneficiary.

NAME OF TRUST OR OTHER	DATE(S) OF	AMOUNT OF MONEY OR DESCRIPTION
DEVICE	TRANSFER(S)	AND VALUE OF PROPERTY OR DEBTOR'S
		INTEREST IN PROPERTY

11. Closed financial accounts

None
□
List all financial accounts and instruments held in the name of the debtor or for the benefit of the debtor which were closed, sold, or otherwise transferred within **one year** immediately preceding the commencement of this case. Include checking, savings, or other financial accounts, certificates of deposit, or other instruments; shares and share accounts held in banks, credit unions, pension funds, cooperatives, associations, brokerage houses and other financial institutions. (Married debtors filing under chapter 12 or chapter 13 must include information concerning accounts or instruments held by or for either or both spouses whether or not a joint petition is filed, unless the spouses are separated and a joint petition is not filed.)

	TYPE OF ACCOUNT, LAST FOUR	AMOUNT AND
NAME AND ADDRESS	DIGITS OF ACCOUNT NUMBER,	DATE OF SALE
OF INSTITUTION	AND AMOUNT OF FINAL BALANCE	OR CLOSING

12. Safe deposit boxes

None
□
List each safe deposit or other box or depository in which the debtor has or had securities, cash, or other valuables within **one year** immediately preceding the commencement of this case. (Married debtors filing under chapter 12 or chapter 13 must include boxes or depositories of either or both spouses whether or not a joint petition is filed, unless the spouses are separated and a joint petition is not filed.)

NAME AND ADDRESS	NAMES AND ADDRESSES	DESCRIPTION	DATE OF TRANSFER
OF BANK OR	OF THOSE WITH ACCESS	OF	OR SURRENDER,
OTHER DEPOSITORY	TO BOX OR DEPOSITORY	CONTENTS	IF ANY

13. Setoffs

6

None
□   List all setoffs made by any creditor, including a bank, against a debt or deposit of the debtor within **90 days** preceding the commencement of this case. (Married debtors filing under chapter 12 or chapter 13 must include information concerning either or both spouses whether or not a joint petition is filed, unless the spouses are separated and a joint petition is not filed.)

NAME AND ADDRESS OF CREDITOR	DATE OF SETOFF	AMOUNT OF SETOFF

---

14. Property held for another person

None
□   List all property owned by another person that the debtor holds or controls.

NAME AND ADDRESS OF OWNER	DESCRIPTION AND VALUE OF PROPERTY	LOCATION OF PROPERTY

---

15. Prior address of debtor

None
□   If debtor has moved within **three years** immediately preceding the commencement of this case, list all premises which the debtor occupied during that period and vacated prior to the commencement of this case. If a joint petition is filed, report also any separate address of either spouse.

ADDRESS	NAME USED	DATES OF OCCUPANCY

---

16. Spouses and Former Spouses

None
□   If the debtor resides or resided in a community property state, commonwealth, or territory (including Alaska, Arizona, California, Idaho, Louisiana, Nevada, New Mexico, Puerto Rico, Texas, Washington, or Wisconsin) within **eight years** immediately preceding the commencement of the case, identify the name of the debtor's spouse and of any former spouse who resides or resided with the debtor in the community property state.

NAME

7

17. Environmental Information.

For the purpose of this question, the following definitions apply:

"Environmental Law" means any federal, state, or local statute or regulation regulating pollution, contamination, releases of hazardous or toxic substances, wastes or material into the air, land, soil, surface water, groundwater, or other medium, including, but not limited to, statutes or regulations regulating the cleanup of these substances, wastes, or material.

"Site" means any location, facility, or property as defined under any Environmental Law, whether or not presently or formerly owned or operated by the debtor, including, but not limited to, disposal sites.

"Hazardous Material" means anything defined as a hazardous waste, hazardous substance, toxic substance, hazardous material, pollutant, or contaminant or similar term under an Environmental Law.

None
☐
a. List the name and address of every site for which the debtor has received notice in writing by a governmental unit that it may be liable or potentially liable under or in violation of an Environmental Law. Indicate the governmental unit, the date of the notice, and, if known, the Environmental Law:

SITE NAME AND ADDRESS	NAME AND ADDRESS OF GOVERNMENTAL UNIT	DATE OF NOTICE	ENVIRONMENTAL LAW

None
☐
b. List the name and address of every site for which the debtor provided notice to a governmental unit of a release of Hazardous Material. Indicate the governmental unit to which the notice was sent and the date of the notice.

SITE NAME AND ADDRESS	NAME AND ADDRESS OF GOVERNMENTAL UNIT	DATE OF NOTICE	ENVIRONMENTAL LAW

None
☐
c. List all judicial or administrative proceedings, including settlements or orders, under any Environmental Law with respect to which the debtor is or was a party. Indicate the name and address of the governmental unit that is or was a party to the proceeding, and the docket number.

NAME AND ADDRESS OF GOVERNMENTAL UNIT	DOCKET NUMBER	STATUS OR DISPOSITION

18 . Nature, location and name of business

None
☐
a. *If the debtor is an individual*, list the names, addresses, taxpayer identification numbers, nature of the businesses, and beginning and ending dates of all businesses in which the debtor was an officer, director, partner, or managing executive of a corporation, partner in a partnership, sole proprietor, or was self-employed in a trade, profession, or other activity either full- or part-time within **six years** immediately preceding the commencement of this case, or in which the debtor owned 5 percent or more of the voting or equity securities within **six years** immediately preceding the commencement of this case.

If the debtor is a partnership, list the names, addresses, taxpayer identification numbers, nature of the businesses, and beginning and ending dates of all businesses in which the debtor was a partner or owned 5 percent or more of the voting or equity securities, within **six years** immediately preceding the commencement of this case.

If the debtor is a corporation, list the names, addresses, taxpayer identification numbers, nature of the businesses, and beginning and ending dates of all businesses in which the debtor was a partner or owned 5 percent or more of the voting or equity securities within **six years** immediately preceding the commencement of this case.

8

NAME	LAST FOUR DIGITS OF SOC. SEC. NO./ COMPLETE EIN OR OTHER TAXPAYER I.D. NO.	ADDRESS	NATURE OF BUSINESS	BEGINNING AND ENDING DATES

None ☐   b. Identify any business listed in response to subdivision a., above, that is "single asset real estate" as defined in 11 U.S.C. § 101.

     NAME   ADDRESS

     The following questions are to be completed by every debtor that is a corporation or partnership and by any individual debtor who is or has been, within **six years** immediately preceding the commencement of this case, any of the following: an officer, director, managing executive, or owner of more than 5 percent of the voting or equity securities of a corporation; a partner, other than a limited partner, of a partnership, a sole proprietor, or self-employed in a trade, profession, or other activity, either full- or part-time.

     *(An individual or joint debtor should complete this portion of the statement **only** if the debtor is or has been in business, as defined above, within six years immediately preceding the commencement of this case. A debtor who has not been in business within those six years should go directly to the signature page.)*

19. Books, records and financial statements

None ☐   a. List all bookkeepers and accountants who within **two years** immediately preceding the filing of this bankruptcy case kept or supervised the keeping of books of account and records of the debtor.

     NAME AND ADDRESS   DATES SERVICES RENDERED

None ☐   b. List all firms or individuals who within **two years** immediately preceding the filing of this bankruptcy case have audited the books of account and records, or prepared a financial statement of the debtor.

     NAME   ADDRESS   DATES SERVICES RENDERED

None ☐   c. List all firms or individuals who at the time of the commencement of this case were in possession of the books of account and records of the debtor. If any of the books of account and records are not available, explain.

     NAME   ADDRESS

None ☐   d. List all financial institutions, creditors and other parties, including mercantile and trade agencies, to whom a financial statement was issued by the debtor within **two years** immediately preceding the commencement of this case.

NAME AND ADDRESS   DATE ISSUED

---

20. Inventories

None ☐   a. List the dates of the last two inventories taken of your property, the name of the person who supervised the taking of each inventory, and the dollar amount and basis of each inventory.

		DOLLAR AMOUNT OF INVENTORY
DATE OF INVENTORY	INVENTORY SUPERVISOR	(Specify cost, market or other basis)

None ☐   b. List the name and address of the person having possession of the records of each of the inventories reported in a., above.

	NAME AND ADDRESSES OF CUSTODIAN
DATE OF INVENTORY	OF INVENTORY RECORDS

---

21 . Current Partners, Officers, Directors and Shareholders

None ☐   a. If the debtor is a partnership, list the nature and percentage of partnership interest of each member of the partnership.

NAME AND ADDRESS	NATURE OF INTEREST	PERCENTAGE OF INTEREST

None ☐   b. If the debtor is a corporation, list all officers and directors of the corporation, and each stockholder who directly or indirectly owns, controls, or holds 5 percent or more of the voting or equity securities of the corporation.

NAME AND ADDRESS	TITLE	NATURE AND PERCENTAGE OF STOCK OWNERSHIP

---

22 . Former partners, officers, directors and shareholders

None ☐   a. If the debtor is a partnership, list each member who withdrew from the partnership within **one year** immediately preceding the commencement of this case.

NAME	ADDRESS	DATE OF WITHDRAWAL

None ☐   b.   If the debtor is a corporation, list all officers, or directors whose relationship with the corporation terminated within **one year** immediately preceding the commencement of this case.

       NAME AND ADDRESS   TITLE   DATE OF TERMINATION

23 . Withdrawals from a partnership or distributions by a corporation

None ☐   If the debtor is a partnership or corporation, list all withdrawals or distributions credited or given to an insider, including compensation in any form, bonuses, loans, stock redemptions, options exercised and any other perquisite during **one year** immediately preceding the commencement of this case.

NAME & ADDRESS OF RECIPIENT, RELATIONSHIP TO DEBTOR	DATE AND PURPOSE OF WITHDRAWAL	AMOUNT OF MONEY OR DESCRIPTION AND VALUE OF PROPERTY

24. Tax Consolidation Group.

None ☐   If the debtor is a corporation, list the name and federal taxpayer identification number of the parent corporation of any consolidated group for tax purposes of which the debtor has been a member at any time within **six years** immediately preceding the commencement of the case.

NAME OF PARENT CORPORATION   TAXPAYER IDENTIFICATION NUMBER (EIN)

25. Pension Funds.

None ☐   If the debtor is not an individual, list the name and federal taxpayer identification number of any pension fund to which the debtor, as an employer, has been responsible for contributing at any time within **six years** immediately preceding the commencement of the case.

NAME OF PENSION FUND   TAXPAYER IDENTIFICATION NUMBER (EIN)

*   *   *   *   *   *

[If completed by an individual or individual and spouse]

I declare under penalty of perjury that I have read the answers contained in the foregoing statement of financial affairs and any attachments thereto and that they are true and correct.

Date _____   Signature _____
                                    of Debtor

Date _____   Signature_____
                                    of Joint Debtor
                                    (if any)

[If completed on behalf of a partnership or corporation]

I, declare under penalty of perjury that I have read the answers contained in the foregoing statement of financial affairs and any attachments thereto and that they are true and correct to the best of my knowledge, information and belief.

Date _____   Signature _____

                                    _____
                                    Print Name and Title

[An individual signing on behalf of a partnership or corporation must indicate position or relationship to debtor.]

_____ continuation sheets attached

Penalty for making a false statement: Fine of up to $500,000 or imprisonment for up to 5 years, or both. 18 U.S.C. §§ 152 and 3571

DECLARATION AND SIGNATURE OF NON-ATTORNEY BANKRUPTCY PETITION PREPARER (See 11 U.S.C. § 110)

I declare under penalty of perjury that: (1) I am a bankruptcy petition preparer as defined in 11 U.S.C. § 110; (2) I prepared this document for compensation and have provided the debtor with a copy of this document and the notices and information required under 11 U.S.C. §§ 110(b), 110(h), and 342(b); and, (3) if rules or guidelines have been promulgated pursuant to 11 U.S.C. § 110(h) setting a maximum fee for services chargeable by bankruptcy petition preparers, I have given the debtor notice of the maximum amount before preparing any document for filing for a debtor or accepting any fee from the debtor, as required by that section.

_____   _____
Printed or Typed Name and Title, if any, of Bankruptcy Petition Preparer   Social Security No.(Required by 11 U.S.C. § 110.)

If the bankruptcy petition preparer is not an individual, state the name, title (if any), address, and social security number of the officer, principal, responsible person, or partner who signs this document.
_____

_____
Address

X _____   _____
Signature of Bankruptcy Petition Preparer   Date

Names and Social Security numbers of all other individuals who prepared or assisted in preparing this document unless the bankruptcy petition preparer is not an individual:

If more than one person prepared this document, attach additional signed sheets conforming to the appropriate Official Form for each person.

A bankruptcy petition preparer's failure to comply with the provisions of title 11 and the Federal Rules of Bankruptcy Procedure may result in fines or imprisonment or both. 18 U.S.C. § 156.

Official Form 22A (Chapter 7) (04/07)

In re _____
                    Debtor(s)

Case Number: _____
                    (If known)

According to the calculations required by this statement:
☐ **The presumption arises.**
☐ **The presumption does not arise.**
(Check the box as directed in Parts I, III, and VI of this statement.)

CHAPTER 7 STATEMENT OF CURRENT MONTHLY INCOME
AND MEANS-TEST CALCULATION

In addition to Schedule I and J, this statement must be completed by every individual Chapter 7 debtor, whether or not filing jointly, whose debts are primarily consumer debts. Joint debtors may complete one statement only.

Part I. EXCLUSION FOR DISABLED VETERANS

1 | If you are a disabled veteran described in the Veteran's Declaration in this Part I, (1) check the box at the beginning of the Veteran's Declaration, (2) check the box for "The presumption does not arise" at the top of this statement, and (3) complete the verification in Part VIII. Do not complete any of the remaining parts of this statement.

☐ **Veteran's Declaration.** By checking this box, I declare under penalty of perjury that I am a disabled veteran (as defined in 38 U.S.C. § 3741(1)) whose indebtedness occurred primarily during a period in which I was on active duty (as defined in 10 U.S.C. § 101(d)(1)) or while I was performing a homeland defense activity (as defined in 32 U.S.C. §901(1)).

Part II. CALCULATION OF MONTHLY INCOME FOR § 707(b)(7) EXCLUSION

2 | **Marital/filing status.** Check the box that applies and complete the balance of this part of this statement as directed.

a. ☐ Unmarried. **Complete only Column A ("Debtor's Income") for Lines 3-11.**

b. ☐ Married, not filing jointly, with declaration of separate households. By checking this box, debtor declares under penalty of perjury: "My spouse and I are legally separated under applicable non-bankruptcy law or my spouse and I are living apart other than for the purpose of evading the requirements of § 707(b)(2)(A) of the Bankruptcy Code." **Complete only Column A ("Debtor's Income") for Lines 3-11.**

c. ☐ Married, not filing jointly, without the declaration of separate households set out in Line 2.b above. **Complete both Column A ("Debtor's Income") and Column B (Spouse's Income) for Lines 3-11.**

d. ☐ Married, filing jointly. **Complete both Column A ("Debtor's Income") and Column B ("Spouse's Income") for Lines 3-11.**

All figures must reflect average monthly income received from all sources, derived during the six calendar months prior to filing the bankruptcy case, ending on the last day of the month before the filing. If the amount of monthly income varied during the six months, you must divide the six-month total by six, and enter the result on the appropriate line.	Column A Debtor's Income	Column B Spouse's Income
3	**Gross wages, salary, tips, bonuses, overtime, commissions.**	$	$

4 | **Income from the operation of a business, profession or farm.** Subtract Line b from Line a and enter the difference in the appropriate column(s) of Line 4. Do not enter a number less than zero. **Do not include any part of the business expenses entered Line b as a deduction in Part V.**

			Column A	Column B
a.	Gross receipts	$		
b.	Ordinary and necessary business expenses	$		
c.	Business income	Subtract Line b from Line a	$	$

5 | **Rent and other real property income.** Subtract Line b from Line a and enter the difference in the appropriate column(s) of Line 5. Do not enter a number less than zero. **Do not include any part of the operating expenses entered on Line b as a deduction in Part V.**

			Column A	Column B
a.	Gross receipts	$		
b.	Ordinary and necessary operating expenses	$		
c.	Rent and other real property income	Subtract Line b from Line a	$	$

6	**Interest, dividends and royalties.**	$	$
7	**Pension and retirement income.**	$	$
8	**Any amounts paid by another person or entity, on a regular basis, for the household expenses of the debtor or the debtor's dependents, including child or spousal support.** Do not include amounts paid by the debtor's spouse if Column B is completed.	$	$

Official Form 22A (Chapter 7) (04/07) – Cont.   2

9	**Unemployment compensation.** Enter the amount in the appropriate column(s) of Line 9. However, if you contend that unemployment compensation received by you or your spouse was a benefit under the Social Security Act, do not list the amount of such compensation in Column A or B, but instead state the amount in the space below: Unemployment compensation claimed to be a benefit under the Social Security Act Debtor $ _____ Spouse $ _____	$	$
10	**Income from all other sources.** If necessary, list additional sources on a separate page. **Do not include** any benefits received under the Social Security Act or payments received as a victim of a war crime, crime against humanity, or as a victim of international or domestic terrorism. Specify source and amount. a. _____ $ ____ b. _____ $ ____ Total and enter on Line 10	$	$
11	**Subtotal of Current Monthly Income for § 707(b)(7).** Add Lines 3 thru 10 in Column A, and, if Column B is completed, add Lines 3 through 10 in Column B. Enter the total(s).	$	$
12	**Total Current Monthly Income for § 707(b)(7).** If Column B has been completed, add Line 11, Column A to Line 11, Column B, and enter the total. If Column B has not been completed, enter the amount from Line 11, Column A.	$	

Part III. APPLICATION OF § 707(b)(7) EXCLUSION

13	**Annualized Current Monthly Income for § 707(b)(7).** Multiply the amount from Line 12 by the number 12 and enter the result.	$
14	**Applicable median family income.** Enter the median family income for the applicable state and household size. (This information is available by family size at www.usdoj.gov/ust/ or from the clerk of the bankruptcy court.) a. Enter debtor's state of residence: _____ b. Enter debtor's household size: _____	$
15	**Application of Section 707(b)(7).** Check the applicable box and proceed as directed. ☐ **The amount on Line 13 is less than or equal to the amount on Line 14.** Check the box for "The presumption does not arise" at the top of page 1 of this statement, and complete Part VIII; do not complete Parts IV, V, VI or VII. ☐ **The amount on Line 13 is more than the amount on Line 14.** Complete the remaining parts of this statement.	

Complete Parts IV, V, VI, and VII of this statement only if required. (See Line 15.)

Part IV. CALCULATION OF CURRENT MONTHLY INCOME FOR § 707(b)(2)

16	**Enter the amount from Line 12.**	$
17	**Marital adjustment.** If you checked the box at Line 2.c, enter the amount of the income listed in Line 11, Column B that was NOT paid on a regular basis for the household expenses of the debtor or the debtor's dependents. If you did not check box at Line 2.c, enter zero.	$
18	**Current monthly income for § 707(b)(2).** Subtract Line 17 from Line 16 and enter the result.	$

Part V. CALCULATION OF DEDUCTIONS ALLOWED UNDER § 707(b)(2)

Subpart A: Deductions under Standards of the Internal Revenue Service (IRS)

19	**National Standards: food, clothing, household supplies, personal care, and miscellaneous.** Enter "Total" amount from IRS National Standards for Allowable Living Expenses for the applicable family size and income level. (This information is available at www.usdoj.gov/ust/ or from the clerk of the bankruptcy court.)	$
20A	**Local Standards: housing and utilities; non-mortgage expenses.** Enter the amount of the IRS Housing and Utilities Standards; non-mortgage expenses for the applicable county and family size. (This information is available at www.usdoj.gov/ust/ or from the clerk of the bankruptcy court).	$

Official Form 22A (Chapter 7) (01/07)   Cont.   3

20B	**Local Standards: housing and utilities; mortgage/rent expense.** Enter, in Line a below, the amount of the IRS Housing and Utilities Standards; mortgage/rent expense for your county and family size (this information is available at www.usdoj.gov/ust/ or from the clerk of the bankruptcy court); enter on Line b the total of the Average Monthly Payments for any debts secured by your home, as stated in Line 42; subtract Line b from Line a and enter the result in Line 20B. **Do not enter an amount less than zero.**		$

	a.	IRS Housing and Utilities Standards; mortgage/rental expense	$
	b.	Average Monthly Payment for any debts secured by your home, if any, as stated in Line 42	$
	c.	Net mortgage/rental expense	Subtract Line b from Line a.

21	**Local Standards: housing and utilities; adjustment.** if you contend that the process set out in Lines 20A and 20B does not accurately compute the allowance to which you are entitled under the IRS Housing and Utilities Standards, enter any additional amount to which you contend you are entitled, and state the basis for your contention in the space below:	$

22	**Local Standards: transportation; vehicle operation/public transportation expense.** You are entitled to an expense allowance in this category regardless of whether you pay the expenses of operating a vehicle and regardless of whether you use public transportation. Check the number of vehicles for which you pay the operating expenses or for which the operating expenses are included as a contribution to your household expenses in Line 8. ☐ 0 ☐ 1 ☐ 2 or more. Enter the amount from IRS Transportation Standards, Operating Costs & Public Transportation Costs for the applicable number of vehicles in the applicable Metropolitan Statistical Area or Census Region. (This information is available at www.usdoj.gov/ust/ or from the clerk of the bankruptcy court.)	$

23	**Local Standards: transportation ownership/lease expense; Vehicle 1.** Check the number of vehicles for which you claim an ownership/lease expense. (You may not claim an ownership/lease expense for more than two vehicles.) ☐ 1 ☐ 2 or more. Enter, in Line a below, the amount of the IRS Transportation Standards, Ownership Costs, First Car (available at www.usdoj.gov/ust/ or from the clerk of the bankruptcy court); enter in Line b the total of the Average Monthly Payments for any debts secured by Vehicle 1, as stated in Line 42; subtract Line b from Line a and enter the result in Line 23. **Do not enter an amount less than zero.**	$

	a.	IRS Transportation Standards, Ownership Costs, First Car	$
	b.	Average Monthly Payment for any debts secured by Vehicle 1, as stated in Line 42	$
	c.	Net ownership/lease expense for Vehicle 1	Subtract Line b from Line a.

24	**Local Standards: transportation ownership/lease expense; Vehicle 2.** Complete this Line only if you checked the "2 or more" Box in Line 23. Enter, in Line a below, the amount of the IRS Transportation Standards, Ownership Costs, Second Car (available at www.usdoj.gov/ust/ or from the clerk of the bankruptcy court); enter in Line b the total of the Average Monthly Payments for any debts secured by Vehicle 2, as stated in Line 42; subtract Line b from Line a and enter the result in Line 24. **Do not enter an amount less than zero.**	$

	a.	IRS Transportation Standards, Ownership Costs, Second Car	$
	b.	Average Monthly Payment for any debts secured by Vehicle 2, as stated in Line 42	$
	c.	Net ownership/lease expense for Vehicle 2	Subtract Line b from Line a.

25	**Other Necessary Expenses: taxes.** Enter the total average monthly expense that you actually incur for all federal, state and local taxes, other than real estate and sales taxes, such as income taxes, self employment taxes, social security taxes, and Medicare taxes. **Do not include real estate or sales taxes.**	

26	**Other Necessary Expenses: mandatory payroll deductions.** Enter the total average monthly payroll deductions that are required for your employment, such as mandatory retirement contributions, union dues, and uniform costs. **Do not include discretionary amounts, such as non-mandatory 401(k) contributions.**	$

Official Form 22A (Chapter 7) (04/07) – Cont. 4

27	**Other Necessary Expenses: life insurance.** Enter average monthly premiums that you actually pay for term life insurance for yourself. **Do not include premiums for insurance on your dependents, for whole life or for any other form of insurance.**	$
28	**Other Necessary Expenses: court-ordered payments.** Enter the total monthly amount that you are required to pay pursuant to court order, such as spousal or child support payments. **Do not include payments on past due support obligations included in Line 44.**	$
29	**Other Necessary Expenses: education for employment or for a physically or mentally challenged child.** Enter the total monthly amount that you actually expend for education that is a condition of employment and for education that is required for a physically or mentally challenged dependent child for whom no public education providing similar services is available.	$
30	**Other Necessary Expenses: childcare.** Enter the average monthly amount that you actually expend on childcare—such as baby-sitting, day care, nursery and preschool. **Do not include other educational payments.**	$
31	**Other Necessary Expenses: health care.** Enter the average monthly amount that you actually expend on health care expenses that are not reimbursed by insurance or paid by a health savings account. **Do not include payments for health insurance or health savings accounts listed in Line 34.**	$
32	**Other Necessary Expenses: telecommunication services.** Enter the average monthly amount that you actually pay for telecommunication services other than your basic home telephone service—such as cell phones, pagers, call waiting, caller id, special long distance, or internet service—to the extent necessary for your health and welfare or that of your dependents. **Do not include any amount previously deducted.**	$
33	**Total Expenses Allowed under IRS Standards.** Enter the total of Lines 19 through 32.	$

Subpart B: Additional Expense Deductions under § 707(b)
Note: Do not include any expenses that you have listed in Lines 19-32

34	**Health Insurance, Disability Insurance, and Health Savings Account Expenses.** List and total the average monthly amounts that you actually pay for yourself, your spouse, or your dependents in the following categories.			
		a.	Health Insurance	$
		b.	Disability Insurance	$
		c.	Health Savings Account	$
			Total: Add Lines a, b and c	$
35	**Continued contributions to the care of household or family members.** Enter the actual monthly expenses that you will continue to pay for the reasonable and necessary care and support of an elderly, chronically ill, or disabled member of your household or member of your immediate family who is unable to pay for such expenses.			$
36	**Protection against family violence.** Enter any average monthly expenses that you actually incurred to maintain the safety of your family under the Family Violence Prevention and Services Act or other applicable federal law. The nature of these expenses is required to be kept confidential by the court.			$
37	**Home energy costs.** Enter the average monthly amount, in excess of the allowance specified by IRS Local Standards for Housing and Utilities, that you actually expend for home energy costs. **You must provide your case trustee with documentation demonstrating that the additional amount claimed is reasonable and necessary.**			$
38	**Education expenses for dependent children less than 18.** Enter the average monthly expenses that you actually incur, not to exceed $137.50 per child, in providing elementary and secondary education for your dependent children less than 18 years of age. **You must provide your case trustee with documentation demonstrating that the amount claimed is reasonable and necessary and not already accounted for in the IRS Standards.**			$
39	**Additional food and clothing expense.** Enter the average monthly amount by which your food and clothing expenses exceed the combined allowances for food and apparel in the IRS National Standards, not to exceed five percent of those combined allowances. (This information is available at www.usdoj.gov/ust/ or from the clerk of the bankruptcy court.) **You must provide your case trustee with documentation demonstrating that the additional amount claimed is reasonable and necessary.**			$
40	**Continued charitable contributions.** Enter the amount that you will continue to contribute in the form of cash or financial instruments to a charitable organization as defined in 26 U.S.C. § 170(c)(1)-(2).			$
41	**Total Additional Expense Deductions under § 707(b).** Enter the total of Lines 34 through 40			$

Official Form 22A (Chapter 7) (04/07) – Cont.　　　　　　　　　　　　　　　　　5

	Subpart C: Deductions for Debt Payment			
42	**Future payments on secured claims.** For each of your debts that is secured by an interest in property that you own, list the name of the creditor, identify the property securing the debt, and state the Average Monthly Payment. The Average Monthly Payment is the total of all amounts contractually due to each Secured Creditor in the 60 months following the filing of the bankruptcy case, divided by 60. Mortgage debts should include payments of taxes and insurance required by the mortgage. If necessary, list additional entries on a separate page.			

	Name of Creditor	Property Securing the Debt	60-month Average Payment	
a.			$	
b.			$	
c.			$	
			Total: Add Lines a, b and c.	$

	Other payments on secured claims. If any of debts listed in Line 42 are secured by your primary residence, a motor vehicle, or other property necessary for your support or the support of your dependents, you may include in your deduction 1/60th of any amount (the "cure amount") that you must pay the creditor in addition to the payments listed in Line 42, in order to maintain possession of the property. The cure amount would include any sums in default that must be paid in order to avoid repossession or foreclosure. List and total any such amounts in the following chart. If necessary, list additional entries on a separate page.

	Name of Creditor	Property Securing the Debt	1/60th of the Cure Amount	
a.			$	
b.			$	
c.			$	
			Total: Add Lines a, b and c	$

44	**Payments on priority claims.** Enter the total amount of all priority claims (including priority child support and alimony claims), divided by 60.	$

45	**Chapter 13 administrative expenses.** If you are eligible to file a case under Chapter 13, complete the following chart, multiply the amount in line a by the amount in line b, and enter the resulting administrative expense.	

a.	Projected average monthly Chapter 13 plan payment.	$	
b.	Current multiplier for your district as determined under schedules issued by the Executive Office for United States Trustees. (This information is available at www.usdoj.gov/ust/ or from the clerk of the bankruptcy court.)	x	
c.	Average monthly administrative expense of Chapter 13 case	Total: Multiply Lines a and b	$

46	**Total Deductions for Debt Payment.** Enter the total of Lines 42 through 45.	$

	Subpart D: Total Deductions Allowed under § 707(b)(2)	
47	**Total of all deductions allowed under § 707(b)(2).** Enter the total of Lines 33, 41, and 46.	$

Part VI. DETERMINATION OF § 707(b)(2) PRESUMPTION

48	**Enter the amount from Line 18 (Current monthly income for § 707(b)(2))**	$
49	**Enter the amount from Line 47 (Total of all deductions allowed under § 707(b)(2))**	$
50	**Monthly disposable income under § 707(b)(2).** Subtract Line 49 from Line 48 and enter the result	$
51	**60-month disposable income under § 707(b)(2).** Multiply the amount in Line 50 by the number 60 and enter the result.	$

Official Form 22A (Chapter 7) (04/07) – Cont.   6

52	**Initial presumption determination.** Check the applicable box and proceed as directed. ☐ **The amount on Line 51 is less than $6,575** Check the box for "The presumption does not arise" at the top of page 1 of this statement, and complete the verification in Part VIII. Do not complete the remainder of Part VI. ☐ **The amount set forth on Line 51 is more than $10,950.** Check the box for "The presumption arises" at the top of page 1 of this statement, and complete the verification in Part VIII. You may also complete Part VII. Do not complete the remainder of Part VI. ☐ **The amount on Line 51 is at least $6,575, but not more than $10,950.** Complete the remainder of Part VI (Lines 53 through 55).
53	**Enter the amount of your total non-priority unsecured debt** $
54	**Threshold debt payment amount.** Multiply the amount in Line 53 by the number 0.25 and enter the result. $
55	**Secondary presumption determination.** Check the applicable box and proceed as directed. ☐ **The amount on Line 51 is less than the amount on Line 54.** Check the box for "The presumption does not arise" at the top of page 1 of this statement, and complete the verification in Part VIII. ☐ **The amount on Line 51 is equal to or greater than the amount on Line 54.** Check the box for "The presumption arises" at the top of page 1 of this statement, and complete the verification in Part VIII. You may also complete Part VII.

Part VII: ADDITIONAL EXPENSE CLAIMS

56	**Other Expenses.** List and describe any monthly expenses, not otherwise stated in this form, that are required for the health and welfare of you and your family and that you contend should be an additional deduction from your current monthly income under § 707(b)(2)(A)(ii)(I). If necessary, list additional sources on a separate page. All figures should reflect your average monthly expense for each item. Total the expenses.

	Expense Description	Monthly Amount
a.		$
b.		$
c.		$
	Total: Add Lines a, b and c	$

Part VIII: VERIFICATION

57	I declare under penalty of perjury that the information provided in this statement is true and correct. *(If this is a joint case, both debtors must sign.)*
	
	Date: _____ Signature: _____
	                                                                    (Debtor)
	
	Date: _____ Signature: _____
	                                                                    (Joint Debtor, if any)

Official Form 22C (Chapter 13) (01/07)

In re _____
                Debtor(s)

Case Number: _____
                (If known)

According to the calculations required by this statement:
☐ **The applicable commitment period is 3 years.**
☐ **The applicable commitment period is 5 years.**
☐ **Disposable income is determined under § 1325(b)(3).**
☐ **Disposable income is not determined under § 1325(b)(3).**
(Check the boxes as directed in Lines 17 and 23 of this statement.)

CHAPTER 13 STATEMENT OF CURRENT MONTHLY INCOME
AND CALCULATION OF COMMITMENT PERIOD AND DISPOSABLE INCOME

In addition to Schedules I and J, this statement must be completed by every individual Chapter 13 debtor, whether or not filing jointly. Joint debtors may complete one statement only.

	Part I. REPORT OF INCOME		
1	**Marital/filing status.** Check the box that applies and complete the balance of this part of this statement as directed. a. ☐ Unmarried. **Complete only Column A ("Debtor's Income") for Lines 2-10.** b. ☐ Married. **Complete both Column A ("Debtor's Income") and Column B ("Spouse's Income") for Lines 2-10.**		
	All figures must reflect average monthly income received from all sources, derived during the six calendar months prior to filing the bankruptcy case, ending on the last day of the month before the filing. If the amount of monthly income varied during the six months, you must divide the six-month total by six, and enter the result on the appropriate line.	**Column A** Debtor's Income	**Column B** Spouse's Income
2	**Gross wages, salary, tips, bonuses, overtime, commissions.**	$	$
3	**Income from the operation of a business, profession, or farm.** Subtract Line b from Line a and enter the difference in the appropriate column(s) of Line 3. Do not enter a number less than zero. **Do not include any part of the business expenses entered on Line b as a deduction in Part IV.** a. Gross receipts $ b. Ordinary and necessary business expenses $ c. Business income Subtract Line b from Line a	$	$
4	**Rent and other real property income.** Subtract Line b from Line a and enter the difference in the appropriate column(s) of Line 4. Do not enter a number less than zero. **Do not include any part of the operating expenses entered on Line b as a deduction in Part IV.** a. Gross receipts $ b. Ordinary and necessary operating expenses $ c. Rent and other real property income Subtract Line b from Line a	$	$
5	**Interest, dividends, and royalties.**	$	$
6	**Pension and retirement income.**	$	$
7	**Any amounts paid by another person or entity, on a regular basis, for the household expenses of the debtor or the debtor's dependents, including child or spousal support.** Do not include amounts paid by the debtor's spouse.	$	$
8	**Unemployment compensation.** Enter the amount in the appropriate column(s) of Line 8. However, if you contend that unemployment compensation received by you or your spouse was a benefit under the Social Security Act, do not list the amount of such compensation in Column A or B, but instead state the amount in the space below: Unemployment compensation claimed to be a benefit under the Social Security Act Debtor $ _____ Spouse $ _____	$	$
9	**Income from all other sources.** Specify source and amount. If necessary, list additional sources on a separate page. Total and enter on Line 9. **Do not include** any benefits received under the Social Security Act or payments received as a victim of a war crime, crime against humanity, or as a victim of international or domestic terrorism. a. _____ $ b. _____ $	$	$
10	**Subtotal.** Add Lines 2 thru 9 in Column A, and, if Column B is completed, add Lines 2 through 9 in Column B. Enter the total(s).	$	$
11	**Total.** If Column B has been completed, add Line 10, Column A to Line 10, Column B, and enter the total. If Column B has not been completed, enter the amount from Line 10, Column A.	$	

Official Form 22C (Chapter 13) (04/07) – Cont.   2

	Part II. CALCULATION OF § 1325(b)(4) COMMITMENT PERIOD	
12	**Enter the amount from Line 11.**	
13	**Marital adjustment.** If you are married, but are not filing jointly with your spouse, AND if you contend that calculation of the commitment period under § 1325(b)(4) does not require inclusion of the income of your spouse, enter the amount of the income listed in Line 10, Column B that was NOT paid on a regular basis for the household expenses of you or your dependents. Otherwise, enter zero.	
14	**Subtract Line 13 from Line 12 and enter the result.**	
15	**Annualized current monthly income for § 1325(b)(4).** Multiply the amount from Line 14 by the number 12 and enter the result.	$
16	**Applicable median family income.** Enter the median family income for applicable state and household size. (This information is available by family size at www.usdoj.gov/ust/ or from the clerk of the bankruptcy court.) a. Enter debtor's state of residence: _____ b. Enter debtor's household size: _____	$
17	**Application of § 1325(b)(4).** Check the applicable box and proceed as directed. ☐ **The amount on Line 15 is less than the amount on Line 16.** Check the box for "The applicable commitment period is 3 years" at the top of page 1 of this statement and continue with this statement. ☐ **The amount on Line 15 is not less than the amount on Line 16.** Check the box for "The applicable commitment period is 5 years" at the top of page 1 of this statement and continue with this statement.	

	Part III. APPLICATION OF § 1325(b)(3) FOR DETERMINING DISPOSABLE INCOME	
18	**Enter the amount from Line 11.**	$
19	**Marital adjustment.** If you are married, but are not filing jointly with your spouse, enter the amount of the income listed in Line 10, Column B that was NOT paid on a regular basis for the household expenses of you or your dependents. If you are unmarried or married and filing jointly with your spouse, enter zero.	$
20	**Current monthly income for § 1325(b)(3).** Subtract Line 19 from Line 18 and enter the result.	
21	**Annualized current monthly income for § 1325(b)(3).** Multiply the amount from Line 20 by the number 12 and enter the result.	$
22	**Applicable median family income.** Enter the amount from Line 16.	$
23	**Application of § 1325(b)(3).** Check the applicable box and proceed as directed. ☐ **The amount on Line 21 is more than the amount on Line 22.** Check the box for "Disposable income is determined under § 1325(b)(3)" at the top of page 1 of this statement and complete the remaining parts of this statement. ☐ **The amount on Line 21 is not more than the amount on Line 22.** Check the box for "Disposable income is not determined under § 1325(b)(3)" at the top of page 1 of this statement and complete Part VII of this statement. **Do not complete Parts IV, V, or VI.**	

	Part IV. CALCULATION OF DEDUCTIONS ALLOWED UNDER § 707(b)(2)	
	Subpart A: Deductions under Standards of the Internal Revenue Service (IRS)	
24	**National Standards: food, clothing, household supplies, personal care, and miscellaneous.** Enter the "Total" amount from IRS National Standards for Allowable Living Expenses for the applicable family size and income level. (This information is available at www.usdoj.gov/ust/ or from the clerk of the bankruptcy court.)	$
25A	**Local Standards: housing and utilities; non-mortgage expenses.** Enter the amount of the IRS Housing and Utilities Standards; non-mortgage expenses for the applicable county and family size. (This information is available at www.usdoj.gov/ust/ or from the clerk of the bankruptcy court).	$

Official Form 22C (Chapter 13) (04/07) – Cont.   3

25B	**Local Standards: housing and utilities; mortgage/rent expense.** Enter, in Line a below, the amount of the IRS Housing and Utilities Standards; mortgage/rent expense for your county and family size (this information is available at www.usdoj.gov/ust/ or from the clerk of the bankruptcy court); enter on Line b the total of the Average Monthly Payments for any debts secured by your home, as stated in Line 47; subtract Line b from Line a and enter the result in Line 25B. **Do not enter an amount less than zero.**		
	a.	IRS Housing and Utilities Standards; mortgage/rent Expense	$
	b.	Average Monthly Payment for any debts secured by your home, if any, as stated in Line 47	$
	c.	Net mortgage/rental expense	Subtract Line b from Line a.
			$

26	**Local Standards: housing and utilities; adjustment.** if you contend that the process set out in Lines 25A and 25B does not accurately compute the allowance to which you are entitled under the IRS Housing and Utilities Standards, enter any additional amount to which you contend you are entitled, and state the basis for your contention in the space below: _____ _____
	$

27	**Local Standards: transportation; vehicle operation/public transportation expense.** You are entitled to an expense allowance in this category regardless of whether you pay the expenses of operating a vehicle and regardless of whether you use public transportation. Check the number of vehicles for which you pay the operating expenses or for which the operating expenses are included as a contribution to your household expenses in Line 7. ☐ 0 ☐ 1 ☐ 2 or more. Enter the amount from IRS Transportation Standards, Operating Costs & Public Transportation Costs for the applicable number of vehicles in the applicable Metropolitan Statistical Area or Census Region. (This information is available at www.usdoj.gov/ust/ or from the clerk of the bankruptcy court.)
	$

28	**Local Standards: transportation ownership/lease expense; Vehicle 1.** Check the number of vehicles for which you claim an ownership/lease expense. (You may not claim an ownership/lease expense for more than two vehicles.) ☐ 1 ☐ 2 or more. Enter, in Line a below, the amount of the IRS Transportation Standards, Ownership Costs, First Car (available at www.usdoj.gov/ust/ or from the clerk of the bankruptcy court); enter in Line b the total of the Average Monthly Payments for any debts secured by Vehicle 1, as stated in Line 47; subtract Line b from Line a and enter the result in Line 28. **Do not enter an amount less than zero.**		
	a.	IRS Transportation Standards, Ownership Costs, First Car	$
	b.	Average Monthly Payment for any debts secured by Vehicle 1, as stated in Line 47	$
	c.	Net ownership/lease expense for Vehicle 1	Subtract Line b from Line a.
			$

29	**Local Standards: transportation ownership/lease expense; Vehicle 2.** Complete this Line only if you checked the "2 or more" Box in Line 28. Enter, in Line a below, the amount of the IRS Transportation Standards, Ownership Costs, Second Car (available at www.usdoj.gov/ust/ or from the clerk of the bankruptcy court); enter in Line b the total of the Average Monthly Payments for any debts secured by Vehicle 2, as stated in Line 47; subtract Line b from Line a and enter the result in Line 29. **Do not enter an amount less than zero.**		
	a.	IRS Transportation Standards, Ownership Costs, Second Car	$
	b.	Average Monthly Payment for any debts secured by Vehicle 2, as stated in Line 47	$
	c.	Net ownership/lease expense for Vehicle 2	Subtract Line b from Line a.
			$

30	**Other Necessary Expenses: taxes.** Enter the total average monthly expense that you actually incur for all federal, state, and local taxes, other than real estate and sales taxes, such as income taxes, self employment taxes, social security taxes, and Medicare taxes. **Do not include real estate or sales taxes.**
	$

31	**Other Necessary Expenses: mandatory payroll deductions.** Enter the total average monthly payroll deductions that are required for your employment, such as mandatory retirement contributions, union dues, and uniform costs. **Do not include discretionary amounts, such as non-mandatory 401(k) contributions.**
	$

Official Form 22C (Chapter 13) (04/07) – Cont.   4

32	**Other Necessary Expenses: life insurance.** Enter average monthly premiums that you actually pay for term life insurance for yourself. **Do not include premiums for insurance on your dependents, for whole life or for any other form of insurance.**	$
33	**Other Necessary Expenses: court-ordered payments.** Enter the total monthly amount that you are required to pay pursuant to court order, such as spousal or child support payments. **Do not include payments on past due support obligations included in Line 49.**	$
34	**Other Necessary Expenses: education for employment or for a physically or mentally challenged child.** Enter the total monthly amount that you actually expend for education that is a condition of employment and for education that is required for a physically or mentally challenged dependent child for whom no public education providing similar services is available.	
35	**Other Necessary Expenses: childcare.** Enter the average monthly amount that you actually expend on childcare—such as baby-sitting, day care, nursery and preschool. **Do not include other educational payments.**	$
36	**Other Necessary Expenses: health care.** Enter the average monthly amount that you actually expend on health care expenses that are not reimbursed by insurance or paid by a health savings account. **Do not include payments for health insurance or health savings accounts listed in Line 39.**	$
37	**Other Necessary Expenses: telecommunication services.** Enter the average monthly amount that you actually pay for telecommunication services other than your basic home telephone service—such as cell phones, pagers, call waiting, caller id, special long distance, or internet service—to the extent necessary for your health and welfare or that of your dependents. **Do not include any amount previously deducted.**	$
38	**Total Expenses Allowed under IRS Standards.** Enter the total of Lines 24 through 37.	$

Subpart B: Additional Expense Deductions under § 707(b)		
Note: Do not include any expenses that you have listed in Lines 24-37		

39	**Health Insurance, Disability Insurance, and Health Savings Account Expenses.** List and total the average monthly amounts that you actually pay for yourself, your spouse, or your dependents in the following categories.		
	a.	Health Insurance	$
	b.	Disability Insurance	$
	c.	Health Savings Account	$
		Total: Add Lines a, b, and c	$

40	**Continued contributions to the care of household or family members.** Enter the actual monthly expenses that you will continue to pay for the reasonable and necessary care and support of an elderly, chronically ill, or disabled member of your household or member of your immediate family who is unable to pay for such expenses. **Do not include payments listed in Line 34.**	$
41	**Protection against family violence.** Enter any average monthly expenses that you actually incurred to maintain the safety of your family under the Family Violence Prevention and Services Act or other applicable federal law. The nature of these expenses is required to be kept confidential by the court.	$
42	**Home energy costs.** Enter the average monthly amount, in excess of the allowance specified by IRS Local Standards for Housing and Utilities, that you actually expend for home energy costs. **You must provide your case trustee with documentation demonstrating that the additional amount claimed is reasonable and necessary.**	$
43	**Education expenses for dependent children under 18.** Enter the average monthly expenses that you actually incur, not to exceed $137.50 per child, in providing elementary and secondary education for your dependent children less than 18 years of age. **You must provide your case trustee with documentation demonstrating that the amount claimed is reasonable and necessary and not already accounted for in the IRS Standards.**	$
44	**Additional food and clothing expense.** Enter the average monthly amount by which your food and clothing expenses exceed the combined allowances for food and apparel in the IRS National Standards, not to exceed five percent of those combined allowances. (This information is available at www.usdoj.gov/ust/ or from the clerk of the bankruptcy court.) **You must provide your case trustee with documentation demonstrating that the additional amount claimed is reasonable and necessary.**	$
45	**Continued charitable contributions.** Enter the amount that you will continue to contribute in the form of cash or financial instruments to a charitable organization as defined in 26 U.S.C. § 170(c)(1)-(2).	$
46	**Total Additional Expense Deductions under § 707(b).** Enter the total of Lines 39 through 45.	$

Official Form 22C (Chapter 13) (04/07) - Cont.   5

	Subpart C: Deductions for Debt Payment		
47	**Future payments on secured claims.** For each of your debts that is secured by an interest in property that you own, list the name of the creditor, identify the property securing the debt, and state the Average Monthly Payment. The Average Monthly Payment is the total of all amounts contractually due to each Secured Creditor in the 60 months following the filing of the bankruptcy case, divided by 60. Mortgage debts should include payments of taxes and insurance required by the mortgage. If necessary, list additional entries on a separate page.		

	Name of Creditor	Property Securing the Debt	60-month Average Payment
a.			$
b.			$
c.			$
			Total: Add Lines a, b, and c $

| 48 | **Other payments on secured claims.** If any of debts listed in Line 47 are secured by your primary residence, a motor vehicle, or other property necessary for your support or the support of your dependents, you may include in your deduction 1/60th of any amount (the "cure amount") that you must pay the creditor in addition to the payments listed in Line 47, in order to maintain possession of the property. The cure amount would include any sums in default that must be paid in order to avoid repossession or foreclosure. List and total any such amounts in the following chart. If necessary, list additional entries on a separate page. |

	Name of Creditor	Property Securing the Debt	1/60th of the Cure Amount
a.			$
b.			$
c.			$
			Total: Add Lines a, b, and c $

| 49 | **Payments on priority claims.** Enter the total amount of all priority claims (including priority child support and alimony claims), divided by 60. | $ |

50	**Chapter 13 administrative expenses.** Multiply the amount in Line a by the amount in Line b, and enter the resulting administrative expense.	
	a. Projected average monthly Chapter 13 plan payment.	$
	b. Current multiplier for your district as determined under schedules issued by the Executive Office for United States Trustees. (This information is available at www.usdoj.gov/ust/ or from the clerk of the bankruptcy court.)	x
	c. Average monthly administrative expense of Chapter 13 case	Total: Multiply Lines a and b $

| 51 | **Total Deductions for Debt Payment.** Enter the total of Lines 47 through 50. | $ |

	Subpart D: Total Deductions Allowed under § 707(b)(2)	
52	**Total of all deductions allowed under § 707(b)(2).** Enter the total of Lines 38, 46, and 51.	$

Part V. DETERMINATION OF DISPOSABLE INCOME UNDER § 1325(b)(2)

53	**Total current monthly income.** Enter the amount from Line 20.	$
54	**Support income.** Enter the monthly average of any child support payments, foster care payments, or disability payments for a dependent child, included in Line 7, that you received in accordance with applicable nonbankruptcy law, to the extent reasonably necessary to be expended for such child.	$
55	**Qualified retirement deductions.** Enter the monthly average of (a) all contributions or wage deductions made to qualified retirement plans, as specified in § 541(b)(7) and (b) all repayments of loans from retirement plans, as specified in § 362(b)(19).	$
56	**Total of all deductions allowed under § 707(b)(2).** Enter the amount from Line 52.	$
57	**Total adjustments to determine disposable income.** Add the amounts on Lines 54, 55, and 56 and enter the result.	$

Official Form 22C (Chapter 13) (04/07) – Cont.   6

| 58 | **Monthly Disposable Income Under § 1325(b)(2).** Subtract Line 57 from Line 53 and enter the result. | $ |

Part VI: ADDITIONAL EXPENSE CLAIMS

| 59 | **Other Expenses.** List and describe any monthly expenses, not otherwise stated in this form, that are required for the health and welfare of you and your family and that you contend should be an additional deduction from your current monthly income under § 707(b)(2)(A)(ii)(I). If necessary, list additional sources on a separate page. All figures should reflect your average monthly expense for each item. Total the expenses. |

	Expense Description	Monthly Amount
a.		$
b.		$
c.		$
	Total: Add Lines a, b, and c	$

Part VII: VERIFICATION

| 60 | I declare under penalty of perjury that the information provided in this statement is true and correct. *(If this is a joint case, both debtors must sign.)*

Date: _____   Signature: _____
                                              (Debtor)

Date: _____   Signature: _____
                                              (Joint Debtor, if any) |

Index

About the Author

John Ventura is a nationally known bankruptcy attorney and author who has been writing about issues related to consumer financial and legal issues for more than 15 years. He currently serves as Director of the Texas Consumer Complaint Center at the University of Houston Law School in Texas and is also an adjunct professor at the law school.

Ventura has been a guest on CNN, CNBC, PBS, and National Public Radio, among other national TV and radio media and has been quoted in such publications as *The Wall Street Journal, Kiplinger's Personal Finance, Money, Newsweek, Black Enterprise, Entrepreneur, U.S. News and World Report, Maxim, Good Housekeeping, Martha Stewart's Living,* the *Chicago Tribune,* the *LA Times,* and *The Dallas Morning News,* among other media outlets. He has been quoted about issues related to bankruptcy, debt and credit rebuilding at CBSMarketWatch.com, Office.com, Bankrate.com, *USA Today, MSN Money, The Dallas Morning News, The Detroit Free Press,* the *Baltimore Sun,* the *Indianapolis Star,* and *Black Enterprise Magazine.*